the Path of Truth

Volume 9

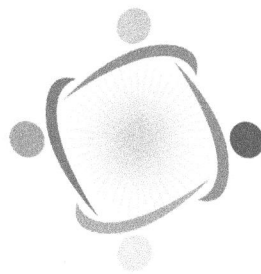

Mesoamerica Region

The Path of Truth, Vol 9

Published by:
Mesoamerica Region Discipleship Ministries
www.Discipleship.MesoamericaRegion.org
www.SdmiResources.MesoamericaRegion.org

Cover design: Slater Joel Chavez
Interior Design: Slater Joel Chavez

Translated into English from Spanish by:
Dr. Dorothy Bullon

ISBN:978-1-63580-109-5

Table of Contents

Presentation

Each year, we have a new challenge when preparing to teach. In the area of Christian teaching, we prepare ourselves not only to share knowledge of the Word of God; but also to share testimonies, experiences, anecdotes, and thus form lives in what it means to be a Christian.

So, it is important to highlight education as an essential tool for the development of the Christian life, taking into account that this is one of the factors that most influences how God's people grow as disciples of Christ.

We also need to observe that we live in a world that challenges us to strive more and more to put Christian values into practice, and thus, to show Christ in our lives. We must remember, then, that as Christians, we must be forgers of a healthy coexistence; a mutual respect where the practice of Christian values is not a coincidence; but a conviction, that is, a change of life which we assume.

Therefore, it is important that through teaching, you can read and study the Word in depth, underscoring how we should live day by day, contributing to the transformation of people who live in a society that constantly is losing out on good values. This edition of The Path of Truth, like all previous editions, aims to always help you in this work of discipleship.

However, it is imperative that each day we commit ourselves to guiding and motivating the disciples to show Christ in our daily lives. In this way, we will be helping to form a more just, more productive and more equitable society where Christians shine and show how to live differently, which will motivate others to seek God.

It is our prayer that God will guide and accompany you in this wonderful work of forming disciples in the image and likeness of Christ. Cheer up! God is with you! "...for the gracious hand of his God was on him. For Ezra had devoted himself to the study and observance of the Law of the Lord, and to teaching its decrees and laws in Israel" (Ezra 7:9b-10).

Patricia Picavea
Literature Coordinator - SAM Region

Recommendations

Preparation of the lesson:

1. Pray to the Lord asking for wisdom and discernment to understand the biblical passages as you study, and to be able to apply them first to your life. Also, pray for your students to be receptive to the teaching of the Word of God.

2. Prepare a place without distractions to study the lesson, where you have a table or desk. It is important to have some tools such as paper, pens, pencils, eraser, etc.

3. As far as possible, in addition to the book The Path of Truth, have a dictionary, a Bible Dictionary and some good biblical commentaries.

4. Read the lesson of The Path of Truth as many times as necessary at the beginning of the week. This will help you prepare the materials you may need for the class, and be aware of news and other information that you might include in the lesson you are preparing.

5. Search the Bible and read each passage indicated.

6. Read the objective of the lesson to know where to direct your students.

7. Write on a sheet the name of the lesson, the points that you will develop, then write the title of the first point and develop your own summary as you study the lesson. Write and highlight the Bible quotations that will be read during the class.

8. Write down the meaning of words you do not know and look them up in the dictionary so you can understand the lesson better to explain it to the members of your class who may ask you questions.

9. If you do research on the Internet, be careful to get information from reliable pages that support the information. Remember that the Internet is an open space where all people can upload the information they want. Unfortunately, not all the information found there is true and reliable.

10. Prepare the lesson as dynamic and participatory as possible. This is a very special time where sharing experiences will help to enrich the learning process. By doing so, people will be more interested in the class; They will remember more of what they participated in or did together, and will appreciate being heard and taken into account.

11. Go through the Optional Questions that are provided at the end of each lesson. This will allow you to make the class more participatory. Select in what time you will be answering the questions.

PRESENTATION OF THE LESSON:

1. Arrive early at your classroom. It is important that when the first person arrives you are already there.

2. Change the position of the chairs (semicircle, circle, groups, etc.). This will make the group feel more comfortable to participate and thus break the monotony.

3. Before beginning the lesson, welcome your students. This will allow you to create a pleasant study environment. Be interested in people and you can pray for those who have needs.

4. Begin the class with a prayer, asking the Lord that He will allow you to understand His Word and give you the willingness to obey it.

5. Write on the board: The title of the lesson and the memory verse. Read the memory verse with your students several times. Once you start the lesson, write the main points of the lesson on one side of the board. This will allow you to keep in view the sequence of points you will teach.

6. Make the introduction as attractive as possible. Try to vary it in each class.

7. Keep an order in the development of the topic. Write the title of the first point and begin to explain it. Use the blackboard as a teaching resource to write down key words, answers to questions, etc. When the first point ends, write the title of second point and so on.

8. As you explain each point, you can guide your students to answer the questions. Allow them to provide answers and raise questions.

9. You can form working groups to answer questions. This will allow everyone to participate. Do not force anyone to participate, but make sure everyone knows that you want and appreciate their contributions. On the other hand, do not let a person dominate the session. In a kind manner, lead the class to listen to the opinion of other people.

10. Take a few minutes to discuss how we will apply biblical truths to our daily lives.

11. Read the conclusion and encourage your students to study the biblical texts of the lesson at home during the following week. Invite them to attend next Sunday. Encourage them to invite other people to the Sunday School class. Finish the class with a prayer.

Other suggestions:

1. Goals and Prizes: You can offer a simple prize for the students who during each trimester learn all the memory verses and say them to the class.

2. Certificate: If you want, for the students who were faithful or did not miss more than one or two classes in the quarter, you can give them a certificate. This can motivate others to attend faithfully.

The Sermon on the Mount Today

First Quarter

Salt and light in this world

The law of God

The law of true love

Jesus and sexual sins

The value of sincerity

Love your enemies

Generosity without praise

Prayer acceptable to God

The model of prayer and fasting

Treasures: in heaven or on earth?

Solution for worry and anxiety

Relationships that transcend

Triple wake-up call

Salt and Light in this World

Amparo Álvarez (Ecuador)

Memory verse: "Let your light so shine before men, that they may see your good works, and glorify your Father who is in heaven" (Matthew 5:16).

Lesson Aim: To learn that we should live as people who have received the life of Christ, like salt which enhances flavors. We must avoid the corruption of the world. At the same time, we need to manifest the light of Christ by doing good works so that the world will believe in Him.

Introduction

In the sermon on the mount, Jesus answered the disciple's questions and taught them many things (Matt. 5:1-2). He told them they were to be like salt and light. In a world full of sin and corruption, both in Jesus' day as well as our times, values are often reversed; evil becomes good, and good evil. In this lesson, we will study Matthew 5:13-16.

I. We are salt for the world

In Matt. 5:13, we read, "You are the salt of the earth." The Greek text says, "You and only you are the salt of the earth."

Jesus told them that, although the world is corrupt and lost, as His followers they should function as salt in the world, preserving it. Christians have a message that can transform lives, bringing salvation to this world. We can really make a difference. So, Christians are like salt because we have new life in Christ and the Holy Spirit dwells in us. We must live to transform our society which does not live according to God's commandments, and each day moves further away from Him.

A. What is so special about salt?

"You are the salt of the earth. But if the salt loses its saltiness, how can it be made salty again? It is no longer good for anything, except to be thrown out and trampled underfoot" (v.13). In this brief statement, Jesus was warning his disciples that they should not commit two very important mistakes:

In the first place, they were not to leave the world and enter into monasteries. Salt is often used to preserve meat, especially in places where there are no fridges. This was the case in Jesus' day. The people around us in the metaphor are the 'meat.' If there was no salt, the meat would rot. It is only as

salt is added that it fulfills its antiseptic function. We must be in the world so that it can benefit from our influence and we can make a difference, showing with our daily actions that we can live correctly in the midst of sinfulness.

Secondly, he told them that Christians also had to avoid being joined to the world, accepting its values and ideologies. God's children must be different and help to preserve true values, just as salt is used to help the meat from going bad. In order for the world to receive our help, we have to be different.

The words of Jesus, "Only you are the salt of the earth", constitute great praise on the lips of the sovereign Lord of the universe. This affirmation gives us as Christians great dignity and self-esteem. Therefore, if we are trying to be like the world in our way of speaking, of dressing, values, manners, etc., we cannot make a difference. On the contrary, in trying to conform to the patterns of this world, we are passing unnoticed like salt that has lost its saltiness in the midst of a world that is lost.

B. The purpose of salt

Jesus didn't say to his disciples, 'You are like sugar', but, 'You are salt'. Let's examine then what is the purpose of salt and how is it that we Christians have to function as this element.

In the first place, salt works as a preservative. In tropical countries where there is no refrigeration, people salt the meat so that it does not spoil. In the same way, when Christians come into contact with people who live in sin they can have a transformative affect, bringing benefits to secular society. Without its presence, the world would degenerate at a greater speed.

Secondly, salt is necessary to highlight the flavor of the meals. Without the presence and practice of Christians and the proclamation of the gospel, this world would be a much more insipid place. This world lacks a genuine and true flavor. There is also no real joy. Following Jesus gives meaning and purpose to life. We can verify this by examining the situations that occur today. We see people looking for solutions to their problems in drugs, alcohol, crime, abortion, etc. As Christians, we need to provide purpose to the world that is lost without Christ. The gospel of Jesus Christ is the power of God for the salvation of everyone who believes.

Third, salt is white, a symbol of purity. Christians must live lives that are free from contamination and sin. As mentioned earlier, Christians must have different values than the world. Each Christian is a citizen of Heaven, and while we live in this lost world, we need to be a blessing and a redeeming factor. As such, we urgently need to resist constantly the temptation to become worldly and, instead, become like the Lord Jesus Christ. In James 4:4b, we read: "anyone who chooses to be a friend of the world becomes an enemy of God." As the salt of the earth, we must be holy, pure, and different from the world. In Romans 12:2, Paul says, "Do not conform to the pattern of this world." Me must be like salt and not lose our purity by conforming to the world's standards and values.

Fourth, salt has also been used as fertilizer. Christians must function in such a way that we promote the growth of what is good for society. Always stimulating good for humanity, repressing evil and being promoters of good.

Fifth, salt causes thirst. In the same way, we must cause people to be thirsty for Jesus Christ and his gospel. If as Christians we live daily only for the glory of God, the world will observe us and want to know about Jesus Christ. The good testimony of Christians will attract people to be thirsty to know God. They will want to know why we are different; how we are full of hope, peace and joy, in spite of having problems. When they ask us we can tell them about Jesus. John 7:37 says, "Jesus stood and said in a loud voice, 'Let anyone who is thirsty come to me and drink'."

Jesus said that if salt loses its saltiness, it becomes useless and worthless. By welcoming today's worldly values and putting aside Kingdom values, we stop being salt.

II. We are the light of this world

In Matthew 5:14-16, Jesus also told his disciples, *"You are the light of the world."* The Greek text says, *"You and only you are the light of the world."* In Proverbs 4:19, we read:, *"But the way of the wicked is like deep darkness; they do not know what makes them stumble."*

A. God Gives Light

In Ephesians 5:8, Paul says, "For you were once darkness, but now you are light in the Lord. Live as children of light." We were in darkness before, but now we are light of the Lord. How should we live as children of light? Jesus said that He is the light of the world and then He told his disciples that now they were to light up the world. Why are we here? To bring glory to God but we cannot help the world when we do not shine. Peter says in 1 Peter 2:9, "But you are a chosen people, a royal priesthood, a holy nation, God's special possession, that you may declare the praises of him who called you out of darkness into his wonderful light." Shining is not optional.

B. The Light Illuminates

How do we function as light? First, by exposing the reality of evil. Jesus, as the light of the world, exposed the corruption that was in his time (Matthew 16:6,11-12, 22:15). The psalmist said, "Your word is a lamp for my feet, a light on my path." The gospel exposes evil and leads us to know God. Light opens the eyes of the spiritually blind who cannot see because of sin. The Creator who ordered light in the darkness when he created the heavens and the earth, now works in creating that light in the depths of our hearts.

How can we let our light shine before a faithless world? We can make a difference in the world by living holy lives, that are based on biblical values; being filled with the Holy Spirit. How will we achieve this? By not accepting bribes to obtain benefits, by paying all fines and taxes due, by not taking anything that is not ours, by not speaking injudiciously, and by not overcharging folks (among others).

III. What is the purpose of living as salt and as light?

Firstly, we should be salt and light so that the world will see our good works. We want the folk around us to observe something that is different in us. Unbelievers who work around us, our schoolmates, those who live in our neighborhoods, will observe us and realize our good works. Paul says, "For we are God's handiwork, created in Christ Jesus to do good works, which God prepared in advance for us to do" (Ephesians 2:10).

The second reason Jesus gives is that the world might praise the Father who is in heaven. In Matthew 6:1, 5, 16, we read that the Pharisees did everything to be seen by others and thus be glorified by man. Our purpose is different, to bring glory to our Father who is in heaven.

Let's examine how we can implement these teachings in our lives. Is our witness insipid like tasteless salt and dark without light? If we are to be salt and light, we will be different in our way of thinking, acting, and feeling. The world will easily realize this. We must live in the world, but not belong to it. We should not try to escape from the world; Where there is no light, there will be darkness in the world. When light shines, darkness goes away. Salt, on the other hand, preserves and enhances flavor. As salt we will help to preserve the world from sin and highlight Jesus in a damaged society.

It is important to do our best in all aspects of our lives. We must be cordial, pleasant, correct and irreproachable to attract the attention of people who live without Christ. As Christians, we must always bear in mind that we can only be the salt of the earth and the light of the world when we represent Jesus Christ, who is the hope for a lost world.

Optional Questions

1. We are salt for the world
- What does it mean for you to be the salt of the earth?
- What examples of daily life show that we are salt?
- Can the Christian lose his saltiness? How?

2. We are the light of this world
- What did Jesus mean by what he expressed in Matthew 5:14-16?
- What is a practical example of how to be light.

3. What is the purpose of living as salt and as light?
- Do you believe that you are being "light of the world"? Why?

Conclusion

Let's examine our lives, and if we realize that we are not being light and salt, let us ask the Lord Jesus to forgive us and sanctify us. Only then will Jesus transform us and help us fulfill His purpose in our lives.

Notes:

Lesson 2

The Law of God

Jessica Rojas (Argentina)

> **Memory verse:** "For I tell you that unless your righteousness surpasses that of the Pharisees and the teachers of the law, you will certainly not enter the kingdom of heaven" (Matthew 5:20).
>
> **Lesson Aim:** That the students might understand the meaning of the Mosaic Law in the teachings of Jesus, and their application today.

Introduction

Laws, rules and regulations are part of all our everyday life; from the life of a baby, to that of the elderly; from Adam and Eve, to you and me. However, some rules seem to be not as important in comparison with other laws which represent the difference between life and death. Take a few minutes of the class to reflect on some laws, rules and norms common to your environment. Think of some of those for children, young people and adults. Then, reflect together on which ones seem important and which ones, not so important. Next, read the passage from the lesson: Matthew 5:17-20.

I. The Mosaic Law

Matthew 5:7-18 says, "Do not think that I have come to abolish the Law or the Prophets; I have not come to abolish them but to fulfill them. For truly I tell you, until heaven and earth disappear, not the smallest letter, not the least stroke of a pen, will by any means disappear from the Law until everything is accomplished." Matthew tells us that Jesus made references to the Old Testament where there were different laws to guide the people.

A. Ceremonial Law

These are laws that specifically relate to how the people of Israel needed to make their offerings: "Speak to the Israelites and say to them, 'When anyone among you brings an offering to the Lord, bring as your offering an animal from either the herd or the flock. If the offering is a burnt offering from the herd, you are to offer a male without defect. You must present it at the entrance to the tent of meeting so that it will be acceptable to the Lord" (Leviticus 1:2-3). The primary purpose of this law was to point to Jesus Christ (the perfect offering); therefore, these laws were no longer necessary after Jesus' death and resurrection. However, we must consider that although we are no longer bound by these ceremonial laws, the principles behind them (worshiping and loving a holy God) still apply. Jesus was accused many times for violating ceremonial laws.

Deuteronomy 12:2-3 says, "Destroy completely all the places on the high mountains, on the hills and under every spreading tree, where the nations you are dispossessing worship their gods. Break down their altars, smash their sacred stones and burn their Asherah poles in the fire; cut down the idols of their gods and wipe out their names from those places."

This shows the importance of worshiping God and God alone. Possibly there are no idols of Asherah today, but there are others 'gods' that could take the place of God in our lives, such as, television programs, addictions, family, full agenda, etc. ... anything that takes first place in our life.

B. Civil Law

These laws applied to daily life in Israel (Deuteronomy 24:10-11). Modern society and culture are radically different from Biblical time; as a result, we cannot follow all these rules to the letter of the law. However, the principles behind these commandments are eternal and should guide our behavior. Jesus demonstrated these principles throughout his life.

Next, let's look at some examples of civil law and the principles that can still guide us today:

- Deuteronomy 22:8 says, "When you build a new house, make a parapet around your roof so that you may not bring the guilt of bloodshed on your house if someone falls from the roof."

Principle: Take the necessary precautions to prevent accidents. In this way, we take care of our family and our neighbor.

- In Deuteronomy 22:13-30, we can read about many rules about sexual sins. This also guides our life today, because sexual sins destroy people, families, churches and society. They ruin the climate of respect, trust and credibility that are essential for a strong marriage and the safe raising of children.

- Deuteronomy 23:7-8 reads as follows, "Do not despise an Edomite, for the Edomites are related to you. Do not despise an Egyptian, because you resided as foreigners in their country. The third generation of children born to them may enter the assembly of the Lord."

Principle: Currently, migration from one country to another is very common. We also know that cultures from country to country, even from one province to another within the same country, can be very diverse. God shows his compassion for foreigners and demands that we also extend compassion and love for them. Before the Lord, we are all people created in his image and likeness, and there is no acceptable excuse for mistreating those who are different from us.

- More civil laws are found in chapters 17 to 26 of Deuteronomy.

C. Moral Law

These laws (found in passages like the Ten Commandments) come as direct commands of God, and require strict obedience. For example, "You shall not murder" (Exodus 20:13). The moral laws reveal the nature and will of God, and still apply today. Jesus obeyed the moral law completely. In comparison to this, everything in our lives changes: technology, culture, ways of speaking, music, loved ones that have passed on etc.; but God's moral law does not change. The Ten Commandments are still valid today. Certainly, they are the basis of our daily walk with God.

II. Discipleship

To explain clearly, Jesus gives us two angles to ensure that we have grasped what he teaches us in Matthew 5:19 which states, "Therefore anyone who sets aside one of the least of these commands and teaches others accordingly will be called least in the kingdom of heaven, but whoever practices and teaches these commands will be called great in the kingdom of heaven."

First, He addresses what should not be done; breaking 'one of the least of these commands', then he goes on to warn that those who teach others to break the law will be called the least in the Kingdom of heaven. The consequence will be serious. Here we have to evaluate more thoroughly what 'least in the kingdom of heaven' means. This may give the idea that they will still be part of this Kingdom. According to the Beacon Bible commentary "the correct way to interpret this phrase is 'in relation to the kingdom of heaven', that is that they will left out" (Volume 6, 2008 p. 76).

Now, Jesus addresses the same concept on the positive side, i.e. what should be done. It shows what happens when a person fulfills his teaching: "... whoever practices and teaches these commands will be called great in the kingdom of heaven" (v. 19b). There is much to be learned from this short sentence. Let's look at the order of the mandate: 'practices and teaches' these laws. The conclusion here is that we must first practice or obey, and only after can we teach. If our life does not show the fruit of having practiced the commandments of God, we are not worthy or prepared to teach them to others.

Another rich teaching that we can glean is the concept of discipleship as the constant practice of receiving, retaining and distributing.

- Receive: we receive instruction and teaching in our spiritual lives through preaching, Bible classes, Bible reading, etc.

- Retain: we retain what we were taught. As we apply biblical truths to our lives, we make changes, and can see the fruit of everything we have received.

- Share: We can share what we have received and retained in our spiritual lives. We share our testimonies, teach Bible classes and discipleship classes, and serve in different capacities within the body of Christ.

When practicing this cycle, there is no way to reach a stalemate. On the contrary, there will be fluidity and growth in our spiritual life. It is not enough just to receive the teaching and retain it. You always have to share it with others. We can avoid being spiritually 'overfed' if we keep these three concepts in balance (receiving, retaining, distributing). When we do this, we are fulfilling one of Jesus' most important commandments: the great commission (Matthew 28:19-20).

III. The Law of Christ

Now let's consider the key verse of the Sermon on the Mount. Matthew 5:20 tells us, "For I tell you that unless your righteousness surpasses that of the Pharisees and the teachers of the law, you will certainly not enter the kingdom of heaven." The Pharisees and the scribes, whom Jesus uses as a standard of comparison, were the religious authorities. They were the ones who knew the Holy Scriptures best and therefore, were the teachers of the people of Israel. Jesus said that the righteousness of his hearers must 'surpass' that of the scribes and Pharisees; surely the people were surprised. They may well have asked themselves, "Is it possible to reach this level of righteousness?"

However, we must analyze the sort of righteousness Jesus asked for; he was referring to inner, moral and spiritual righteousness. The righteousness of the teachers of the law was exterior, ceremonial, and legalistic. "The problem of the Pharisees," says Martin Lloyd-Jones, "was that they were interested in details rather than principles, in actions rather than motives, and were more interested in doing than in being" (Beacon Bible Commentary), Volume 6, 2008, p. 76).

Faced with this, it might be easy to want to throw stones at the Scribes and Pharisees of the New Testament; but we need to be careful before bending down to look for a few stones. Today, we are still human with the same faults that the teachers of the law had. For this reason, it is important to constantly evaluate our motivation. It is easy, as time goes by, to fall into routines, traditions and rules even when the motivation may have been correct at the beginning. Hence, walking with Christ requires sincere analysis. It is much easier to maintain an exterior, ceremonial and legalistic righteousness, but that is not what Jesus is asking for. For example, Jesus requires us to keep the laws, not only words (external) but also in our thoughts (inner beings).

We find a good example in Matthew 5:27-28: "You have heard that it was said, 'You shall not commit adultery.' But I tell you that anyone who looks at a woman lustfully has already committed adultery with her in his heart." Jesus tells us that we should not only abstain from (external) adultery; but also, of lustful looks (interior). "Keeping the law of Christ is a greater requirement than the observance of the law of Moses" (Beacon Biblical Commentary, Volume 6, 2008, p. 76).

Optional Questions

I. The Mosaic Law

- Think of a ceremonial rule that you practice. Evaluate if this rule brings you closer to God, or if you have fallen into the trap of just doing things through routine or obeying blindly in a legalistic fashion (Matthew 5:17-18).

- In addition to the Ten Commandments, what are some other examples of moral laws that we find in the Word of God?

II. Discipleship

- Explain why it is important to follow the order of actions Jesus presents to us in Matthew 5:19: to practice and then teach.

- Think of your life and how you are fulfilling these three concepts. Is there an area of your life where you think God asks for more?

  ◊ Receive (I am filled with the Word of God)

  ◊ Retain (I apply the Word of God to my life, I make changes)

  ◊ Share (I share the Word of God with others)

III. The law of Christ (v. 20)

- Think of one or two areas of your life where it is easier to follow a 'law' to maintain appearances.

Conclusion

After understanding more about the system of laws that governed the life of the people of Israel, we can fully appreciate Jesus' teachings and understand why He did not strictly follow all the laws, as well as the religious leaders of His day. Jesus is our greatest example of how to please God; it is not just about fulfilling a long list of rules and regulations or maintaining outward piety. Walking with Christ produces a transformation in our hearts, and that is where a desire to share this good news with others comes from.

The Law of True Love

Mabel de Rodríguez (Uruguay)

Introduction

After making clear his position regarding the law, Jesus began a series of teachings in clear contrast to the interpretations that the ancient rabbis had given the law of God (Matthew 5:21-26). For the Israelites, the law was considered to be divine and holy, so its interpretation had to be by men consecrated for such a function. This implied that no one dared to give their personal interpretation of the Holy Scriptures, not even the most outstanding rabbis, contemporaries of Jesus.

When one of them explained a part of the law, they would refer to the interpretation that a former rabbi had made; nobody ever dared to give their own interpretation. Therefore, it was shocking to hear Jesus say, "You have heard that it was said to the people long ago..." referring to what the ancient rabbis had said about the law. Then, He gave His own interpretation by saying, "But I tell you that..."

This must have caused astonishment in the audience, but it certainly showed the great authority that the holy Rabbi had when citing the correct interpretation of the sacred text, something that for the Pharisees and Scribes was very daring. On the other hand, the town people were amazed at the authority with which He spoke.

I. Anger, a sin as serious as murder

A. The Law in the Old Testament

When Jesus said, "You have heard that it was said to the people long ago, 'You shall not murder'..." (Matthew 5:21a), he was referring to one of the Ten Commandments that Moses had given to the people on Mount Sinai. According to this law, if someone was accused of killing a person, they should be brought to trial and judged by a jury chosen by the people for these cases. If found guilty, the death sentence was to be pronounced. In the minds of the Jews, there was no doubt that this sin was so serious that the punishment should be death. But the divine Teacher took the interpretation of the law to another level, saying that anger is a sin as serious as murder.

Jesus shows how the law can be badly applied as well as providing us with His own interpretation of God's intentions. The law said "you shall not murder" (Exodus 20:13), referring only to physical death, without specifying anything about the treatment of our neighbor. It was about killing someone. For the interpreters of the law, it was enough to say, 'anyone who commits murder will be judged and punished.' In Israel, many people took these words literally. So, the general idea was that It did not matter how they treated others, as long as they did not kill anyone. Jesus taught that this commandment goes much deeper.

Generally, we classify some sins as mild and others as serious. For example, we talk about sins such as resentment, lying, murmuring, taking folders or paper clips from the office without permission, or abusing the time and resources of the company (which in the end is stealing) as minor sins. Some folk do not even consider that they are sins. But every sin is serious and deserves the same eternal punishment as homicide, rape, homosexuality, etc. Remember what James says, "For whoever keeps the whole law and yet stumbles at just one point is guilty of breaking all of it" (James 2:10).

B. The Application of the Law in the New Testament

In the New Testament, there are two words in Greek which are most used to refer to anger. The first is thumós (θυμός), which refers to an anger that arises suddenly, and which goes away fast. The other Greek word for anger is the one that appears in this text and is the one Jesus uses: orgídso (ὀργίζω), which describes an anger that manifests as the most intense of all human passions. Orgidso (ὀργίζω) is less sudden that thumós (θυμός), but more durable. This is the anger that we keep in our hearts and which does not go away; that is, the one that produces permanent resentment and hatred.

C. The Practice of This New Law

This anger that is stored in the heart is what Jesus condemns as murder, and says that those who feel this way will be guilty of judgment (Matthew 5:21b). This judgment to which Jesus refers is the local court formed by the elders of the people who were in charge of judging the matters within their jurisdiction. The anger that the Bible condemns is that which we harbor in our hearts. Therefore, remember what Paul mentions in Ephesians 4:26, "Be angry, but do not sin, do not let the sun go down on your anger" (Ephesians 4:26). James adds in his epistle, "because human anger does not produce the righteousness that God desires."

In both texts, the Greek word for anger is orgidso (ὀργίζω). Later, Jesus goes on to speak of two cases where the anger that is stored in the heart is manifested with insulting words.

The first is a fool (Matthew 5:22); that is raká (ῥακά) in Greek, which in the Bible is used to refer to those people who deny the existence of God through their deeds and words. Such a person will be guilty before the council. The council was the Sanhedrin, the council of great authority among the Jews, and which consisted of the priests and elders of greater renown who were in charge of judging the cases considered most serious at the national level.

In God, love for our neighbor is paramount. Every person who gets angry with his brother must be prosecuted. The person who says 'fool' to his brother must justify himself before the tribunal of God; and the person who says 'idiot' to his neighbor is worthy of hell. The Jewish concept clashed strongly with the words of Jesus; for they show us how God takes treating each other without love very seriously. Angry shouting hurts our neighbors; Jesus demands love in all our dealings with others.

With this, our Lord meant that the sin of uncontrolled anger is bad; but it is worse when it comes to complete contempt, expressed in harsh words. This sort of behavior deserves to be judged not by a local court; but by the highest legal power of the nation. He also said that anyone who would say 'you fool' or 'idiot'; that is moros (μωρός) in Greek, will be exposed to the fire of hell, or the Greek original says, "will be exposed to the flames of the gehenna (γέεννα)".

The term gehenna is the Greek transliteration of the Hebrew gai jinnom, better known in the Old Testament as the Valley of Ben Hinnom which was located south of Jerusalem (Joshua 15:8). It was in that valley of Hinnom where Solomon erected high places to Moloch (1 Kings 11:7), and Ahaz and Manasseh sacrificed their sons (2 Kings 16:3; 2 Chronicles 28:3; 33:6; Jeremiah 32:35).

To put an end to these abominations, Josiah desecrated the site with human bones and other contaminations, and converted it into a crematorium where the garbage was thrown out of the city (2 Kings 23:10,13; 2 Chronicles 34:4), thus turning this place into a symbol of horror and dishonor where fire permanently destroyed the garbage and the worms moved in the midst of it. Thus, our Lord Jesus says that people who in anger slander and denigrate the name and reputation of another person is worthy of eternal punishment in the flames of hell.

II. Called to Be In Complete Peace

Jesus concludes this teaching by making them see the importance of being completely reconciled with everyone at the time of making offerings to God (Going to church) (Matthew 5:23). While it is true that through the sacrifice of Christ we can be reconciled to God and be in complete peace with Him, it is also important to be at peace with our fellow men.

In Israel, offerings were given by the people through the priests in order to atone for the sins, or in thankfulness and communion. However, Jesus tells them that it is useless for them to offer their offerings to God if they are not completely reconciled with their fellow men. Jesus said, "Settle matters quickly with your adversary who is taking you to court. Do it while you are still together on the way, or your adversary may hand you over to the judge, and the judge may hand you over to the officer, and you may be thrown into prison. Truly I tell you, you will not get out until you have paid the last penny" (Matthew 5:25-26). When we get to the judgment day, it will be too late to make peace with our neighbor. We have to do it now.

III. A Christian Practice of True Peace

Jesus said, "... if you are offering your gift at the altar and there remember that your brother or sister has something against you, leave your gift there in front of the altar. First go and be reconciled to them; then come and offer your gift" (Matthew 5:23-24). It does not matter who started the dispute or who is right, before going to church together they both need to be reconciled. They need to apologize for what happened, regardless of whether the other party accepts it or not. Jesus is clear, we need to obey and be free of guilt, and then present the offerings to God.

This does not mean that we will always manage to be reconciled with everyone, or reach mutual agreements. On some occasions, our Christian principles will be against the worldly systems, which has been the churches experience throughout history. Therefore, Paul wrote, "If it is possible, as far as it depends on you, live at peace with everyone" (Romans 12:18). Paul exhorted the believers to be at peace with all people to the extent that it depended on them; that is, as long as it is possible. This means that we cannot always be in complete peace with everyone, as sometimes Christian principles will cause discontent in the world and this will provoke opposition, criticism and, sometimes persecution. But as far as we are concerned, we must be willing to forgive and be messengers of peace.

Here Jesus teaches us an important lesson by explaining the true spirit of the law; anger, contempt and hatred are as serious as murder which will be punished in hell. Also, if we remember that our brother has something against us, we need to seek reconciliation with them before we go to church to worship God. We might say, 'The past is the past', but God asks us to be reconciled with our brother or sister. Then we can go to God to ask for his forgiveness. We need to learn, because otherwise, we must remember that we have to face the highest and only true judge: God himself.

Optional Questions

I. Anger, a sin as serious as murder

- Is murder only a physical crime? In what other ways can the commandment "you shall not murder" (Matthew 5:21) be breached today?
- How would you define the two words that Matthew 5:22 describes as insults?

II. Called to be in complete peace

- What important aspect should we take into account when making our offering (worshipping in church)? (Matt 5:23-24)
- Comment on some experiences when you have forgiven someone who has offended you.

III. A Christian practice on true peace

- Is it possible to be at peace with all people? Why?
- What should we do when we know that a person has done something against us, even though we feel that we did not do anything wrong against them?

Conclusion

One day in Heaven, we will all love one another perfectly. For now, we put our love to the test learning now to treat our neighbors well.

Notes:

Jesus and Sexual Sins

Lesson 4

Elí Porras (Peru)

Memory verse: "But I tell you that anyone who looks at a woman lustfully has already committed adultery with her in his heart" (Matthew 5:28).

Lesson Aim: That the students might understand that sin goes beyond the physical act, for its root is in the heart; because of this, we need to take the appropriate measures.

Introduction

Martin Luther said a famous thought, "I cannot prevent the birds from flying over my head, but I can prevent them from nesting on it." Ask your students to comment on this thought. As you prepare the lesson, you can find and cut out images of people who show inappropriate attitudes. For example, images of men in the street who fix lascivious glances on ladies who cross by their side, or vice versa.

Ask your students to continue commenting and reflecting on what Jesus said about this in the Sermon on the Mount (Matthew 5:27-30).

I. Adultery as a very serious matter

What is adultery? It is sexual relations with a person that is not their spouse.

A. An Old Commandment

Jesus said, "You have heard that it was said..." The Jews knew the law or Torah. Adultery was forbidden. Thus, we find the following recorded in Exodus 20:14: "You shall not commit adultery." And in verse 17, in the prohibition of greed, there is talk of coveting the neighbor's wife: "You shall not covet your neighbor's house. You shall not covet your neighbor's wife, or his male or female servant, his ox or donkey, or anything that belongs to your neighbor."

In our fallen world, it is common for married couples to commit acts of infidelity. This is the biggest cause of separation and divorce in the world. God's commandment was given with the purpose of caring for marriage, the family and our spiritual health.

B. The Prohibition of Polygamy

God's intention for the people of Israel was that they should be different from the other neighboring and pagan peoples whose characteristic was polygamy. Adultery was forbidden in the Jewish moral code and taught emphatically within the commandments. This prohibition also reaches the new Israel of God, the church. Paul says, "It is God's will that you should be sanctified; that you should avoid sexual immorality; that each of you should learn to control your own body in a way that is holy and honorable, not in passionate lust like the pagans, who do not know God" (1 Thessalonians 4:3-5).

C. Adultery Was Punished

The moral teachers of Jesus' time emphasized this commandment and even punished adulterers by stoning them. Jesus saw an adulterous woman whom they were about to judge. They tested him. "Teacher, this woman was caught in the act of adultery. In the Law, Moses commanded us to stone such women. Now what do you say?" (John 8:4-5) They tried to trick Jesus by claiming that Moses commanded them to stone people who committed this sin. The Jews, in this scene, made reference to what was established. Leviticus 20:10 says, "If a man commits adultery with another man's wife—with the wife of his neighbor—both the adulterer and the adulteress are to be put to death."

We know what the outcome was for adulterous woman. Jesus challenged them to stone her if they were innocent. When they all went away, he told her, "Go now and leave your life of sin" (John 8:11b). Even when Jesus forgave her, He made it clear that she was to stop committing this sin. This commandment was taken very seriously, but the

Jews limited adultery to the concrete act itself. For this reason, Jesus makes an interpretation that went beyond the physical act.

II. New Scope of Adultery

Jesus had the authority to interpret and expand God's commandments. He said with authority, "But I tell you…" (Matthew 5:28a). Apparently, the concept of adultery was very limited, since it applied only to the act itself. But in the Sermon on the Mount, Jesus surprised his hearers with a higher concept.

A. New Moral Scope

Let's look at this. Jesus said, "… who looks at a woman lustfully has already committed adultery with her in his heart" (Matthew 5:28). Notice that Jesus goes beyond the physical act itself, for He speaks of greed, and this has more implications. In the first place, Jesus extends the scope of this commandment. The expression "anyone who looks …" includes married couples, those who are single, and includes both men and women.

In the second place, Jesus defines the problem as greed, which can be defined as 'the desire or appetite to possess material goods and riches'. Applying the above to adultery, Jesus is talking about the lustful desire to possess a person with immoral intentions. So Jesus in the Sermon on the Mount goes beyond the common definition of adultery. He says that it's possible to commit adultery in our thoughts.

B. A Matter of the Mind

Jesus is not saying 'do not look at a woman.' He is talking about lustful and inappropriate thoughts. With this new interpretation, the Jewish moralists of that time, and those of our time, cannot be justified by saying, 'I have never committed adultery, or I have never been unfaithful to my spouse'. Some might judge this concept to be a bit over the top, but this is how Jesus dealt with the subject of adultery.

It is for this reason that the apostle Paul advises the Philippians, "Finally, brothers and sisters, whatever is true, whatever is noble, whatever is right, whatever is pure, whatever is lovely, whatever is admirable— if anything is excellent or praiseworthy—think about such things" (Philippians 4:8).

In our times, we see in the mass media ill-intentioned phrases of a sensual nature that can spark sexual fantasies with impure intentions. The saying, "The idle mind is the workshop of the devil" hits the nail on the head. Mental lustful fantasies may lead to impure acts. This is also a matter of the human heart.

C. A Matter of the Heart

Here we are not talking about the organ that pumps our blood around. Metaphorically, the heart is the very center of the human mind and will. Jesus, speaking of mental adultery, is making reference to the spiritual nature that has been affected by sin. Of course, Jesus also said, "For it is from within, out of a person's heart, that evil thoughts come—sexual immorality, theft, murder" (Mark 7:21). James calls this our own 'evil desires' or excessive inclination to sexual pleasures and in a disorderly manner. Let us see the following verse, "but each person is tempted when they are dragged away by their own evil desire and enticed. Then, after desire has conceived, it gives birth to sin; and sin, when it is full-grown, gives birth to death" (James 1:14-15). When our hearts are not healthy, they can produce a nest of thoughts and evil desires that then turn into acts that displease the Lord. What can we do to prevent this? Jesus puts some radical measures into his speech.

III. Measures Against Adultery

The passage in Matthew 5:19-30 needs to be interpreted carefully, since one can fall into errors if one takes the literal point of view. For this, we need to make use of hermeneutics (science of the interpretation of biblical texts). This discipline teaches us that the Bible sometimes has 'idioms', figures and phrases typical of the New Testament time that should be considered carefully. Examining the new concept, regarding adultery and bad thoughts, we can affirm the following recommendations of Christ:

A. Spiritual Self-Evaluation

Jesus said, "If your right eye causes you to stumble, gouge it out and throw it away. It is better for you to lose one part of your body than for your whole body to be thrown into hell. And if your right hand causes you to stumble, cut it off and throw it away. It is better for you to lose one part of your body than for your whole body to go into hell" (Matthew 5:29-30).

The phrase: 'if your right eye … or your right hand causes you to stumble …' calls for a self-examination of conscience. By studying in depth the original meaning, we understand that the phrase 'causes you to stumble' has to do with the 'traps' that seduce the human being towards the very act of sin.

The eye makes us imagine wrong things, and the hand has to do with actions that range from the small acts of adultery transgressing the law of God. Jesus' followers must evaluate whether their eyes or hands are inclined to commit an impurity. There are traps which can make us fall spiritually.

One of the traps or ways of passing time is becoming 'slaves' to the power of pornography. The pornographic industry invests millions and millions of dollars by feeding the lustful minds of people who have become enslaved by their sexual fantasies and, in many cases, have become addicted.

B. Take Radical Steps

To understand the expression, 'Cut it off and throw it away', we must again make use of hermeneutics. This tells us that a rhetorical figure very common in the time of Jesus was hyperbole which is a figure of speech that uses exaggeration; We should not take Jesus expression literally. He sought to create awareness of how radical our measures should be. For example, when we get home, and we are very tired from the work of the day, we often say expressions like, 'I am dead tired.' Are we really dead? Obviously not; it is an idiomatic way of expressing ourselves to refer to intense physical exhaustion.

Something similar happened in the time of our Lord Jesus Christ. He was not saying, 'Be half blind or just have one hand' as some fanatics have understood in the story. What Jesus was saying and is saying is, get away from the temptation or get rid of the thing that leads us to sin. We need to stop ourselves from indulging in lustful looks or circumstances that could lead us to commit a sinful act; this is what taking radical measures means.

On one occasion, a young man had to decide to end an entertainment that took him towards pornography; and he did it by disciplining his free time in things that kept him busy.

Christians must make drastic decisions when they are exposed to sin. This requires sacrifices in our lifestyles, separating ourselves from any kind of spiritual traps, and being self-controlled in our actions. A sanctified heart is the solution, and in some cases a specialist should be asked for help.

C. Consider the Eternal Consequences

Let's look carefully at the following verse: "...It is better for you to lose one part of your body than for your whole body to go to hell" (v. 29b). Jesus' intention is clear: Christian should deprive themselves or make sacrifices for the sake of their soul, always bearing in mind that not doing so, not having a clean heart before God, can bring bad consequences. The writer of Hebrews says, "Marriage should be honored by all, and the marriage bed kept pure, for God will judge the adulterer and all the sexually immoral" (Hebrews 13:4). The only way to have a salvific encounter with God is with a clean and pure heart, since without holiness no one will see the Lord. Otherwise, the consequences or destiny of adulterers will be eternal damnation (1 Corinthians 6:9).

Optional Questions:

I. Adultery as a very serious matter

- Why is this commandment: "You will not commit adultery" very serious? (Exodus 20:14)

- How was adultery punished in ancient times?

II. New Scope of Adultery

- What did Jesus consider to be adultery?

- How do you relate sexual immorality to the subject of adultery? (James 1:14-15)

III. Measures against adultery

- What do you think is the correct interpretation of the phrase about the eye: "... gouge it out and throw it away", or the hand: "... cut it off and throw it away?"

- Please give an example of a radical measure that a believer can take to avoid falling into the sin of adultery.

Conclusion

Adultery is a serious problem that is not limited only to the sexual act. According to the teaching of Christ, we can commit adultery in our minds and hearts. Faced with this situation, the believer must take radical measures and allow God's Spirit to perform surgery on the sinful heart.

The Value of Sincerity

Joel Castro (Spain)

Memory verse: "All you need to say is simply 'Yes' or 'No'; anything beyond this comes from the evil one" (Matthew 5:37).

Lesson Aim: That the students understand the true value of saying 'yes' and 'no'.

Introduction

Have you ever heard someone say, 'I swear, by my mother', or other expressions like 'I swear, for what I love most, that...', 'I promise you, by the cross of Christ, that I will not do it again' (among others)? 'An oath is a solemn promise, often invoking a divine witness, regarding one's future action or behavior' (on-line dictionary). Do we really need oaths to seek credibility? Is it correct to swear oaths?

Let's see what the Word of God tells us about oaths and their validity. Let us listen to the counsel of the Lord Jesus so as not to fall further into trivial oaths. Already the eighteenth-century preacher, John Wesley said, 'I am as afraid of murmuring as of oaths and blasphemies.'

In what follows, we will paraphrase our biblical passage from Matthew 5:33-37 to find the teaching of our Lord Jesus.

I. "... you have heard that it was said to the people long ago..." (Matthew 5:33)

Many theologians agree that the Sermon on the Mount is Jesus' greatest sermon. Matthew expands it more than Luke (Luke 6:20-49). Matthew wished that his recipients, the Jews (original readers of this gospel), could understand the true spirit of the law.

Jesus began his dissertation on the law from Matthew 5:17-20. He makes three clarifications regarding the law. First, He declares that He is the fulfillment of the law (v. 17); Secondly, the law has a purpose and must be fulfilled (vv. 18-19), and in third place, the law must be fulfilled according to God's pleasure and not merely as the Pharisees and Scribes understood it (v. 20).

Based on this last point, many were a little confused because the people believed that what the Scribes and Pharisees taught was perfect. In light of this, Jesus declared to them the practical way of understanding and practicing the law covering five topics: anger (vv. 21-26), adultery (vv. 27-30), divorce. (vv. 31-32), the oaths (vv. 33-37); and love towards enemies (vv. 38-48).

What is then the true teaching and interpretation with regard to making oaths? With the phrase 'you have heard that is was said ...', Jesus went back to the first part of the Bible, the Pentateuch, which is the set of five books of the Bible. From there, he reminds them of what had been stated before in three passages of the Old Testament that are very important: "Do not swear falsely by my name and so profane the name of your God. I am the Lord" (Leviticus 19:12), "When a man makes a vow to the Lord or takes an oath to obligate himself by a pledge, he must not break his word but must do everything he said" (Numbers 30:2), and "If you make a vow to the Lord your God, do not be slow to pay it, for the Lord your God will certainly demand it of you and you will be guilty of sin" (Deuteronomy 23:21).

According to these original commands, the oaths added a spirit of truthfulness and fidelity to the promise. No matter what the person has promised, he must intend to fulfill it. God does not want us to profane his name, because together with the oath, we bind our soul with obligations. Therefore, we should not delay in fulfilling it. These verses go against any unfulfilled promise whether or not the oath is carried out in God's name or not.

II. "But I tell you…"

Unfortunately, the religious leaders had profaned this commandment by practicing it in their own way and by failing to be sincere and honest (Matthew 5:34-36). In fact, they had failed to act honestly not only from the time of Jesus, but from much earlier. The prophet Jeremiah (Jeremiah 5:1-2) gives us the sad spiritual reality of those leaders: "Go up and down the streets of Jerusalem, look around and consider, search through her squares. If you can find but one person who deals honestly and seeks the truth, I will forgive this city. Although they say, 'As surely as the Lord lives,' still they are swearing falsely."

Jesus wants to warn us not to fall into the same religiosity of the Jewish leaders, who by acting falsely were not only a bad testimony, but also their hypocrisy led them to eternal death. So Jesus said, "But I tell you"; that is to say, in order not to follow the distorted teachings of the Pharisees, his hearers had to act differently.

The statement continues, "… do not swear an oath at all" (v. 34). This statement has two important connotations: one negative and one positive. Let's start with its positive connotation. With this phrase, Jesus does not condemn the serious and necessary oath. Long after the exhortation of Jesus, the New Testament records some serious oaths. For example, in Hebrews 6:13, we are told of the promise that God made to Abraham by swearing by himself. In 2 Corinthians 1:23, Galatians 1:20, and Philippians 1:8, the apostle Paul put God as a witness in many of his affirmations. Finally, in Revelation 10:5-7, we see the angel of the Lord taking an oath. These examples make us see that a serious oath has validity.

It is also valid if we have to testify under oath before a civil court. As disciples of Christ, our testimony should be enough for us to be believed; but if the secular judicial systems ask us to make an oath, we must obey. Often in civil courts oaths are made with a hand on the Bible, implying that the oath is before God.

From a negative point of view, when Jesus, expressed: "do not swear an oath at all", He is exhorting the people not to take the name of God lightly, because the initial spirit of the oath had lost its essence. God hated oaths made in hypocrisy. It is clear that a heart that does not fear God becomes indifferent to sincerity and honesty. Such a person seeks selfishly his own benefit without caring about his neighbor.

Nowadays, we live in a world that swears and vows it will change. If we were to ask a lady who has been mistreated time after time to comment, very likely she will say, 'But he swore to me that he would not do it anymore, for the sake of our children.' However, likely as not her life be snatched away by a violent man who swore he would change. Because of falsehood and hypocrisy, the words of many people are no longer valid and have lost all credibility.

As Christians, we must take care of what we promise. We have to comply, we have to be reliable. Sincerity will speak a lot about our personality, and if we get used to failing, we will be acting like the Pharisees and as a result we will incur severe condemnation.

Jesus knew very well the hypocritical heart of the Pharisees. They had classified the oaths into two classes: those that directly named the name of God, and others that related to sacred things. The first ones were of greater commitment, that is, they had to be fulfilled because they had mentioned the name of God. But with the latter, they had some freedom to break the oath, because they had not pronounced the name of God directly. Jesus was blunt in the face of this classification that the Pharisees had made in oaths; therefore, he said to them, "do not swear an oath at all: either by heaven, for it is God's throne; or by the earth, for it is his footstool; or by Jerusalem, for it is the city of the Great King. And do not swear by your head, for you cannot make even one hair white or black. All you need to say is simply 'Yes' or 'No'; anything beyond this comes from the evil one" (vv. 34-37).

The Pharisees believed that swearing by 'the temple', 'the altar', 'the sky', 'God's throne', 'the earth' and 'Jerusalem' was a light thing; nevertheless, Jesus makes them notice that it is the same, and even if they swear by their own head, because it is part of the life that God has given us.

So, some people have the habit of swearing an oath. Maybe they do not take the name of God, but they do swear by their mother or by another being or thing they want most in life. In order to be believed, they also swear by some sacred thing like 'the cross of Christ', 'the church', 'the blood of

Christ' (among others). God does not want this pharisaical attitude for his children. It is wrong to hide our apparent sincerity in certain things, or to try to convince others by using His name in vain.

We must take note, Jesus does not want to give us the same condemnation he gave to the religious guides of his time. Matthew 23:16-19 reports, "Woe to you, blind guides! You say, 'If anyone swears by the temple, it means nothing; but anyone who swears by the gold of the temple is bound by that oath.' You blind fools! Which is greater: the gold, or the temple that makes the gold sacred? You also say, 'If anyone swears by the altar, it means nothing; but anyone who swears by the gift on the altar is bound by that oath.' You blind men! Which is greater: the gift, or the altar that makes the gift sacred?"

For God there are no levels or ranges of oaths. Each one is equally serious and must be kept. We cannot swear oaths to justify vanity and hypocrisy. Jesus wants to show us a different path than vain oaths. He mentions this in verse 37.

III. "All you need to say is..."

A. "Yes, yes; no, no"

Jesus helps us not to fall into a mere religion by giving us a simple formula, "all you need to say is simply 'Yes' or 'No'..." (Matthew 5:37). For this reason, we teach within our Christian circles that a disciple of Christ, in order to be believed, does not need to swear by God or anything else when he or she makes a promise.

As sons and daughters of God, our testimony will speak louder than arguments and attitudes, and a good, sincere testimony we will gain credibility and confidence. We are called to be men and women of our word without having to use oaths. At the beginning of the third century, Clement of Alexandria said that 'Christians should live in such a way - that is, in holiness - and show such a character that no one would dare to demand an oath'.

B. "Anything beyond this comes from the evil one"

Swearing does not do us any good, and it can lead to condemnation. If we want to swear an oath by the name of God our Creator, we must realize that is not the will of our heavenly Father, but of the evil one. The Message version says, "When you manipulate words to get your own way, you go wrong" (v. 37). James exhorts us, "Above all,

my brothers and sisters, do not swear—not by heaven or by earth or by anything else. All you need to say is a simple "Yes" or "No." Otherwise you will be condemned" (James 5:12). According to the historian Josephus, the Essenes believed that whoever swore to be believed was self-condemning, because every promise that is made and not fulfilled brings condemnation. In closing, I share with you the following counsel of the Preacher in Ecclesiastes 5:1-7.

Optional Questions:

I. "... you have heard that it was said to the people long ago..."

- According to Matthew 5:17-19, what are the teachings regarding the law?

- What are the three passages of the Old Testament to which Jesus referred in this first section.

- What is the spirit of the oaths according to the previous verses of the Old Testament?

II. "But I tell you ..." (Matthew 5:34-36)

- Explain the two connotations of the phrase: "... Do not swear in any way ...".

  ◊ Negatively:

  ◊ Positively:

- Why did the Pharisees swear by heaven, by earth or by Jerusalem?

III. "All you need to say is..." (Matt. 5:37)

A. Simply 'Yes' or 'No'

- According to this affirmation of our Lord Jesus, where should our words or promises be?

- Read Matthew 5:37; James 5:12; Ecclesiastes 5.1-7 and explain why we should not swear when making our promises.

Conclusion

Every oath is in vain if our word is valid; and if our word is valid, it does not need an oath to be reinforced. Let us take care to be responsible with our promises to gain confidences and thus not fall into our own condemnation. The oath fulfills its purpose of making us hypocrites; Let us renounce this bad habit and practice sincerity, which is a purely Christian value. A sincere person does not need to resort to oaths.

Love Your Enemies

Wilmar Rojas (Argentina)

Memory verse: "Be perfect, therefore, as your heavenly Father is perfect" (Matthew 5:48).

Lesson Aim: To encourage the students to develop the character of the Father through forgiveness and practical love.

Introduction

Is the Sermon on the Mount still valid? Does it apply to our days? Do we put it into practice now? In the Sermon on the Mount, Jesus gives instructions on how His disciples should behave; that is, he describes the kind of life that God's children should live. Jesus initiates His teaching by emphasizing who the happy ones are, then, he explains the function and purpose of His disciples on this earth, and finally, he enters into the questions of the law and warns His hearers, "Do not think that I have come to abolish the Law or the Prophets; I have not come to abolish them but to fulfill them" (Matthew 5:17). Jesus came to show us the correct way to live.

The theme of life or death came up in the middle of this discussion. Ask your students to think about these questions. What does it mean to really love our enemies? Would we forgive the offender? That person who may have put our life or that of our loved ones in danger? Or the one who murdered a loved one or a friend? This is a crossroads where the choice is the path of revenge or the path of forgiveness ... Which would we choose? Here are two examples that can help to clarify the issue.

Good Guy

The Latin American international preacher, Yiye Avila, forgave his daughter's murderer. He was traveling on a plane when he was informed that his daughter had just died. He closed his eyes and raised a prayer to God. However, he suspected that there was more information ... and the truth was that his daughter had been brutally killed by her husband ... Yiye stopped breathing. He raised his hands, fell to his knees, wept and prayed ... When he got off the plane, there were many journalists who argued, "Your daughter's murderer deserves the death penalty, what do you think?" He answered, "I do not ask God to take his life, God will forgive him, as I forgive him." Despite the pain, Yiye did not hold a grudge in his heart. Later he said, "people have to coexist with evil, which is inevitable. There are wicked people, but there are more who are good."

Another Example

Peter was a police agent. He was recognized among his comrades for being very tough against criminals. However, betrayal knocked on his door. One day he found his wife with another man in his own bed. His chest cringed, anger made his blood boil, he put his hand to his waist where he had his revolver. His wife expected the worst, and the one next to her was terrified. Peter cried, he does not know if it was anger or pain or both. He left his gun where it was and turned around.

The people asked him, "Why did you not kill them?" This policeman replied, "I am not a bad man ... I could not justify my wife's action or forgive her, but I realized that if I was a good man, I had to forgive ... What greater harm I would have caused my children if I had killed their mother. Today I feel proud that I didn't kill them, although in the eyes of my companions I should have done it. But I did not do it even though he was my best friend. Peter was another good guy.

I. The law says,,"eye for eye, tooth for tooth, hand for hand, foot for foot"(Exodus 21:24).

Leviticus 24:20 and Deuteronomy 19:21 address this same topic. And in the face of this question, we have to ask ourselves, is Jesus promoting passive resistance? Is it alright to let thieves steal our property? Would not letting them take advantage of us be an embarrassment to us?

To answer these questions, we need to focus more on the purpose of our talk: Jesus is asking that personal relationships be valued more than possessions (Matthew 5:38-48). In some way, all of us, when we think or feel that our rights are being violated, seek to put the perpetrators in their place so that they might learn the message "don't try to mess with me." However, the Old Testament 'eye for an eye' law was not given to incite revenge; rather, it limited the vengeance by demanding exact compensation for an injury without doing more harm than the other person deserved.

For example, Exodus 21 talks about the fact that if someone hurt their neighbor, they should die in the same way ... and not kill the whole family, as happened in many cases, where two families have killed each other until they become extinct.

Jesus is inviting us to take proactive steps, that is, to anticipate what is coming, prepare before the situation arises, so problems do not take us by surprise. I believe that Jesus is urging His hearers to take care of their actions.

- "Give to the one who asks you…" (Matthew 5:42a). In other words, before he steals from you, be kind to the one who asks for your help.

- "…and do not turn away from the one who wants to borrow from you…" (Matthew 5:42b). In other words, lend, be helpful, do not be greedy. Do not take advantage of the needy to take away the few possessions from others through the interests of a loan. If you have the power to do good, do it!

Let's be generous and compassionate!

II. Beyond the Law

Abraham Lincoln said, "Do I not destroy my enemies when I make them my friends?" Matthew 5:43b says, "You have heard that it was said, 'Love your neighbor and hate your enemy'". However, in the law (its statutes and commandments).the second part of this statement was never contemplated. In fact, it was added later by the Jewish rabbis. Those they considered as their brothers, 'their neighbors', were only those of their country.

Apparently, this also happened with many other parts of the law. For this reason, Jesus spoke against them for widening their robes to put more phylacteries (boxes or wrappings with passages of the Scriptures) in their garments. Jesus did not condemn so much that they had added to Scripture, but rather the fact that they did not comply with the law although they demanded vehemently that others keep it (Matthew 23:1-5).

The natural thing is to love those who love us, and reject and judge those who are hostile to us. Faced with this, God says, "Good people obtain favor from the Lord, but he condemns those who devise wicked schemes" (Proverbs 12:2). Therefore, God is responsible for judging; it's His job, He knows every heart.

But Jesus says to us, "… But I tell you, love your enemies and pray for those who persecute you" (Matthew 5:44).

God is just. If He forgives us, He also wants us to forgive those who commit evil actions. We deserve death. Nevertheless, God gave us life. God wants to share that same life with those who need it. Paul says, "Our Scriptures tell us that if you see your enemy hungry, go buy that person lunch, or if he's thirsty, get him a drink. Your generosity will surprise him with goodness. Don't let evil get the best of you; get the best of evil by doing good" (Romans 12:20 MSG).

Let's think about how many neighborhood battles would end right now if we were just obedient to one of the commandments contemplated in the law: "Do not seek revenge or bear a grudge against anyone among your people, but love your neighbor as yourself. I am the Lord" (Leviticus 19:18).

III. The true purpose of the law

On one occasion, speaking with an individual about the plan of salvation, a man declared: "I know that God wants to save me and that there is a better life in Him, but I cannot follow Him, because if I follow Him, I must obey what He says. And God says that I must forgive my enemy ... and I cannot forgive Luis, he is a wretch, a liar, a usurer and a thief."

Loving an enemy is something distinctive of Christian life. God respects all people and He shows it by giving us all the rain that falls on everyone. In the same way, we must act by granting forgiveness to those who offend us. In this way people will see that we are true children of God. Is it easy? No way, but it is possible when the Holy Spirit dwells in us.

Ask the students if they have encountered people who, after forgiving someone, have begun to heal? Haven't we noticed that when we get angry, our muscles and joints get tense? Doctors tell us that when we get angry, our body reacts negatively producing harmful substances that affect our body.

Forgiveness has eternal reward as well as peace now. Many people, after forgiving someone, have received peace and health, and above all things, the one who forgives is freed from bitterness and shows the Father's love in his life. There are still more rewards:

- A clear distinction is established in the life of the believer.

- God is glorified. If a family rejoices when two of its members are reconciled, can you imagine the face of God when two individuals are reconciled?

- And above all, our character begins to look more like that of the Father. This is the supreme purpose: to be like the Father … Perfect! Perfect in unity, perfect in the same feeling, perfect during the test, being perfected through it.

In the Bible, there are two marked historical periods: the period of the law and the period of grace. The period of the law was inaugurated through Moses on Mount Sinai; and the period of grace was inaugurated through Jesus Christ on Calvary.

However, we must bear in mind that the period of the law has not disappeared (the moral law, not the ceremonial law of Israel), because it is still in force. The following commandments, "You shall not murder…You shall not steal. You shall not give false testimony against your neighbor" (Exodus 20:13-16) even today are punishable by law.

In relation to the above, the issue is not to comply with or not comply with the law. Certainly, this must always be fulfilled. The difference is that now, as Jesus dwells in us, we are enabled from within to fulfill the law, through the new covenant, sealed with the sacrifice and shedding of the blood of the Lord Jesus Christ on Calvary. He is the one who produces in us the desire to do God's will. He who saved us is faithful, and He helps us to fulfill the law if we live in the power of his Spirit.

It is impossible to achieve it by ourselves, we need to be in continuous contact with God and filled with the Holy Spirit so that together we can fulfill our mission. In this way, we will be ambassadors, agents of God's grace and love. And we do not do this out of duty, but we do it out of love for the Lord who gave everything for us.

Emmanuel means 'God with us.' It is wonderful to know that Jesus comes to dwell with us! What does He demand of us? That we love our neighbor, and that we forgive those who offends us.

Ask the students to write on a piece of paper the name of a relative or person who may have hurt them. We need to read the name on the paper several times and that way we can get rid of the weight in our hearts caused by the pain. When we see those who have offended us, give them a big hug and tell them how much we love them and that we forgive them. The result will surprise us.

We should not be discouraged if we are rejected. The point is that in healing others, we heal our own souls.

Optional Questions

I. The law says, "eye for eye, tooth for tooth, hand for hand, foot for foot."

- What is the teaching in these verses: Exodus 21:24, Leviticus 24:20, and Deuteronomy 19:21?

- What was the purpose of the commandments mentioned above?

- How are the verses in question contrasted with the teachings of our Lord Jesus as indicated in Matthew 5:38-48?

II. Beyond the law

- How can we put into practice each day Matthew 5:44: "But I tell you, love your enemies and pray for those who persecute you?"

III. The true purpose of the law

- Being honest with yourself, and evaluating difficult situations that you have had to live, do you really believe that it is possible to forgive? Why or why not?

- What benefits do you find in forgiving?

Conclusion

Do we really want to forgive our enemies? The best solution is not to have any! We need to remember too that we have been "crucified with Christ." The dead have no rights; and if we do not have rights, they cannot be violated.

Generosity Without Praise

Myriam Pozzi (Argentina)

> **Memory verse:** "Each of you should give what you have decided in your heart to give, not reluctantly or under compulsion, for God loves a cheerful giver" (2 Corinthians 9:7).
>
> **Lesson Aim:** To learn the correct attitude and manner in which God wants us to help the needy.

Introduction

The following command, "But when you give to the needy, do not let your left hand know what your right hand is doing" (Matthew 6:3b), has become a popular saying so much so that many people do not even know its origin. Ask one or two of your students to share briefly how they interpret the command.

The media usually gives notoriety to artists, athletes, TV presenters, celebrities, etc. who dedicate their lives to charitable works. For example, Michael Jackson devoted much of his efforts and financial resources to humanitarian aid. For this reason, the Guinness Book of Records described him as the artist who donated the most money to charities in history. Shakira is a Goodwill Ambassador for UNICEF and has her own Foundation called 'Pies Descalzos' (bare feet), which has donated ten thousand pairs of shoes to poor children from Barranquilla, her hometown in Colombia.

Angelina Jolie is a UNHCR Goodwill Ambassador, and an advocate for the human rights of war or poverty of refugees in Darfur, Sierra Leone, Tanzania and Pakistan, among others, for whom she donates a lot of money. Oprah Winfrey donated more than 50 million dollars for charity. Ask your students if "But when you give to the needy, do not let your left hand know what your right hand is doing" (Matthew 6:3b) is true in the case of these celebrities?

I. The wrong way: looking for human recognition

From the examples in the introduction, can we infer that there is an incorrect way to help other people? If the goal is to help, does it matter or not how we do it? The Word of God is clear and warns us about the following:

A. Giving alms as the hypocrites

The dictionary defines hypocrisy as, "the practice of claiming to have moral standards or beliefs to which one's own behavior does not conform; pretense". Hypocrisy is a subtle sin. Jesus denounced the hypocrisy of the scribes and Pharisees who did things to be seen by men.

Let's look at following passages:

Mark 12:38-40 says, "As he taught, Jesus said, 'Watch out for the teachers of the law. They like to walk around in flowing robes and be greeted with respect in the marketplaces and have the most important seats in the synagogues and the places of honor at banquets. They devour widows' houses and for a show make lengthy prayers. These men will be punished most severely'."

Luke 11:43 says, "Woe to you Pharisees, because you love the most important seats in the synagogues and respectful greetings in the marketplaces."

Luke 20:46 says, "Beware of the teachers of the law. They like to walk around in flowing robes and love to be greeted with respect in the marketplaces and have the most important seats in the synagogues and the places of honor at banquets."

Ask your students: what were Pharisees, scribes and leaders of the synagogues doing that Jesus had accused them of being hypocrites?

There are two issues here to be taken into account as Christian followers: giving to the needy and the attitude of the giver. In fact, giving to the needy is a duty in which all the disciples of Christ must take part without exception. But what is important is not so much the amount, some people do not earn much, but rather the attitude of the person who is giving to others.

Giving for those in need is a kind action born of compassion and mercy for the unfortunate that appears repeatedly in the law of Moses. God has special consideration for the poor, and ordered His people to take care of foreigners, orphans and widows, who in those times represented the most destitute and despised.

Leviticus 25:35 talks about how the poor should be treated. Deuteronomy 15:7-8 talks about actions for the needy, and Deuteronomy 26:12 refers to how to care for Levites, foreigners, orphans and widows.

It is true that giving to the poor and needy will not take us to heaven; but it is also true that we cannot go to heaven without good works. In fact, compassionate caring for others is part of the pure religion of which James speaks (1:27).

Jesus approved of the practice of giving to the needy but he cautioned against doing it for selfish reasons or with lack of sincerity. Our Lord encourages us to be generous to the poor, even to the point of real personal sacrifice, as proof of Christian character and integrity.

B. Giving to the poor to seek praise

The worldly mentality of the scribes and Pharisees whom Jesus confronted led them to have a hypocritical attitude. They gave their offerings to seek approval and be praised for their generosity without taking into account God's approval. Giving to the needy, prayer and fasting are three Christian duties with which Christians pay homage and service to God. In prayer, the soul is involved; in fasting, the body; and in giving, our resources. So as children of God, we should not just turn away from evil; but we must do good, and do it well. That is, without hypocrisy and without seeking to be approved and praised by others. The three elements mentioned, prayer, fasting and giving alms, go together if we want to serve and honor God and men.

C. Giving alms for the wrong reasons

They say that there was a custom in olden times in the East where water was scarce. In many places it had to be bought. When a person wanted to do a good deed, and bring blessing on his family, he would address the water carrier and in a loud voice would tell him: 'Give a drink to the thirsty!' The water carrier filled the wineskin and went to the water market. 'Oh, thirsty one,' he would cry out, 'come drink out of grace!' The generous one, who was at his side, said, 'Bless me, because I am the one who offers you this gift.'

This is a clear example of incorrect motivations, such as pride, ostentation and a desire to get the interest or esteem of the people, and to be praised. The religious leaders in Jesus' time did their prayers on the streets and in the synagogue so that they could be observed and recognized as good men.

Neither should we give with sadness but with joy. Some give reluctantly, with real regret and pain. Once a pastor said, 'If you feel that you are giving too much and that it hurts, you must ask God to lower His income needs.'

II. The right way: God's way

The passage in Matthew 6:1-4 clearly invites us to give in a different way to how the world often acts. We must do it in obedience to God, for love and compassion for the poor. We must remember the promise given to those who are sincere and humble as they give to the needy.

A. Our good deeds are observed

Jesus said, 'Let your alms be a secret, and then your Father who sees in secret will reward you.' We may not even be recognized for our good actions, but God sees both our good as well as our bad deeds. He sees them all. God also sees when injustices are done to us (Psalm 38:14-15). He sees the good done by us even when we do not observe the consequences of our actions.

In this part of the lesson, it would be interesting if a student who has seen the movie 'Pay it forward' can comment on the unsuspected results that a good action can have.

God sees hypocritical actions which will bring their own consequences. Sincere Christians can be assured of consolation and hope. But this is not all, God does not just see, He also rewards us.

B. He rewards us

Jesus not only observes and praises the correct way of giving to the poor and needy, but He Himself will reward such actions openly. Hebrews 11:6 says, "And without faith it is impossible to please God, because anyone who comes to him must believe that he exists and that he rewards those who earnestly seek him."

The reward comes from God. The right way to be a cheerful giver also has to do with surrendering to Him. God will reward us as our Father, not as a teacher or patron who gives to his servant what they have earned, what is just and nothing else. As a father, He gives abundantly and without restrictions to His child who serves him.

The reward that God gives is not only abundant, it is also open to all children receiving it without distinction. It is not just for the present, but it will also be for the future, in the great day. He himself will give us the reward He promised to Abraham in the beginning (Genesis 15:1).

C. There are different types of rewards

A reward is an incentive that is offered to someone for the accomplishment of a task.

According to Proverbs 11:24-25, we are sometimes rewarded in abundance with material things, "It is possible to give away and become richer! It is also possible to hold on too tightly and lose everything. Yes, the generous person shall be rich! By watering others, he waters himself."

At other times, we are rewarded with security in times of adversity or need, "The wicked borrow and do not repay, but the righteous give generously; those the Lord blesses will inherit the land, but those he curses will be destroyed. The Lord makes firm the steps of the one who delights in him; though he may stumble, he will not fall, for the Lord upholds him with his hand. I was young and now I am old, yet I have never seen the righteous forsaken or their children begging bread" (Psalm 37:21-25).

Psalm 41:1-2 says that our reward is help in anguish, and Psalm 112:9 states that they who have freely scattered their gifts to the poor, their righteousness endures forever; their horn will be lifted high in honor.

In Luke 14:14, it says that we will be rewarded in the resurrection of the righteous with eternal riches. We will receive different rewards; but equally, we will all receive rewards.

III. It is a duty that we cannot avoid

A. We always need to give

Jesus warned us that we would always have the poor with us. There is a saying that, 'The riches that you give to others is the only form of wealth that you will always keep.' We need to show compassion to those who are poor and needy. God himself is compassionate and we must be His imitators.

Alms is a word that has almost stopped being used. Formerly, beggars in the streets or at the doors of churches stretched out their hands and said, "Alms, please." "Alms" comes from a Greek word meaning "compassion, mercy or mercy."

We could say today that alms are food, money or objects that we give to the poor as an act of charity.

God was the first to show gestures of charity with mankind. In material help to the needy, we must be imitators of God.

B. As we proposed in our heart

When Paul says to the Corinthians, "Each of you should give what you have decided in your heart to give..." (2 Corinthians 9:7), he was not forcing them to give or pressuring them to do so. He took for granted that in the hearts of those Christians there was already the desire to give.

The gift needs to be well thought out, planned. This involves the idea of having thought of two things: first, of the need of the brother or sister; and second, on how it can be given. That is to say, what steps can be taken to meet this need.

C. God loves the cheerful giver

Joy is the right attitude for the one who gives. Obviously, we cannot hide our joy. Whoever receives will also be joyful. Whether we give our money, resources, time or feelings, let us do it with joy, giving free rein to what God puts in our hearts. Charles Spurgeon said, 'One thing I know, a cheerful giver always wants to be able to give ten times more than he is able to give.'

How can we hide what the left hand does from the right if both belong to the same body? It is a hyperbole without doubt that involves hiding as much as possible; that is, keeping our works private without the need to publish them. The meaning is that we should not be concerned about what other people think of how we have helped others, so as not to run the risk of falling into pride.

Optional Questions
I. The wrong way: looking for human recognition
- Who would be the destitute and despised today?
- Think about the characteristics of the groups mentioned above.

II. The right way: God's way
- What do these passages teach us about giving to the needy? (Proverb 11:24- 25, Psalm 37:21-25, Psalm 41:1-2)
- What do you think should be the greatest motivation we should have to give?

III. It is a duty that we cannot avoid
- Do you consider that when we give, we should expect a reward?
- What benefits can we receive if we give to those in need in the way that God asks us; that is, without expecting anything in return?

Conclusion
We give because we must do it, because it flows from a heart that wants to please God, and we renounce helping to be noticed by others. We hide our actions not only from others, but also in humility we hide them from our own ego. The right hand can be used to help the poor, and the left also. Let us place our hands at the service of the needy.

Prayer Acceptable to God

Litzy Vidaurre (Spain)

<table>
<tr><td>Lesson
8</td></tr>
</table>

Memory verse: "The eyes of the Lord are on the righteous, and his ears are attentive to their cry" (Psalm 34:15).

Lesson Aim: To realize that God is interested in our attitude and intention when we pray.

Introduction

Many of us were taught prayers when we were children. Ask the students to remember and share some of those prayers they were taught and that we teach our children now. For example, saying grace before meals, or before going to bed: "In peace I will lie down and sleep, for you alone, Lord, make me dwell in safety" (Psalm 4:8). This is a Psalm that we often use as a prayer to go to sleep. Many of these sentences are mechanical phrases that we learn and repeat almost daily. Ask the students to share with the class some of these prayers that they themselves use.

In this lesson, we will see how Jesus instructs his disciples on what sort of prayer is acceptable to God. First, we will see what the Pharisees and Gentiles did in their prayers, and what God disapproved of in light of Matthew 6:5-8.

I. The prayer that is unacceptable to God

The first thing we must highlight about this passage is that Jesus assumes that all his disciples pray: "And when you pray, do not be like the hypocrites, for they love to pray standing in the synagogues and on the street corners to be seen by others. Truly I tell you, they have received their reward in full" (Matthew 6:5). This verse helps us to understand that prayer was a common practice among the Jews; therefore, here he is not telling them to pray, but he is giving them specific guidelines on how they should pray. At this point, Jesus teaches them about how they should not pray and who they should not imitate.

A. Do not pray like the Pharisees

1. The Problem of Hypocrisy

The first warning that Jesus gives his disciples in this passage is 'do not be like the hypocrites.' Jesus does not make it clear who he refers to as hypocrites,

but it goes without saying that he was talking about the Pharisees of his time. The word "hypocrite" (Gr. Hippocrites) denotes an actor on stage. It was the custom among Greek and Roman actors to speak in large masks with mechanical devices to increase the power of the voice. Hence this term came to be used to denote a deceiver, a hypocrite. On stage, the actors left their true identity to play a role in the play. In this sense, we cannot say that the actors were being deceitful, pretending to be who they were not.

However, the problem with the religious hypocrite is that he does deceive deliberately. This is what Jesus really condemns: pretending to be pious in public to receive applause. To receive the praise and recognition of the public around them was for them the most important thing ... the reward they wanted to receive.

2. The problem of showing off

Actually, it was not so important to pray in this or that place, or whether they prayed standing or kneeling. In fact, it was common to pray standing in the synagogues or on the street. Jesus does not condemn either the position or the place of prayer. He does not condemn praying in public either, since on several occasions we see that he himself went to the synagogue to pray. The problem can be identified when Jesus says that they 'love to pray standing in the synagogues and on the street corners to be seen by others.' Hypocrites loved the most public places where there were more people to admire their piety. So, they made the streets and synagogues their theaters. The emphasis is placed on the intention at the time of prayer. It was evident that the Pharisees did not love to pray to speak with God, but rather to 'be seen' by people. They wanted to flaunt a false pity before others, preferring the admiration and approval of those around them rather than receiving God's approval.

B. Do not pray like the Gentiles

1. They used vain repetitions

In the second part of Matthew 6:7, Jesus points out the unnecessary practice of the Gentiles in praying ... they said vain repetitions. It is worth clarifying that Jesus does not condemn repeating a prayer, for in Gethsemane we see that Jesus repeated the same prayer three times: "So he left them and went away once more and prayed the third time, saying the same thing" (Matthew 26:44).

In Luke 18:1-8, Jesus even praised the widow's persistence, leaving her attitude as an example of prayer: "…In a certain town there was a judge who neither feared God nor cared what people thought. And there was a widow in that town who kept coming to him with the plea, 'Grant me justice against my adversary.' For some time, he refused. But finally, he said to himself, 'Even though I don't fear God or care what people think, yet because this widow keeps bothering me, I will see that she gets justice, so that she won't eventually come and attack me!' And the Lord said, 'Listen to what the unjust judge says. And will not God bring about justice for his chosen ones, who cry out to him day and night? Will he keep putting them off? I tell you, he will see that they get justice, and quickly. However, when the Son of Man comes, will he find faith on the earth?"

We can also see how Paul repeated a prayer three times since it had not been answered as he expected. In 2 Cor. 12:8 Paul states, "Three times I pleaded with the Lord to take it away from me." However, the emphasis is on the word "vain." So, it is not acceptable to God for us to use words which are meaningless.

The Gentiles had the habit of praying the same prayers to their pagan gods, shouting and shouting while repeating the name of their deity again and again. It made sense for them to do it, because they prayed to gods who 'had ears but could not hear.' In other words, their prayers were mere senseless noises.

2. They did not pray with the right attitude

Jesus also points out that they must not be like the Pagans: "…when you pray, do not keep on babbling like pagans, for they think they will be heard because of their many words" (Mat. 6:7).

Our Father knows what we need even before we ask Him. This does not mean that we should not be specific in our prayers; but God, like every loving Father, delights in satisfying the needs of his children. Therefore, it was not necessary to use so much 'babblings' to convince God to grant our requests.

Once again, the Gentile prayer was not carried out with the right attitude. Jesus disapproves of this behavior and practice and puts the emphasis on the relationship with God (our Father), and not in religiosity, much less in what we can obtain from Him.

Gentiles believed that the more times they repeated the same phrases without sense or meaning, the sooner their requests would be answered. They approached their gods with the attitude opposite to Jesus' teaching about establishing a personal relationship with our Father.

II. Prayer acceptable to God

Jesus not only instructs them about how they should not pray, but he goes further and teach them how to pray, giving them a pattern of prayer in the verses of Matthew 6:9-13. The Lord encourages his disciples to practice private prayer in intimacy with the heavenly Father. The center of ostentatious prayer before men is to get praise from the public, not to reach intimacy or the favor of God. It is possible to deceive men with that kind of prayer, but not God.

In contrast to the prayers of the Pharisees and the Gentiles, Jesus leaves us a pattern of prayer full of simplicity and profound intimacy with our Father.

A. "Go into your room"

As we have already seen, Jesus does not condemn public prayer, but condemns prayers made for audiences rather than establishing contact with our heavenly father. In fact, secret prayer is the best training for public prayers. Jesus knew this, so he instructed them by saying, "But when you pray, go into your room, close the door and pray to your Father, who is unseen…" (Matthew 6:6a). So, the best way to pray in public is to have intimacy with the Father in secret first. Prayer, in secret or in private, produces in us the necessary intimacy that enables us to pray in public and guide our brothers and sisters to establish the same relationship with God.

Jewish houses did not have private rooms. The only room that had a door and was private was the pantry or cellar. It was the only place with a door and without windows where they could be truly alone, without interruptions or distractions from outside. There only God could see them.

B. "Pray to your Father"

God must be the only and main reason for praying. Prayer should be directed exclusively to God and with the desire to please Him, and not for other people. In both public and private prayer, we must address only our heavenly Father with the sincere and pure motive of seeking His approval.

Believers should be clear that God must be at the center of our prayers, and we should only address Him. When we find that intimacy with our Father in secret, we will be truly able to pray in public as well. We must not approach God as any god; Jesus closes the doors and invites us to enter into an intimacy with our Father. With God, we can be ourselves, without masks or hypocrisies.

Likewise, in prayer, nothing more should be sought than the approval and acceptance of the Father. In fact, our prayer will reflect the kind of intimacy we have with God, and this will be reflected on the outside. Actually, there is nothing we do in secret with God that is not reflected in our actions, attitudes and words. Jesus calls this a reward in the second part of Matthew 6:6, but this is a reward of grace and not of merit: "Then your Father, who sees what is done in secret, will reward you." Are you seeking God's approval in your prayer? Or are you content with the applause of people?

Optional Questions

I. Prayer that is not acceptable to God

- What were the two problems of the Pharisee's prayer in the time of Jesus?

- Explain briefly each of the problems you just mentioned.

- What Gentile practice is referred to as "vain repetitions"?

- What was the real attitude of the Gentiles in praying?

II. Prayer acceptable to God

- What instructions does Jesus give us to make a prayer acceptable to God?

- What should I change so that my prayer is acceptable to God?

Conclusion

Jesus says, "when you pray" and not "if you pray". Therefore, He expects each of His sons and daughters to pray. However, we must remember that Jesus condemns praying to be seen and heard by men. Also consider that the place or position we use when praying is not so important. Prayers should not be vain repetitions. What Jesus really cares about is that our intentions and attitudes in prayer are pure and sincere. Our Father is willing to assist us if we approach seeking intimacy in his presence.

Notes:

The Model of Prayer and Fasting

Lesson 9

Eudo Prado (Venezuela)

> **Memory verse:** "But when you fast, put oil on your head and wash your face, so that it will not be obvious to others that you are fasting, but only to your Father, who is unseen; and your Father, who sees what is done in secret, will reward you" (Matthew 6:17-18).
>
> **Lesson Aim:** To learn how to apply Jesus' model for personal prayer and fasting in our constant communion with God.

Introduction

Prayer is one of the most important occupations of the Christian. It is not just a religious duty, but also a deep personal need. On one occasion, the disciples asked Jesus to teach them to pray. As a result, He taught them the Lord's Prayer.

By studying the prayer model of Matthew 6:9-13 we can learn how to talk to God daily according to His will. Along with his teaching on prayer, Jesus instructed about secret or personal fasting in Matthew 6:16-18. God is interested in us worshiping Him in a genuine way, not seeking the approval of men, but exclusively to please Him.

I. The Lord's prayer

Jesus' model prayer can be found in Matthew 6:9-15 (see also Luke 11:2-4). This is one of the most beautiful and well-known portions of the Sermon on the Mount. Throughout Christian history, the Lord's prayer has had great transcendence in many aspects of the life of the church. A Swiss theologian Ulrich Luz said, "The constant use of the Lord's Prayer has meant that there is hardly a Christian text with such a wide influence on spirituality, divine worship, instruction and dogmatism" (Ulrich Luz, 1993, p. 472).

But this influence has not really affected the dynamic of daily prayers following this model prayer, but rather, it has signaled other aspects of the life of the church, such as, for example, its liturgy and theology. The prayer model of the Lord is a guide or pattern to help us pray according to God's will.

A. A Model for Daily Prayer

The Lord's Prayer relates prayer to daily life. In Jesus' time, prayer was one of the three most important daily religious practices, along with almsgiving and fasting. But in practice it had completely detracted from the biblical sense. The scribes and Pharisees, for example, liked to make long prayers in public places in order to pretend to have piety before the people (Matthew 6:5, 23:14).

For Jesus, prayer was not a mere religious exercise; it meant daily communion with the Father. It was on one occasion when Jesus was apart praying that one of his disciples said to him, "Lord, teach us to pray" (Luke 11:1). The disciples were motivated to learn how to pray properly because Jesus had modeled His dependence on the Father in His daily and secret prayer (Matthew 14:23, Mark 1:35, Luke 6:12, 9:28, 22:41).

He then instructed them on the correct way to talk to the Father: "This, then, is how you should pray..." (Matthew 6:9). In his teaching, we can see that Christian prayer is distinguished from the various religious forms of invocation to God. He gave them a model of prayer fully consistent with the main themes of his preaching. This can be clearly seen in the various requests that it included. The Lord's Prayer (Also know and "Our Father" prayer) touches on themes such as the Kingdom of God, His omniscience, providence, justice, mercy, sovereignty, etc. Let us not worry about adorning our prayers with great rhetoric, but rather, let's be sure that our prayers are coherent with Christian theology and practice.

In addition, daily personal prayer is as important as public or congregational prayer.

The habit of praying only in congregational activities is not God's will for our life. He wants us to have a disciplined and fervent personal prayer life. The main reason is because prayer pleases God and keeps us bound to His will. It also has to do with one of the main needs we face, maintaining our communion with God.

B. The 'invocation' of the Lord's Prayer

Now, let us consider the structure of the Lord's Prayer. In the first place, it begins with what some have called 'the invocation': "Our Father in heaven, hallowed be your name" (v.9). For His children, God is not a punishing judge, but a loving and merciful Father. Here, Jesus spoke of filial trust. We have been reconciled with the Father through the sacrifice of Christ, and we have also received adoption as His children. The main guarantee of our adoption is the wonderful gift of the Holy Spirit (Romans 5:11, 8:15-16, 2 Corinthians 1:22).

The expression "Our Father in heaven" reminds us of the transcendence of God. The transcendence of God means that He is totally above all the created. Some prayers are of excessive familiarity and informality when addressing the most high and holy God. The Scriptures often speak to us of His majesty and infinity. In comparison all the attributes of finite man pale.

The following clause of Jesus' prayer, "hallowed be your name" alludes to the purity and respect with which we should give the name of God when praying. To ask that the name of God be hallowed is to ask God to make known the glory of his power and unequaled perfection. This model of Jesus' prayer leads us to a full certainty and admiration of the attributes of God. It is up to us to ask ourselves seriously if we are approaching God in the way Jesus taught the disciples.

C. What our Father wants us to ask for

Four basic requests follow the beautiful invocation (Matthew 6:10-15). Notice that they are in plural form. This makes us see that we should not pray in a selfish way, but also pray for the needs of others. These requests could be simply defined as follows:

1. The will of God is expressed in the following phrase: "your kingdom come, your will be done, on earth as it is in heaven" (v. 10). May the will of God be fulfilled and not that of the person who is praying. Some of our prayers seem to start with an excessive interest in the favors of God, rather than in his Person, or the fulfillment of his sovereign will. Jesus taught that all prayer should begin with reverence and be characterized by the recognition of God's absolute sovereignty.

2. The daily sustenance (v. 11). God is the giver of all good things and provides us with our material needs. He gives us the necessary bread in a timely manner. Therefore, we should not worry about our needs, but put them daily into the hands of God (Matthew 6:25-34). Paul says, "Do not be anxious about anything, but in every situation, by prayer and petition, with thanksgiving, present your requests to God" (Philippians 4:6).

3. Divine forgiveness (v. 12). Divine forgiveness is conditioned on us also forgiving offenses by our neighbor. The Greek word translated here as debt is "opheilema", which is often used to refer to moral or spiritual debts (vv. 14-15). Sometimes, it refers to a debt that we do not have the capacity to pay. Thus,

it reminds us of the unpayable debt of our previous sins. God has forgiven us by pure grace. In our prayer, we must express our personal incapacity for justice, in addition to the grace of God (1 John 1:5-10).

4. Personal sanctity (v. 13). The last request of the prayer model is help to face temptation and sin. In Luke 22:46, after his agonizing prayer in Gethsemane, Jesus found his disciples sleeping because of sadness, and he said to them, "Get up and pray so that you will not fall into temptation." Our firmness depends on clinging to the sufficiency of God's grace, because humanly, we cannot deal with sin. Therefore, asking for the holiness of God must be one of the main requests of the daily prayer of every Christian.

The prayer closes with a brief doxology: "for yours is the kingdom, and the power, and the glory, for all ages. Amen" (Matthew 6:13). This is a final confession of confidence in the perfection and sovereignty of God on which our faith rests. The model of the Lord's Prayer begins and ends with exalting God for his perfection and absolute sovereignty.

II. The power of secret fasting

The second part of our lesson is based on the same passage from Matthew 6:16-18 and contains Jesus' teaching about secret (private) fasting. Fasting is a special time of communion with God that is expressed in the abstinence of food, and that usually includes prayer. Fasting is looking exclusively for the spiritual bread of the Word and the presence of God.

The Old Testament fast was accompanied by various forms of dejection (Nehemiah 1:4, 9:1-2). He concentrated more on the physical expressions of pain that reflected repentance. In the New Testament, and particularly in the practice of Jesus and the early church, fasting is deeply attached to prayer as a form of worship and seeking the will of God (Acts 13:1-3).

A. Fasting is for God

In the time of Jesus, when the religious fasted they "disfigured" their faces so that people would consider them to be pious (Matthew 6:16). This means that they changed their appearance on purpose. Their pretended outward piety was only a mask to cover the breakdown of their inner moral condition (Matthew 23:25).

Although the Pharisees fasted strictly twice a week, their motives were not correct (Luke 18:12a). Thus, fasting by pure asceticism has no value before God. Much less if it is proclaimed to 'the four winds'. In this passage from Matthew 6:16-18, Jesus taught his disciples how to fast correctly. They were not to do anything to show they were fasting, but on the contrary, they were to disguise their fast well. The reasons and the manner of the fast were to be a secret between them and God (v. 17-18a).

Of course, it is difficult to hide the fact that we are fasting, and even more so when we are expected to participate in a normal meal. However, as soon as possible, we must literally observe Jesus' instruction to fast in secret. Finally, fasting seeks exclusively the glory and praise of God.

B. God's reward for fasting

When we fast, we usually seek an answer from God. Sometimes, it is about requests for material matters, and on other occasions, for spiritual blessings. God knows our words even before they are in our mouths, and only He knows what we really need. Therefore, He will always respond to us timely and adequately.

Fasting is not a meritorious work to force God to answer us about something. Fasting is a genuine act of worship. The teaching of Jesus in verse 16 of Matthew 5 indicates that the fasting of the hypocrites (probable reference to the scribes and Pharisees), had already gotten its reward. The Greek word that translates as a reward indicates a pay or salary. The 'reward' or payment of the hypocritical fast could well refer to the inconsequential reward of human admiration, or also to the rejection of God. Sincere, humble and secret fasting has great value for God. "and your Father, who sees what is done in secret, will reward you" (v. 18b). Jesus promised the public manifestation of God on our behalf as a reward for our intimate adoration.

Optional Questions

I. The Lord's prayer

- Which do you consider most important: the prayer in the temple or the secret prayer? Why?
- According to Jesus' model of prayer, how should we start our prayers?
- What is the appropriate way to close our prayers?

II. The power of secret fasting

- How was fasting done in the Old Testament, and how was it in the New Testament?
- What is the purpose of fasting in secret?
- What is the reward of the hypocritical fast?
- What does it mean that God will publicly reward secret fasting?

Conclusion

The Bible says that God honors those who honor him (1 Samuel 2:30). When we meet Him in intimacy, what counts is the integrity of our hearts. God honors our secret worship, in public. Both prayer and fasting lose their effectiveness if they are not an exercise of humility and dependence on the grace of God. Do we come to God secretly? Have we experienced God's reward for our secret worship?

Notes:

Treasures: In Heaven or on Earth?

Macario Balcázar (Peru)

Lesson 10

Memory verse: "For where your treasure is, there your heart will be also" (Matthew 6:21).

Lesson Aim: To listen to, understand and decide to follow our Lord Jesus' advice about riches.

Introduction

Who is the richest person in the world? It is likely that you know the answer, but according to divine thought, the richest person in the world is the one who trusts one hundred percent in God. In this lesson we will learn and analyze what Jesus said in Matthew 6:19-21, 24.

I. Where should we have our treasure? (Matt. 6:19-20)

Often people are centered on having money and material goods; that is their treasure. The world is governed by money and the accumulation of earthly goods. The powerful (that is, those who have money and own the resources of the earth) are those who manage the world. Countries arm themselves with money; they buy airplanes, ships, and submarines with money. Tourists move with money, and people in general make diverse moves based on money.

The avaricious accumulate money as treasure. This has been the case through the ages, because in every human being there is a need that must be met, and almost always material goods symbolized by money are sought to fill this need. This situation has led us to the division between rich and poor people on earth, wealthy and disinherited, overweight and malnourished, or where people live in mansions or shacks.

There are powerful countries that dominate, and poor countries with no power; there are bosses and workmen, economic slaves who barely receive enough for each day's food for their families, while others, in an hour, consume liquor equivalent of what a worker earns in a month, and so on and so forth.

The list is very long. In short, there exists a situation of inequality, inequity and injustice greater than the solar system in which we live.

In spite of everything, nobody is really happy with abundance of money. For this reason, the Lord Jesus, aware of this reality, declared, "Do not store up for yourselves treasures on earth…" (Matthew 6:19a).

A. "Do not store up for yourselves treasures on earth"

The Lord's command is for all of our well-being (Matthew 6:19). Jesus said this statement because he knew the heart of the human being, what our most intimate thoughts are, and what decides our daily life and future.

Why did Jesus say that we should not store treasures on earth? Jesus wants us to live up to the height and quality of what God wants for each one of us. He knows that we want to have assets and secure our futures. He knows that we do not want to go hungry or have no clothes. He is aware of how difficult it is when we suffer an accident or get sick. He knows that we try to accumulate treasures in order to meet those needs, but he also knows that everything is ephemeral, that on earth nothing is certain. It is for that reason he tells us what His will is. That does not mean that we should not make provisions for the future, but rather, such provisions must be made on the basis of submitting ourselves to the will of God.

1. On earth, moth and rust corrupt. We all know about moths. They can destroy food, wood clothes, etc. Moths seems so harmless, but their larvae work silently; they are very

destructive. Just like the moth, there are other elements such as rust, industrial acid, fungi and other natural elements that, as soon as we neglect them, destroy our treasures, reducing them to dust which will be thrown away as rubbish. Many accumulated treasures are silently destroyed by these natural or artificial elements, and we lose what we have put aside and have no comfort.

2. On earth, thieves break in and steal. Are there any countries where there are no thieves? Probably not. Even in the countries where stealing receives the death penalty, there are seasoned thieves who are watching to surprise and snatch away other people's treasures. Maybe one of the things thieves steal the most at the moment are cell phones. Thousands are stolen every day. In the news we hear about bank robberies. Every day people great and small are victims of robbery. In Jesus' time, there were no cell phones, but there were many thieves who stole what they could. One of the things that most depresses people is that, after accumulating money or goods for years, in a matter of seconds, everything they have accumulated passes into the hands of thieves who ruthlessly take their possessions and may even kill them. We too could be their victims, which is a possibility.

Our Lord, knowing the terrible insecurity that exists on earth, teaches us not to store our treasures here.

B. Have your treasures in heaven

Earthly insecurity is contrasted with the safety of heaven: "But store up for yourselves treasures in heaven, where moths and vermin do not destroy, and where thieves do not break in and steal" (Matthew 6:20).

1. In heaven, where God is and where we will live if we accept him as our Savior, there is no corruption because He is entirely pure and perfect. Polluting or destructive elements that we know on earth are absent in heaven. Eternity means that nothing is contaminated, destroyed or will deteriorate. Eternity, where we will be with Jesus, is perfect and endless.

2. In heaven, there is no insecurity. When we move into eternity, we will be absolutely safe, without fear. How can there be fear in a place where the Master and Lord of the universe is in charge? Never! On the contrary, thieves, extortionists, and the corrupt will be in hell forever. If we know and believe this truth, then we must live according to it. Not doing it means rebellion, malice and stubbornness. The presence of Christ in the heart and the faithful guidance of the Holy Spirit will make the difference in focus in our daily lives.

3. We can accumulate treasures in heaven. From our earthly present, we can accumulate treasures in heaven. The following are some suggestion about how this is possible:

- Committing our hearts and wills to Christ.
- Practicing the Christian stewardship of the tithes, first fruits and offerings.
- Sharing the Word of God with those who do not have it.
- Helping the needy, etc.

II. Where your treasure is, there your heart will be also

This is a truth that we do not always realize. Jesus states it clearly, "For where your treasure is, there your heart will be also" (Matthew 6:21).

A. The heart is the center of human decisions

The heart is the center of our thoughts and decisions. Everything we think, say and do originates in our heart. God knows it well, and He also knows that at times we attach to the unimportant and seek to accumulate treasures. Material treasure is so attractive, because it is related to our basic and secondary needs. For that reason, money captivates us, it catches us, and under the influence of human temptations, can enslave us. That's what the evil one wants. Satan wants us to crawl through the earth with a heavy load of 'treasures' that will be corrupted and destroyed, and can be snatched away by thieves and delinquents.

B. What we will become depends on the motives of our heart.

If our heart is trapped by material treasure, our life will be centered on earthly things. We will not be able to look towards transcendent eternal happiness. We will remain as slaves to perishable material goods. If accumulating wealth occupies the center of our heart, we may be able to leave a large amount of money or many goods in our will. However, none of this can free us from eternal death, that is, from hell. A lot of people live trapped by money or material treasures. Many of the wars past and present were fought for material gain (for example, the oil wells and refineries of the Middle East). Greed and avarice are often the cause of social conflicts, injustices, lamentations and disgraces so painful that they break our hearts. We humans can be free of that slavery for money and goods just by believing in Jesus and letting Him be the Lord of our lives.

III. We must choose whom to serve

The situation painted by Jesus (Matthew 6:24) is similar to that when Moses, in the fields of Moab, confronted Israel shortly before he died: "See, I set before you today life and prosperity, death and destruction. For I command you today to love the Lord your God, to walk in obedience to him, and to keep his commands, decrees and laws; then you will live and increase, and the Lord your God will bless you in the land you are entering to possess" (Deuteronomy 30 :15-16). Jesus presents two masters: God or riches; there's no others.

A. Riches as a master and oppressor

Who has not seen human struggles because of riches? In the last century, two world wars were the scene for more than a hundred million deaths because of the ambition to dominate wealth. In the present century, the powerful countries and the great transnationals move their pawns, 'horses, bishops, towers and queens' to control the other nations and 'checkmate' them in order to keep the riches of the world. Even in the evangelical churches we find those called great 'apostles, prophets and prophetesses" who with a mantle of piety, and at the same time with a lot of cunning, trick their listeners into giving them their money as they, as self-named 'servants of God' in stately mansions, with the latest expensive models, demonstrate that they are slaves of the god 'riches.'

Unfortunately, all that will end, and if they do not change, when they awaken in eternity they will be so poor and "masters" of the most terrible misery and suffering in the eternal flames of hell.

B. God is a Master who leads us to true happiness

God is a Master that leads us to true happiness. This reality will be ours if we submit to the only Master who can provide for all our needs. The Psalmist says, "I was young and now I am old, yet I have never seen the righteous forsaken or their children begging bread" (Psalm 37:25). As a senior pastor, this text has been part of my experience. Now I'm old, but I can testify that it's true. Instead of putting riches in the first place of my life (Matthew 6:33), I put God there and I am sure that as long as I live, His Word will be fulfilled in me. What do you think and how do you live?

God has not remained silent. He has spoken through his prophets, and very clearly through his only Son, who tells us to love God and despise riches. Again, riches are necessary, but they are second to our dependence on God. If we have received the ability to make wealth, we must remember this: God is the owner of all, and we can be very useful in his Kingdom if we decide to put Him first (Matthew 6:33), and put everything else under his will. If we do this, we will not regret it!

Optional Questions

I. Where should we have our treasure? (Matthew 6:19-20)

- In your opinion, why do treasures accumulate on earth? (Matthew 6:19-20).

- How are you accumulating treasures? What kind are these treasures? Where are you accumulating them?

II. Where your treasure is, there your heart will be also

- Do you know people trapped by earthly treasures? If your answer is affirmative, describe how they behave (Matthew 6:21).

- Write a brief testimony of how you are free in Christ of greed.

III. We must choose whom to serve

- Who are now masters, and how do they exercise that attribution? (Matthew 6:24)

- Mention three reasons to submit to God as the Master of your life.

Conclusion

The difference between happiness and unhappiness, insecurity and security, is about obeying what Jesus, the King and Owner of everything, commands. Let us make the decision to obey Him and experience the difference.

Solutions for Worry and Anxiety

Lesson 11

Macedonio Daza (Bolivia)

Memory verse: "But seek first his kingdom and his righteousness, and all these things will be given to you as well" (Matthew 6:33).

Lesson Aim: To learn that in our order of priorities, God should always be in the first place.

Introduction

Anxiety and depression are mental illnesses that are claiming many lives today. We read in the newspapers of people who commit suicide because they have debts that they could not pay. Many people are living under great anxiety and do not know what to do with their lives! Others have turned to anxiolytics, which leads some of them to become addicts.

Many people too are worried and cannot solve their problems. In this lesson, we will turn to the teachings of Jesus and study how to resolve anxiety according to Matthew 6:25-34.

We all need to be prudent and think ahead. The Bible teaches on the subject: "Ants are creatures of little strength, yet they store up their food in the summer; hyraxes are creatures of little power, yet they make their home in the crags" (Proverbs 30:25-26). Jesus also teaches that we must be good stewards by making wise decisions: "Suppose one of you wants to build a tower. Won't you first sit down and estimate the cost to see if you have enough money to complete it?" (Luke 14:28).

When are worries harmful? When we have wrong priorities. When we allow ourselves to be governed by wrong principles and values and are impatient. In Matthew 6:25, Jesus says, "Therefore I tell you ... You cannot serve both God and money" (v.24). In other words, we need to put God first.

Later on, when he was explaining the parable of the sower, He said, "The seed falling among the thorns refers to someone who hears the word, but the worries of this life and the deceitfulness of wealth choke the word, making it unfruitful" (Matthew 13:22).

I. Do not worry about daily needs

To understand the proposed topic, let's see a brief definition of the word 'anxiety: "a feeling of worry, nervousness, or unease, typically about an imminent event or something with an uncertain outcome" (Online Dictionary). Now that we have the definition of anxiety, Jesus' teaching on the subject will be better understood.

A. Do not worry about food and drink

Food and drink are vital for life and to keep the body in good condition. However, those needs should not mortify God's children. Does worrying do any good? Sometimes we need to be concerned about things, but this should be kept within the normal and natural parameters.

B. Do not worry about your body, what you have to wear

Many people worry about the shape of their body and feel they must follow stereotypes. The West promotes the Miss Universe pageant where the ladies are encouraged to be extremely thin. This idea that thin is beautiful has led many young ladies to the extreme of anorexia.

Men are presented with some very muscular models and to be like them, they undergo very hard body exercises and make economic investments, even to the extent of taking steroids to build up muscles. We are often encouraged to buy fashionable clothes which are often made by very expensive brands. We are encouraged to change our clothes as the new seasonal fashion kicks in. Buying clothes made by certain popular brands is the 'thing.'

Jesus says to all of us, "Do not worry... about your body" (Matthew 6:25). The care of the body is important, it is not bad; but it should not be the priority to blindly follow the latest seasonal fashion trends. The Apostle Paul said later, "For physical training is of some value, but godliness has value for all things, holding promise for both the present life and the life to come" (1 Timothy 4:8).

Paul is affirming that corporal exercise is profitable, although it is no comparison with piety which is important for this life and the life to come. Jesus' call not to worry about the body is not against beauty or aesthetics, because God made the human being perfect and beautiful. Sin is when our priorities are wrong. Many people make their bodies and fashions into gods, investing a lot of their money in these things, rather than in basic needs. Jesus wants to prevent us from the mental and physical illnesses which we expose ourselves to when we exaggerate in the care of our body.

We must make a difference between need and luxury. Necessity is to have clothes to cover the body: luxury is when consumer society pushes us to buy clothes of certain expensive brands. We need to exercise and eat healthily, but we must not exaggerate or make this a top priority.

II. The example of birds and flowers who do not worry

A. Jesus invites us to observe the birds

In Matthew 6:26, we read: "Look at the birds of the air; they do not sow or reap or store away in barns, and yet your heavenly Father feeds them. Are you not much more valuable than they?" If we 'look' at the birds as our Lord suggested we can learn that they get up early and sing as soon as the morning comes; they fly around searching for food; in adverse seasons, they migrate to other areas; they build their nests with such care and patience; they dig for worms; and they also bring food to their chicks which they have kept in their beaks. Wonderful!

Without a doubt, after looking at the birds' activities, we can see that Jesus motivated His listeners to be diligent and responsible. Birds are such busy animals that we can never learn laziness from them.

We are the crown of God's creation and of course, have more value than birds. Therefore, if we have our priorities right, we need not worry. God will provide when His children live responsibly, consecrated to their Creator. Let us bear in mind that if we live a life of holiness, we will not be the same as the people who are not Christians.

The Lord says, "Can any one of you by worrying add a single hour to your life?" (V.27). The different translations differ between "stature" and others between "life". To a modest understanding, instead of lengthening life, worries on the contrary can shorten it.

B. Consider the lilies of the field

Jesus, referring to the clothes that cover our bodies, says, "And why do you worry about clothes? See how the flowers of the field grow. They do not labor or spin. Yet I tell you that not even Solomon in all his splendor was dressed like one of these" (28-29).

Jesus is inviting us to reflect. Even if we spend a lot of money, we won't gain natural beauty. Artificial imitations are not the same as God's creation. It is said that the kings of that time wore white clothes which is maybe why he made the reference to the lilies of the field.

Jesus' comparison of King Solomon's dress with flowers leads us to think of an opulent and splendid garment, as well as one which cost a lot, all of which pales beside flowers. If he cares for flowers that are transient, how much more will He do for humanity that has an eternal destination? To those who strive for clothes, Jesus calls them "men of little faith."

III. The right priority in the life of the Christian has a reward

A. God ... the right priority

The Word says, "But seek first his kingdom and his righteousness" (v.33). That is Jesus' teaching; We need to worry about the Kingdom of God; it is a matter of priorities in life. The word "seek" is present imperative (keep on seeking).

Christians must recognize God as their King. He has dominion over His people, and they are heirs of the Kingdom. This implies continual dependence and consecration and absolute confidence: in other words, salvation. Therefore, it is also up to us to live within the values of the Kingdom because God loves justice and repels injustice. Christians must be busy in the expansion of the Kingdom through evangelization. Therefore, there will be a global interest in the missionary witness of the church - to proclaim the good news of salvation beyond its borders.

With regard to righteousness, John Wesley, in writing about the Sermon on the Mount, says, "Righteousness is the fruit of the Lord's reign in the heart. And what is righteousness without love? It is the love of God and all of humanity that flows from faith in Jesus Christ. It is a love that produces humility of mind, meekness, sweetness, resignation, patience and lack of worldliness. With every adequate disposition of heart toward the Lord and toward men will produce all the holy actions; everything that is loving or of good name. Love produces every work of faith and work of love that is acceptable to God and profitable for men" (The Sermon on the Mount, Sermon 24). Physical needs, however legitimate they may be, for a Christian should never supplant their surrender to the Kingdom.

B. Needs are met in addition

1. The promise of satisfaction of needs is for the children of God.

"So, do not worry, saying, 'What shall we eat?' or 'What shall we drink?' or 'What shall we wear?'" (Matthew 6:31). When the priorities are correct, we no longer need to worry about temporary things; because they will be added. When Christians live according to the values of the Kingdom, they are freely submitting themselves to God and, as a result they will have a different lifestyle. They will be organized and diligent. They shine like light in the darkness, and like salt that can preserve society. When we live correctly and in order, our needs will be met in addition.

2. Christians develop their gifts

We need to take advantage of opportunities and extend our influence through surrendering and placing our trust in God. We have the opportunity to witness to those who do not know Christ because we will practice Kingdom spiritual values. Non-Christians do not know God and their motivations are centered on material things; therefore, we must guide them.

C. Live one day at a time

We need to learn to live one day at a time. Concerns about the future should not be pretexts for neglecting present responsibilities. Jesus, teaching about the Lord's Prayer, said, "Give us today our daily bread" (Matthew 6:11). Yes, it is possible to live one day at a time. It is clear that concerns are necessary, but when they are exaggerated and become anxiety, they are harmful and can shorten our lives. The apostle Paul recommends a recipe to stop worrying: "Do not be anxious about anything, but in every situation, by prayer and petition, with thanksgiving, present your requests to God" (Philippians 4:6).

Optional Questions

I. Do not worry about daily needs

- What is anxiety?

- When is it good to be worried?

- When are worries and anxiety harmful?

- Explain the differences between needs and luxury.

II. The example of birds and flowers who do not worry

- Jesus invites us to observe the life of birds. What can we learn from them?

- What can we learn from the lilies of the field? What do you think about this?

III. The right priority in the life of the Christian has a reward

- God first. That is the correct priority. How do you know if your priorities are correct?

- What is God's promise to those who seek first the Kingdom and its righteousness?

- Why is it important to live one day at a time?

Conclusion

Jesus teaches us not to worry. It helps to look at the birds and the flowers that are finite. Let us rest by always giving our worries to God.

Relationships That Transcend

Raúl Soto (CHILE)

> **Memory verse:** "So, in everything, do to others what you would have them do to you, for this sums up the Law and the Prophets" (Matthew 7:12).
>
> **Lesson Aim:** To understand that the victorious Christian life is based on developing correct relationships both with God and with our neighbors.

Introduction

We are facing one of Jesus' most extensive sermons. In this, the Lord gives special emphasis to the relationship that a child of God must have with both their heavenly Father and others, basing such relationship on two important concepts: faith and prayer (Matthew 7:1-12).

Jesus gives clear and definite principles of how we should conduct ourselves in our interpersonal relationships. The passage for our study precisely shows us these two relationships: towards God and others. Jesus taught that the perfect relationship is based on giving love. Remember that love is one of the fruits of the Holy Spirit. Jesus summarized keeping the law in terms of loving God and neighbors. The Sermon on the Mount places us between these two relationships.

Ask your students to, for a moment, do an evaluation of these two relationships in their lives. To do this, they must put a score from 1 to 5, (1 = bad; and 5 = excellent). Taking into account their answers, ask them: What can we do to have excellent relationships?

I. How we give depends on how we receive

Jesus said, "So, in everything, do to others what you would have them do to you, for this sums up the Law and the Prophets" (v.12). For Jesus, victorious relationships are determined by what we give or what we do.

Many Christians have adopted for themselves the worldly humanist philosophy as a philosophy of life that is contrary to the Word of God. They just sit back feeling comfortable saying to themselves, 'I don't steal, or commit murder, etc. so I have a right relationship with God,' while others say, 'I do not get involved with others; I live my own life, that's why I have a good relationship with my neighbors.'

What Jesus really teaches us is that right relationships are full of life and activity; they are dynamic not static. It's not just about not doing what seems to be bad, we need to start doing what is good. As James says, "If anyone, then, knows the good they ought to do and doesn't do it, it is sin for them" (James 4:17). The Bible is clear, a good relationship both with God and with our neighbor depends strictly on what we do and give.

A. How will we be judged?

The Bible says, "For in the same way you judge others, you will be judged…" (Matthew 7:2a). One of the things we do most days is to judge others. We do it in all kinds of situations. This is one of the most deeply rooted problems in our hearts and is something that limits or prevents us from developing a right relationship with God and with our neighbor. The passage mentioned does not tell us that we should not judge, but rather it speaks of the way we express judgment.

The term 'judge' can mean decide, think, believe, consider, affirm after comparing, etc.

What this passage of Matthew teaches us is that we should not judge the internal motives of others in the sense of condemning them. We do not know or understand why another person or a fellow Christian has acted in a certain way. We can only see what they have done. God does not forbid judging good or bad actions. But the fact is that if you are hard on your judgments about others, you will be known as a severe person. The result will be that others will judge us strictly and rigorously. If we are tough in our judgments, what we will reap is censures.

B. How do we measure?

Matthew 7:2b says, "and with the measure you use, it will be measured to you." One of the things that we have lost in our relationships is the ability to put ourselves in other people's shoes.

Many destroy their relationships precisely by making rules too harsh for others and too flexible for themselves. Some people talk of the 'law of the funnel'. A funnel has two ends: one very wide, and one very narrow. The narrow part represents the way we demand others to act. We do not allow them to do anything that we do not believe is right; while the wide part is the way we measure our own lives, giving ourselves a lot of room to allow ourselves to fail and do things that we know are wrong.

Jesus teaches us that we must be righteous. He does not mean that we are to be too flexible but that we must be fair and balanced. Extremes destroy relationships.

C. How do we see others?

The Bible says, "Why do you look at the speck of sawdust in your brother's eye and pay no attention to the plank in your own eye?" (Matthew 7:3). Many of us live with very high standards, and that is not bad, but this can be negative if these standards are only applied to our neighbor.

At some point in our relationship, we have felt free to demand from others what we are not able to fulfill. We set parameters of Christian life very high, and when we see that they are not met by others, we are the first to judge harshly and criticize destructively.

Many Christians think that because they have already received forgiveness for their sins, they have the authority to walk through life looking at the mistakes of others. They are very tough about criticizing others, even their leaders. Typically, these people do not do much and are always criticizing everything.

Let's not forget that we have been called to love and not to criticize or judge. This does not mean that we cannot point out what might be wrong, but when our relationships are based only on criticism, we are in the wrong.

II. We cannot give what we do not have

A. How can you say …

"How can you say to your brother, 'Let me take the speck out of your eye,' when all the time there is a plank in your own eye?" (Matthew 7:4). In general, the one who is in the position of judging others believes that everything has been solved and that he is the solution to their lives. He believes that his words are the solution to the mistakes others might have make.

Many go through life giving solutions and looking at others as if they were sickly, while they consider themselves healthy, qualified to heal the sick. But this is the greatest deception that the devil has put in our hearts.

There is a basic principle of relationships both with God and with our neighbor; this is that we cannot give what we do not have. Let's reflect: How can we help a sick person to heal if we ourselves are sick?

Many make demands on others that they are not able to give. They ask God for fidelity in, for, and with their life, but they are unfaithful. They ask for loyalty in their relationship, but they themselves are disloyal.

B. First take the plank out of your own eye…'

Jesus also said, "You hypocrite, first take the plank out of your own eye, and then you will see clearly to remove the speck from your brother's eye" (Matthew 7:5). Jesus makes the relationship our responsibility. In order for a relationship to work in the right way, we need to change.

Many times, we think is that it is the other person that must change for us to have a good relationship. If we want healthy relationships, we are responsible for changing first, thus contributing in a very positive way.

In order to have a right relationship with God and others we must first change. So, wherever we look at it, we see that we cannot have good relationships if we do not live correctly. We cannot give what we do not have.

C. 'Do not give dogs what is sacred…'

Jesus also points out, "Do not give dogs what is sacred; do not throw your pearls to pigs…" (Matthew 7:6). While it is true that the Lord teaches us that we should not discriminate against people, in this passage, we find useful advice about taking a good look at 'would be' friends. There are many people who, because of their egocentric and proud nature, do not know how to value what we have, and they will end up trampling on what God has given us.

The aforementioned passage also shows us the reality of those who judge unjustly and severely who end up alone as nobody wants to be friends with them.

We must seek inner healing in order to establish healthy and lasting relationships. The psalmist said, "Guide me in your truth and teach me, for you are God my Savior, and my hope is in you all day long" (Psalm 25:5). We must learn to be able to give, keeping in mind that we cannot give what we do not have.

III. Ask, Seek, Knock

A. Ask and it will be given to you

Many see these verses as a key to ask for whatever comes to mind. Yet if we read the context, we will see that Jesus is teaching us one of the greatest problems for a child of God: how to relate to other people. Every day we rub shoulders with people of all social and moral levels. Some need our friendship and help, and we also need them and we should be close to them, while others just want to harm us. Although these verses may apply to other situations, here the three actions of 'asking', 'seeking' and 'knocking' refer to this problem.

Only in God can we find the inexhaustible source of all wisdom so we can learn how to relate correctly to others. We need a lot of God in our lives to be able to give the best we have to others. So, the first thing we must look for in order to reach an excellent relationship with God and with our neighbor is an internal transformation that only comes from a transforming experience of the Holy Spirit.

B. The Father wants to give us the best so that we can give the best

One of the principles of Scripture is that God gives us so that we can give. We have already seen that relationships are based on how we give. Now, the question is what do we have to give? If we want to give the best in our relationships, we need access to the best, and that only comes from a dynamic relationship with God.

The Scriptures shows us that if we, as human parents, want the best for our children, how much more does God, our heavenly Father, wants to give us the best. The point is whether we as children are looking for the best, or are we simply conforming to what we have, and building our relationships on it.

That's where we make big mistakes, because many times what we bring to a relationship is loaded with egocentrism, carnality or sin. This is obviously a bad basis for any relationship which will be affected. The key to this passage is that the Father will give us the ability to establish right relationships with those who ask for them. If we have a good relationship with God, we cannot expect the other party to be the one to take the initiative to be better in this relationship. We are the ones who must take that initiative.

God wants to enable us to develop these healthy relationships, but we must seek His presence as well as the necessary tools. It is interesting to note that Jesus closes by saying that right relationships will result in the fulfillment of the law and the prophets. Because by 'ask', 'seek, and 'knock', looking for God's guidance in prayer, we can live in the light of the 'golden rule'. God guides us so that we can live in such a way that our relationships lead us to live a life according to what is established by Scripture.

Optional Questions:

I. How we give depends on how we receive
- What does humanistic philosophy teach?
- What is Jesus' rule in Matthew 7:12?
- What do you think prevents us from developing the right relationships?

II. We cannot give what we do not have
- What does Jesus ask of us in Matthew 7:5, before we try to criticize others?
- Do you believe that what Jesus says in Matthew 11:29 is necessary for a right relationship? Why?

III. Ask, Seek, Knock (Matthew 7:8)
- According to Jesus, where should we go to find the characteristics we need to have in order to relate excellently with God and with our neighbor? (Matthew 7:7-11)
- How much would you be willing to give to be able to establish right relationships?

Conclusion

We are facing the principle of building lives that fulfill God's purposes. What matters most to us is to be able to fulfill what God's wants. As we have seen in these passages, being able to have right relationships allows us to fulfill the law of God and the Word given by His prophets. The life of a Christian depends on how we relate to God and to our neighbor. Let's reflect on this: do we have what it takes to develop these relationships successfully? Are we looking to God for what we need for these relationships? How much are we willing to give way in order to receive what we need to give?

Triple Wake-up Call

Jessica Nogales (Spain)

Lesson 13

Memory verse: "Not everyone who says to me, 'Lord, Lord,' will enter the kingdom of heaven, but only the one who does the will of my Father who is in heaven" (Matthew 7:21).

Lesson Aim: To understand Jesus' warnings, recognize false doctrines, and learn not to deviate from the truth about Christ.

Introduction

The Sermon on the Mount is cataloged as an exposition of Jesus as a teacher, and in it we find many themes that affect our spirituality. Let us attend to three great walk-up calls Jesus uses warn us.

I. A great warning

When we read Matthew 7:15-23, we realize that the Lord Jesus gives us several warnings; among them, that of watching out for false prophets (Matthew 7:15a). Who are the false prophets? To understand it better, let's search the Bible for some answers.

A. A Biblical Prophet

In the Bible, we can find several men who obeyed God's voice and took His message to their people. In this way, they left everything and gave their whole lives to guide the children of God. Therefore, we can say that a biblical prophet is a ...

1. Servant of God

Being a prophet is not a simple task, nor does it involve usually predicting what will happen in the future, as some think. In Amos 3:7, the prophets of God are called 'servants. In biblical times servants were often slaves. They were people who performed duties for a master or personal employer. A servant of God, then, is someone who submits to God's will and is obedient in everything, does not seek his/her own benefit, but does everything to glorify God.

Let's see some examples from the Bible:

- **Moses** (Exodus 3-4) was called by God to free the people of Israel from slavery in Egypt. He had his fears, but he trusted God.

- **Elijah** (1 Kings 17-19) was used by God to show that God was the only true God. In Elijah's place, any of us would have been frightened to see ourselves alone before so many people against us; but Elijah did what His God had asked of him.

- **Jeremiah** (Jeremiah 1:5). Before he was born, God had already separated him to be his servant, and even in spite of adversities, Jeremiah continued to obey God.

- **John the Baptist** (Matthew 11:7-11) was the last biblical prophet. His mission was to announce the One who would come from heaven to prepare the way of the Lord, although that cost him his life.

The common denominator in all of these men was their obedience to God's voice, no matter how difficult or hard it was to fulfill. All became servants of God by putting aside their fears, seeking to carry out God's plans.

2. Characteristics of true prophets

The Word says, "But the one who prophesies speaks to people for their strengthening, encouraging and comfort" (1 Corinthians 14:3). The Bible also reveals to us clearly what are the characteristics of the true prophets:

- They are builders. They contribute to the development and growth of God's Kingdom, working with God not against Him.

- They are exhorters. The on-line dictionary defines "exhortation" as: "to strongly encourage or urge (someone) to do something." So a true prophet is always encouraging and advising people to seek the will and holiness of God.

- They are comforters. As human beings, we all go through emotional problems. The prophet, as a servant of God, is there to give us those words of encouragement to help us to get ahead or to relieve our pain. They are like shepherds taking care of the sheep: if one is injured, the shepherd treats it and looks after it until it is better. A true prophet, then, is one who gives himself or herself totally to work in favor of the Kingdom of God.

B. False prophets

Jesus also warns us of those who pass themselves off as true prophets and are not. This kind of people has the appearance of people who are dedicated to God's service, but their true interest is selfish.

1. They wear sheep's clothing (Matthew 7:15a)

Jesus says that false prophets are like wolves dressed up as sheep. Matthew 23:28a says, "In the same way, on the outside you appear to people as righteous …" On the outside only they seem to be humble, sincere, apparently servants of God, but the reality is that between appearing to be, and being, there is a lot of difference. They give the impression of being true prophets but they are just pretending.

2. "but inwardly they are ferocious wolves" (Matthew 7:15b)

Why do these people pretend to be sheep or true prophets of God? Philippians 2:21 gives us the answer: "For everyone looks out for their own interests, not those of Jesus Christ." A false prophet only wants to take advantage of the flock of God in order to achieve his own desires. We can see this today where many prophets rise up preaching only what people want to hear. For example, they preach Prosperity Gospel, knowing that the only one who will prosper will be the preacher himself. This was true in the Old Testament. We read Micah 3:11: "Her leaders judge for a bribe, her priests teach for a price, and her prophets tell fortunes for money. Yet they look for the Lord's support and say, "Is not the Lord among us? No disaster will come upon us." Does this sound familiar? Well, Jesus had already warned us that many false prophets would rise up and deceive many (Matthew 24:11).

3. By their fruit you will recognize them (v.16)

It is undeniable that sooner or later the way that these people act will be noticed even if they do not want it to be. Jesus, our great Teacher, told us in the form of a metaphor. So, we cannot ask an orange tree to give us apples, even if we put up a sign that says 'Apple tree', and we paste the apple flowers on the orange tree. Sooner or later, when the time comes around and this tree will start to bear fruit, we will really know what kind of tree it is. The same will happen with the false prophets, because their own attitudes and behavior will betray them. Luke 6:45 clearly says an "evil man brings evil things out of the evil stored up in his heart." Matthew 23:28 says, "In the same way, on the outside you appear to people as righteous but, on the inside, you are full of hypocrisy and wickedness."

II. A Serious Statement

Because of these people who are deceiving and pretending to be what they are not, Jesus makes the statement, "Not everyone who says to me, 'Lord, Lord,' will enter the kingdom of heaven" (Matt. 7:21a).

A. What does the word 'Lord' mean?

The word 'Lord' in the Greek language is Kyrios, and in Hebrew it is Adonay. They mean 'God of the universe.' On the other hand, in the Middle Ages the word 'Lord' was used to give a title of honor to people of the nobility who, in general, had many possessions (lands, animals, etc.). And along with this title, they were given rights that others did not possess. When we say the word 'Lord', we are mentioning someone who is the owner and master of something; in this case, Jesus Christ, absolute owner of everything.

B. What does it mean to say "Lord, Lord"?

1. This is a very important statement.

For all that has been said above, to say Jesus Christ is the Lord is much more than a gesture of respect or a sign of gratitude for having saved us from eternal condemnation. In reality, what we are saying is that He is our Owner and Master. That is, we are his possession and that He has a right over us.

2. Saying 'Lord' implies doing the will of God (v.21b).

It is to profess Jesus, to embrace his teachings, to spread them and to practice them in our daily life in such a way that we inspire others to want to become servants of God as well. Sadly, it is not always like that. In Isaiah 29:13, we see how God complains against His people because they were worshipping Him only with their lips, but their hearts were far from Him. Let's take care that this does not happen to us. Let us be authentic and sincere with our Savior and Lord.

3. To call Jesus 'Lord' is to declare our obedience to Him above all.

He is to be the first in our lives and has authority over us. Luke 6:46 says, "Why do you call me, 'Lord, Lord,' and do not do what I say?" We cannot say that Jesus Christ is our Lord if we are not obeying Him in everything.

We can choose what to do. Joshua 24:15 says, "choose for yourselves this day whom you will serve…" Whom do we want to serve? Are we willing to do what He wants? Never mind what our friends might say. What should we listen to, what world says or what God says?

III. A Big Disappoint

"I never knew you" (Matthew 7:23). How terrible will be the final day if our Savior has to say to us, 'I do not know you, get away from me!' I do not want that to happen to me, and I'm sure you do not want it either. However, our Master warns us that this day of judgment will come and, therefore, we must take care how we are living before God.

A. There will be no excuses

According to Matthew 7:22, "Many will say to me on that day, 'Lord, Lord, did we not prophesy in your name and in your name drive out demons and, in your name, perform many miracles?'" Nobody is going to escape God's judgment; rich and poor; big and little ones; the just and the unjust; we will all give an account to Him. This is also said in 2 Corinthians 5:10, "For we must all appear before the judgment seat of Christ, so that each of us may receive what is due us for the things done while in the body, whether good or bad."

And what might we say to God when we are facing Him? Many will want to excuse themselves mentioning the gifts that were given to them, or the things they did in the name of God: "Many will say to me on that day, 'Lord, Lord, did we not prophesy in your name and in your name drive out demons and, in your name, perform many miracles?'" (Matthew 7:22). However, the Word of God teaches us that salvation is not by works: "For it is by grace you have been saved, through faith—and this is not from yourselves, it is the gift of God—not by works, so that no one can boast (Ephesians 2:8-9). God could not have made it clearer.

B. A very clear message

An example of this is seen in Revelation 2:2-5, in the message that God sends to the church in Ephesus. In verse 2, God tells him, "I know your deeds." One of the attributes of God is omniscience, that is, that He knows everything and there is nothing that is hidden from Him. God knows our effort, dedication and patience; But all this is not enough. In verse 4, God tells him, "You have forsaken the love you had at first."

Before men, we can pretend, but not before God. It will not do us any good to do great works in the name of God, even to do supernatural things, if our heart is far from Him and we do not give Him first place. Finally, God tells the church, "repent ..." (v.5) showing them that could have a new opportunity.

Optional Questions:

I. A Big warning

- What are the prophets of God called according to Amos 3:7?
- What characteristics does a true prophet have? (1 Corinthians 14:3)

II. A serious statement

- Where does the word 'Lord' come from and what does it mean?
- What should it mean to say the word 'Lord' in our life today?
- What did the law mandate regarding your neighbor? (Deut. 14:29; 15:1-11; 19:14; 22:1-4).

III. A Big disappointment

- What does Ephesians 2:8-9 teach us about works and salvation?
- What did God have against the church of Ephesus, and how does it apply to our life?

Conclusion

When Jesus comes back, there will be great surprises, even for those within the church. Where are the false prophets? We must be careful, for we too could be included among them! If we claim to be a Christian who announces or prophesies the coming of Christ, we must make sure we are doing God's will and bearing good fruit. Let us attend promptly to the call of obedience to Christ.

Meeting the Minor Prophets

An encounter with the minor prophets
The Father's Compassion
The mercy of God is within our reach
God's Judgments and blessings
Dealing with stuff now while we can
The power of fasting and prayer
An encounter with Micah
God of love and justice
A cry for justice and a prayer of hope
Zephaniah - God's anger against sin
All hands on deck
A prophecy for today
Which side are we on?

An Encounter With the Minor Prophets

Marco Rocha (Argentina)

Lesson 14

To Memorize: "He has shown you, O mortal, what is good. And what does the Lord require of you? To act justly and to love mercy and to walk humbly with your God" (Micah 6:8).

Lesson Aim: To discover the fundamental principles of the message of the Minor Prophets.

Introduction

One of the most frustrating situations is to try to establish a dialogue with a person who does not speak your language. Ask one or two of your students, who have gone through such an experience, to briefly discuss some details of the circumstances of a similar experience and to express how they felt about it. If none of your class has gone through such an experience, you can ask them to imagine the situation and ask for their reaction.

Start the class by explaining that, to avoid making our encounter with the Minor Prophets a frustrating one, we need to discover their main characteristics and the fundamental principles of the message they proclaimed.

I. A guide for the meeting

Just as missionaries must prepare themselves in the knowledge of the language and general characteristics of a culture in order to be effective in their ministries, we too need to consider different aspects and the context in which the Minor Prophets ministered. Ask your students why they think that most Christians often overlook the reading of the Minor Prophets?

A. Minor, but yes they are important

Minor prophets are not called 'minor' because they are less important within the biblical canon, but this classification refers to the fact that their writings are less extensive than the so-called Major Prophets. There are twelve Minor Prophets: Hosea, Joel, Amos, Obadiah, Jonah, Micah, Nahum, Habakkuk, Zephaniah, Haggai, Zechariah, and Malachi. In their prophecies, we find a message that can challenge us today; their message is very relevant. That is why, even though many of these passages seem difficult to understand, which might frustrate us, we must be willing to understand who they were, their personal characteristics and their immediate context. The Minor Prophets guard great treasures that we can discover for the benefit of our spiritual growth.

B. Getting to know another form of classification

The classification of the Minor Prophets, as we find it in our Bibles, is known as the traditional-canonical one. However, in this guide for our meeting with them, the chronological classification can help us a lot. We will even find some cases where the Minor Prophets coexist with the major ones. The prophets of the 8th century BC were Amos, Hosea, Isaiah and Micah, and it is likely that Joel, Jonah and Obadiah belonged to that period. In the seventh century BC, Zephaniah, Nahum and Habakkuk prophesied; these were contemporaries of Jeremiah. And in the 6th century BC, Haggai and Zechariah challenged the people to rebuild the temple. Finally, in the 5th century BC, Malachi prophesied approximately 400 years earlier the arrival of the promised Messiah and his predecessor John the Baptist. This classification according to the chronological order can be very useful for a better understanding of the historical time in which the Minor Prophets developed their ministry.

II. Exploring their message

A. An encounter with different literary genres

The biblical writings arose in the context of a culture very different from ours, and the Minor Prophets are not the exception. It is for this reason that we need to take into account the different literary genres used by these prophets in their writings.

For example, we will find genres of wisdom in the form of a question, such is the case of Amos 3:3-6; or genres taken from worship, as in Amos 4:4-5; or the judicial scenes, as described in Micah 6:1-8. There are also genres taken from daily life, as in Habakkuk 2:7-8. And finally, those known as strictly prophetic narrative genres, which included as essential elements the denunciation of sin and the announcement of punishment, and which could be directed both towards an individual and a people. This genre was expressed through certain actions or instructions that the prophet gave for others to do, showing those actions as truths that should be communicated, such as the case of Amos 1:5.

B. An encounter with the prophetic ministry

In the prophetic writings we find the result of ministerial work, a service to God, to the community of his time and also to us today. The prophets describe and interpret God's story and proclaim God's plan. During their ministry they were called different things:

1. *Ro'eh* (seer), used eleven times in the Old Testament, which describes the prophet as a man of exceptional spiritual perceptions.

2. *Chozeh*, used twenty-two times in the Old Testament, and also with the meaning of 'seer' but with a connotation of one who leads a contemplative religious life;

3. *Nahbi*, which is found three hundred times in the Old Testament, which emphasizes the strength and importance of the expression of the message and not in the vision; that is, it refers more of the function of the prophet as one proclaiming or announcing.

Both the word 'prophet in English and the word propheetes in Greek refer to a person who speaks on behalf of another. While at first glance throughout the Old Testament many may have the idea that prophets predicted near or remote future events, the function of the prophet was predominantly to be a teacher and preacher as a witness of the Most High and, of course, also as a predictor of the future.

The prophets were also known by other names such as: guardian of the watchtower, man of God, servant of the Lord, messenger of God, interpreter and man of the Spirit. Names or titles were used according to the circumstances and the place where they exercised their ministry. They were recognized for their austere and independent character, that they did not negotiate with men, nor with sin or circumstances.

The prophets were convinced of their call to holiness and that it was God Himself who commanded them. They valued their communion with God and were willing to act when they were needed, even if this resulted in insult and opposition. The prophets as God's ministers were fully aware that God was sovereign over their lives, which became more evident in difficult times. They were consecrated to God and

maintained an irreproachable character. They were also willing to criticize courageously the social ills and injustices of the world before political, religious or military authorities.

The prophets retained a conscious control over themselves, both in receiving and pronouncing the message. They were not unconscious instruments in the service of God, but they exercised their ministry without renouncing their personality and without putting aside their perception of their needs and those of their people. That is to say, the prophets were not passive instruments; they imprinted their personality onto the message of God, and hence the differences between them. The message was divine, but the language and styles were human. Micah, for example, who came from a rural context, received the same message at the same time as Isaiah, but he did not express it with rhetorical and courtly language, but with a brief and popular one.

Another aspect to consider when speaking of prophetic ministry in the Old Testament is its difference with priestly work. Although morality occupied an important place for the priests, they emphasized mostly the question of ritual and worship liturgy. However, the prophet emphasizes conduct and morals first.

For the prophet, behavior is much more important than the ceremonies. That is why they were seen as moral teachers for their times, reformers of behavior, and people who were in constant battle against sin, vices and moral downfalls, in addition to being against those who incited people to sin.

This is why the prophetic ministry is important for us today because it calls us to holiness and to prioritize integrity of heart above anything else. In this same sense, the Minor Prophets transcend their time, bringing us a message that is not only an interpretation of their time, but also challenges us to commit ourselves to the present and look forward to the future.

C. An encounter with men of God

In order to understand more deeply the message of the Minor Prophets, we must also approach the person of the prophet and the purpose of his ministry. Next, we will mention general aspects of each of them.

- Hosea: His name means 'salvation.' He prophesied between 750 and 736 BC. approximately, and his place of ministry was the Kingdom of Israel, in the North. The main theme of the book is the triumph of love. God's message to his people through Hosea is about the love that redeems.

- Joel: His name means 'Jehovah is God.' The time in which he prophesied is uncertain, although perhaps it was in the eighth or fourth centuries BC, and his place of ministry was probably the Kingdom of Judah, in the South. God's message to his people through the prophet Joel could be summarized as - God punishes sin.

- Amos: His name means 'strong' or 'brave'. He is probably the first of the prophets who wrote his messages, and he ministered near 670 BC. in the North of Israel, mainly in Bethel. The message that Amos preached focused on the righteousness of God over his people and the surrounding nations.

- Obadiah: His name means 'worshiper of Jehovah.' He probably prophesied between the eighth and sixth centuries BC. in Judah, and his message is divided between the destruction of Edom and the restoration of Israel.

- Jonah: His name means 'dove' and according to 2 Kings 14:25, he lived in Galilee. He prophesied in Nineveh during the reign of Jeroboam II, who was king of Israel between 787 and 747 BC. The message focused on there being salvation for the nations.

- Micah: His name means 'Who is like Jehovah?', And he lived in Moreset-Gat or Morasti, some 30 km southwest of Jerusalem. He fulfilled his ministry as a contemporary of the prophet Isaiah, between 740 and 700 BC. in the kingdom of Judah. Micah centered his message on presenting Jehovah as the defender of the poor.

- Nahum: His name means 'comforter', and he lived possibly in Ecos, about 30 km southwest of Jerusalem. He prophesied between 633 and 612 BC., and in his short message focused on Jehovah's judgment against cruelty.

- Habakkuk: His name means 'embrace.' He prophesied around 603 BC. in the kingdom of Judah. His message was divided between the punishment of Judah and Babylon, and the prayer of the prophet.

- Zephaniah: His name means 'Jehovah was hidden'. He probably prophesied in Jerusalem about 625 BC. in Judah, and his message described the punishment of Judah and foreign nations, and the salvation of a remnant.

- Haggai: His name means 'festive.' He prophesied around 520 BC. in Jerusalem, and the theme of his message was the exhortation to commitment to the construction of the temple.

- Zechariah: His name means 'Jehovah remembers.' He prophesied between 520 and 518 BC. in Jerusalem. The central theme of his message was the final triumph of holiness.

- Malachi: His name means 'my messenger.' He prophesied about 450 BC. in Jerusalem, and the central theme of his message was the denunciation of sin, the punishment of God and the promise of blessing.

In our encounter with the Minor Prophets, we discover men of God who, although ministering in a specific context, left a message which can resound in our hearts today with the same force.

Optional Questions:

I. A guide for the meeting

- Who are the Minor Prophets and why should they be called that? How else could you classify them?

- What would you say to a person who prefers to overlook the reading of these prophets by saying that they are difficult?

- What should we say to those who say that their message is not applicable to our time?

II. Exploring their message

- How does it help to know the literary genres for the correct interpretation of the writings of the Minor Prophets?

- With which of the Minor Prophets do you identify yourself with best and why?

- In what practical ways are you fulfilling, or intend to fulfill, your mission to preach the gospel?

- In the context we live in today, are you ready to make a difference by living in integrity and justice?

- Are you willing to proclaim the gospel message with courage even if this causes you to experience adverse situations?

Conclusion

God is the same yesterday, today and forever, and the message of justice and redemption that his prophets proclaimed will also help us to live according to His holiness.

The Father's Compassion

Lesson 15

Hernán Massacesi (Argentina)

> **Memory verse:** "I will heal their waywardness and love them freely, for my anger has turned away from them" (Hosea 14.4).
>
> **Lesson Aim:** To understanding the wonderful compassion of our heavenly Father and confess all sinful situations.

Introduction

Have you ever felt cheated? Did you ever give all on your part, and in return receive contempt, rejection, indifference? Did you ever experience the pain of betrayal? Or like Hosea, have we fully confided in someone, surrendered ourselves completely, opened our hearts fully, but the person we loved so much, little by little, began to move away from us, betraying us and exchanging our love for the love of another person?

Our news is full and overcrowded with these painful situations. Since we humans cannot fight them, much less avoid them, we try to live with them, as if they were normal, like the landscape definitely installed in a decadent and painful reality. However, nothing that we can do can hide the pain, the anguish, and the internal pain that betrayal and infidelity provokes.

This was how God felt when he called the prophet Hosea (Hosea 1:2) to live and graphically experience in his own life the pain that the Lord Himself was suffering because of the infidelity of His people Israel, the ten tribes that made up the kingdom of the North.

I. The Contrariety of Israel

- "But the more they were called, the more they went away from me" (Hosea 11:2a).

- "It was I who taught Ephraim to walk, taking them by the arms; but they did not realize it was I who healed them" (Hosea 11:3).

- "they refuse to repent" (Hosea 11:5).

- "My people are determined to turn from me. Even though they call me God Most High, I will by no means exalt them" (Hosea 11:7).

Although it seems contradictory, God's blessings had gradually distanced the people of Israel from God. They began to ignore God's law: "My people are destroyed from lack of knowledge. 'Because you have rejected knowledge, I also reject you as my priests'; 'because you have ignored the law of your God, I also will ignore your children'" (Hosea 4:6). That made them fall into the sensuality of the pagan cults, thus losing good judgment. "Prostitution; old wine and new wine take away their understanding" (Hosea 4:11).

Prosperity made them proud: "Israel's arrogance testifies against them; the Israelites, even Ephraim, stumble in their sin; Judah also stumbles with them. When they go with their flocks and herds to seek the Lord, they will not find him; he has withdrawn himself from them" (Hosea 5:5-6).

The blessings made them unstable and superficial: "What can I do with you, Ephraim? What can I do with you, Judah? Your love is like the morning mist, like the early dew that disappears. Therefore, I cut you in pieces with my prophets, I killed you with the words of my mouth— then my judgments go forth like the sun. For I desire mercy, not sacrifice, and acknowledgment of God rather than burnt offerings" (Hosea 6:4-6).

Abundance divided their hearts: "Israel was a spreading vine; he brought forth fruit for himself. As his fruit increased, he built more altars; as his land prospered, he adorned his sacred stones. Their heart is deceitful, and now they must bear their guilt. The Lord will demolish their altars and destroy their sacred stones" (Hosea 10:1-2).

They fell into the lowest spiritual, moral, political and national corruption: "They have sunk deep into corruption, as in the days of Gibeah. God will remember their wickedness and punish them for their sins" (Hosea 9:9). Hosea began to preach in times of great prosperity and stopped doing so when the nation struggled with the power of anarchy. During his first years, Jeroboam II was the great monarch of Samaria. He headed an arrogant military despotism. In his day, the nation was at the height of its military prosperity, but at the same time, it descended rapidly to a fatal moral corruption. The second book of Kings informs us that upon the death of Jeroboam, there were internal dissensions, rival politicians sacrificed the interests of the nation for their own, the princes were corrupted, they became illegal kings, and power was seriously weakened. The kings were "swept away like a twig on the surface of the waters" (Hosea 10:7).

Conspiracy was the order of the day (see 2 Kings 15). In their despair, therefore, they bowed, first to one direction and then to another seeking foreign help, paying tribute alternately to Assyria and Egypt, until they finally lost their independence and national autonomy. Their decline was rapid after their independence was over. Things went from bad to worse, until the prophet exclaimed, "There is no faithfulness, no love, no acknowledgment of God in the land. There is only cursing, lying and murder, stealing and adultery; they break all bounds, and bloodshed follows bloodshed" (Hosea 4:1-2).

All this national decadence, because of the infractions, infidelities and conspiracies in Israel, broke God's heart. To illustrate this lamentable and painful reality, He called Hosea so that his personal story (Hosea 1:2) would serve as a living mirror of God's love for a blatantly unfaithful people.

II. The reach of God's love

Chapter 11 of the prophecy teaches us that despite our sins, God loves us. We can see how God shows us his compassion throughout our life.

A. He led them out with ties of love (v.4a)

God draws us with unbreakable cords of love, necessary to pull us because we cannot leave our swamp of sin alone. Necessary to pull us even when in principle we resist and refuse to let ourselves be rescued; ropes that reach any place and situation in which we find ourselves. In the past, Israel had been enslaved in Egypt, and there the loving and powerful ropes of God had come to rescue them.

B. He takes away the heavy yoke of our sin

Israel would have been 420 years enslaved under the yoke of Egypt, and we too were enslaved for a long time, or on many occasions, because of our sins, our bad decisions, our pride, our rebellions, our foolishness and our miseries. Only Christ can take away the heavy yoke we carry on our backs. We are unable to do it for ourselves (Isaiah 9:4 and 10:27), only God's forgiveness through the sacrifice of Jesus can free us from the weight of our unforgivable and detestable actions. Nor will he give what we really deserve, because unlike us humans, he only uses his anger to correct (v.9). When the sword has fulfilled its purpose, God will roar like a lion with full authority and power, calling us to return to Him and be led by Him, guided by His love, protection and eternal wisdom. (v.10). God calls us to become meek in His presence.

Without wasting any more time, let us allow ourselves to be pulled by those strings of love:

- Allowing Him to take away the heavy yoke of sin,
- Receiving the food He gives us for a full and abundant life,
- Permitting His sword to finish the work of cleansing and purifying us,
- Allowing ourselves to be healed.

C. He gives us life-giving food (v.4c)

When he brought Israel out of Egypt with a strong arm, he fed them manna from heaven for 40 uninterrupted years in the desert. In our state of weakness and absolute spiritual rickets, we must remember that Jesus said, "I am the bread of life. Whoever comes to me will never go hungry, and whoever believes in me will never be thirsty" (John 6:35).

With his food, advice, encouragement, teachings, confessions, warnings and ear-tugs, He restores us to strength and feeds us with abundant and eternal life. The King of Kings descending to our state of prostration to give us His food of blessing in our mouth.

D. Treats us with the sword of discipline (v.6)

Our setbacks and rebellions demand that the love of God be manifested in discipline: The more he called them, the more they went away (v.2); they did not want to convert (v.5); although he was called the Most High, absolutely no one wanted to exalt him (v.7). As a result, the prophet said, "A sword will flash in their cities; it will devour their false prophets and put an end to their plans" (v.6). This prophecy was fulfilled when they were conquered by Assyria (approximately 722 BC).

When does God have to show us his love through His sword?

- To destroy our strongholds that separate us from Him.
- To wake us up from our numbness.
- To cut and eliminate everything bad and impure in us.

Hebrews 12:5-6 says, "My son, do not make light of the Lord's discipline, and do not lose heart when he rebukes you, because the Lord disciplines the one he loves, and he chastens everyone he accepts as his son." At the beginning, discipline seems painful, but it is "profitable for us to help us to participate in His Holiness. He "gives us the quiet fruit of righteousness" (Hebrews 12:10-11).

E. He rescues us with strong compassion (vv.8-10)

God said to Israel, "My heart is changed within me; all my compassion is aroused" (v.8). Despite our errors, God will not abandon us or completely destroy us. In His grace he will make us blossom, spread out our roots, give us good branches, and perfume like a great forest (Hosea 14:1-9). The one who is wise and prudent will understand this call (Hosea 14:9).

Optional Questions:

I. The Contrariety of Israel

- What were the contradictions in Israel?
- Have you seen those contradictions in your life at some time?
- Israel had been enslaved in Egypt and there came the loving and powerful ropes of God to rescue them. Do you remember where the Lord rescued you and how was he at that time in your life?

II. The reach of God's love

Give practical examples of your life today, referring to these statements:

- He draws us with cords of love (Hosea 11:4a).
- His love takes away the heavy yoke of our sin (Hosea 11:4b).
- It gives us life-giving nourishment (Hosea 11:4c).
- He treats us with the sword of discipline (Hosea 11:6).
- He rescues us with inflamed compassion (Hosea 11:8-10).
- He calls us to turn quickly and meekly to the presence of God (Hosea 11:11).

Conclusion

Whoever has understood the incomparable love of God will return to Him swiftly: As bird (Hosea 11:11), a creature who can fly high and fast to escape the heights of difficulties, fears and problems. He will return to the Lord 'meek as a dove' to live in the place and state where we belong, in the father's house, the house of love, in the paradise of His presence.

Notes :

The mercy of God is within our reach

Mary Prado (Venezuela)

Lesson 16

> **Memory verse:** "Rend your heart and not your garments. Return to the Lord your God, for he is gracious and compassionate, slow to anger and abounding in love, and he relents from sending calamity" (Joel 2:13).
>
> **Lesson Aim:** To understand that the mercy of God is in reach of any repentant heart.

Introduction

All believers are prone to turmoil when we break our relationship with God through disobedience. But as God is just, He is also great in mercy and offers us His forgiveness and restoration. The book of Joel shows us the meaning of God's forgiveness and eternal love for the repentant sinner.

I. The announcement of the impending trial (Joel 1- 2:11)

The news of a natural disaster causes all kinds of unrest in the community. Generally, these events are beyond the control of humans and their arrival implies the loss of many lives. In the Bible, natural catastrophes were seen as signs of divine judgment. Although the prophets usually anticipated this type of calamities, in the case of Joel's prophecy, some commentators think that the judgment was already present, and the intention of the announcement was to move the people to repent and seek God's forgiveness.

The announcement of the trial includes two main themes: Devastation of the land of Judah by the plague of locusts, and the announcement of the 'day of the Lord'. Joel makes a symbolic connection of the devastation by the locusts with the God's judgement day, an event that describes God's final judgment on impenitent sinners.

A. The devastation of the earth by locusts (Joel 1:1-14)

This first section describes a catastrophic scenario with few precedents in the history of the Hebrew nation. It is possible that the image of the locust plague could refer to an invading army: "What the chewing locust left, the gobbling locust ate; What the gobbling locust left, the munching locust ate; What the munching locust left, the chomping locust ate" (Joel 1:4, The Message version). The image clearly describes a complete destruction process. Joel took advantage of the people's crisis to call their attention

see that God could use that circumstance of national disaster to show them His mercy and turn the calamity into a blessing. The plague of locusts was of such great dimensions that the prophet called everyone to bemoan it, but especially to those who were directly affected: drunkards (v.5), priests (v.9), and farmers and vine growers (v.11).

The ministers of God had a crucial role to play in the midst of that terrible juncture: to lead the people to search for God in prayer and repentance. The epicenter of that great national cry should be the house of God, the temple. "Put on sackcloth, you priests, and mourn" (v.13). Obviously, the ministers of the Lord have the great responsibility to be faithful guides of the church on the path of holiness. We must be examples of prayer and intimate encounter with the One who is the source of our victory and strength. Our intercessory prayer must remain on the altar of God as a fundamental part of our Christian ministry (Acts 6:4).

When everything seems lost and we feel disappointed because of difficult circumstances, how important it is to search and humble ourselves before God! Crises are crucial moments that can define our defeat or victory, depending on how we approach our relationship with God. These moments should not be a cause of spiritual decay, but on the contrary, extraordinary opportunities to discern the holy will of God and experience His mercy. They are timely moments to review our spiritual condition and to straighten out what needs to be sorted out in our life.

B. The terrible day of the Lord (Joel 1:15- 2:11)

The next theme in Joel is 'the day of the Lord.' Some commentators believe that this is the core theme of the book. It is also mentioned in some of the Major Prophets and in almost all the Minor Prophets. The phrase 'the day of the Lord' has no reference to a period of chronological time but to a period of divine judgment without equal.

This portion of the prophecy recalls a series of similes that describe the terrible march of insects on earth. For Joel, the invasion becomes a powerful metaphor for the terrible judgment of God. Just as the plague of locusts could not be circumvented, the Day of the Lord is a certainty. Just as this great devastation could not be confronted in any way, the terrible events of God's final judgment will be tough (2:11). The day of the Lord, is a day of punishment for the nations (Ezekiel 30:3). All sinners will be wiped out of the earth (Isaiah 13:9). In the New Testament, besides being called the Day of the Lord, it is designated as the day of the Father and of Christ. It is directly related to the second coming of our Lord Jesus Christ, in the sense that it describes the subsequent judgments that will fall upon humanity. However, both Testaments warn about judgment for the ungodly; the faithful remnant of God will be saved (Obadiah 17:1 Thessalonians 5:1-11).

How can we be prepared as believers for that day? The Word of God teaches us the need to live holy lives before God, living in obedience to His will (2 Peter 3:14).

II. The call to repentance

Joel 2 is a call to repentance. Fortunately, God does not abandon us, leaving us to perish because of our wrong decisions. He urges us to straighten out our path for our own good.

A. Genuine repentance

Some people are confused about what repentance means. "Repentance, (Gk. Metanoia), is a summons to a personal, absolute and ultimate unconditional surrender to God as Sovereign. Though it includes sorrow and regret, it is more than that. ... In repenting, one makes a complete change of direction" (on-line Dictionary). We need to change our intentions to be able to change our way of life. To repent is to feel sadness for what we did wrong, but in addition, we must be determined to change.

In the Old Testament, it was customary to show repentance through bodily signs of mourning and sadness, such as fasting, crying, putting on rough garments, throwing ash on one's head, etc. Sometimes, to make their pain more obvious, people would tear their clothes in public and remain silent and without eating food for some time.

In Joel 2:12-17, an element of greater importance is introduced to the meaning of repentance; heart conversion (vv.12-13). Repentance, in a natural sense and without any understanding of the will of God, can lead to bitterness and all kinds of negative feelings, or to making wrong decisions that do not fix the evil that has been caused at all. Some people even go so far as to end their lives due to their apparent 'repentance'. For example, the Gospel narrates the case of Judas Iscariot

(Matthew 27:3-5). Judas said, "I have sinned… for I have betrayed innocent blood." In addition, he returned the thirty pieces of silver for which he sold the Lord, but then, he went and hung himself. His repentance without knowledge of God's will led him to death.

True repentance from the biblical point of view produces in the soul a burning desire to do the will of God. Paul explains it to the Corinthians, "Godly sorrow brings repentance that leads to salvation and leaves no regret, but worldly sorrow brings death" (2 Corinthians 7:10).

B. True repentance brings forgiveness (Joel 2:18-27)

When the sinner repents, he can have full certainty of reaching God's mercy. Repentance, if genuine, results in the merciful and great demonstration of God's love. The Bible assures us that we will receive forgiveness for any sin committed, and total restoration to communion with God.

This passage deals with this very important issue: The result of genuine repentance is forgiveness. This idea can be seen in verse 18, which would be the key verse of this passage: "Then the Lord was jealous for his land and took pity on his people". God loves his people so much that he would soon grant them forgiveness. But divine forgiveness is not something ethereal but a tangible fact. The following verses of the passage (vv.19-27) show that God's forgiveness results in the removal of the negative conditions that result from sin, but also in the outpouring of innumerable blessings.

C. The promise of the Spirit (Joel 2:28-32)

It can be said that the greatest blessing of forgiveness and communion with God is the presence of the Holy Spirit in our life. Next, we have the passage that speaks of the promise of the outpouring of the Spirit of God (Joel 2:28-32).

The Lord announces through the prophet Joel that in the last days He will pour out of His Spirit in abundance. The word 'pour out' means a future abundant outpouring of His presence. This will come after they have answered the call from the Lord to an attitude of heart searching and consecration. That is, when they are back on good terms with Him.

Like every promise of the Lord, the outpouring of the Spirit has its conditions. The Lord promises to pour out His Spirit and blessings only after they have willingly and repentantly turned to Him. It is not about expressions of empty religiosity that hinder the total consecration. This blessing has universal connotations. It is complete, turning our hearts of stone into hearts of flesh (Ezekiel 11:19), but also, it indicates the outpouring of the Holy Spirit is for all who truly believe.

Matthew Henry says, "The effect of this blessing: They shall prophesy; they shall receive new discoveries of divine things, and that not for their own use only, but for the benefit of the church. They shall interpret scripture, and speak of things secret, distant, and future, which by the utmost sagacity of reason, and their natural powers, they could not have any insight into nor foresight of" (https://www.biblegateway.com/resources/matthew-henry/Joel). The apostle Peter referred to the fulfillment of this promise in the outpouring of the Holy Spirit on the day of Pentecost in Acts 2:14-21, 38-39.

III. The blessings of repentance (Joel 3:1-21)

Chapter 3 of Joel is a message of hope for afflicted people. The prospect of the devastation that Judah had suffered had filled them with confusion and discouragement, but God always has a word of hope for the sorrowful hearts of his children.

A. Redemption and restitution (Joel 3:1-5)

The first part of this chapter shows us the promise of redemption and restitution. God promises to "restore the fortunes of Judah and Jerusalem" (v.1). The prospect of being taken captive by an enemy army meant pain and suffering. On several occasions the people of God in the Old Testament suffered such circumstances. The captivity of Israel represents the bondage of sin from which Christ came to set us free (Luke 4:18).

The Lord in His mercy will be the just judge of all those who seek Him from the heart and serve him. He himself will take care of giving them back everything that has been taken from them, and He will avenge all the affronts made by their enemies. We can rest confident in His justice and leave vengeance in the hands of the Lord (Deut. 32:35, Rom. 12:19, Heb. 10:30).

B. Protection of God and eternal prosperity

"The Lord will roar from Zion and thunder from Jerusalem; the earth and the heavens will tremble. But the Lord will be a refuge for his people, a stronghold for the people of Israel" (Joel 3:16). The image of God as a lion roaring for His people was of singular importance for Judah. The tribe of Judah had as its symbol the lion, which represents dignity, strength and victory. Jesus Christ is called the 'Lion of the tribe of Judah' (Revelation 5:5). He is our helper who fights on our behalf.

The presence of God in our favor constitutes our strength and security in the face of adversity. Paul says, "If God is for us, who can be against us?" (Rom. 8:31b).

"In that day the mountains will drip new wine, and the hills will flow with milk; all the ravines of Judah will run with water. A fountain will flow out of the Lord's house and will water the valley of acacias" (Joel 3:18).

Although at that time the inhabitants of Judah were completely devastated, repentance and the search for God would bring back their blessings. This promised prosperity is both spiritual and material. "The ravines of Judah" were apparently known for their dryness and sterility, but God promises that "A fountain will flow out of the Lord's house and will water the valley of acacias" (v. 18). This is a possible reference to revival as a result of renewed communion with God.

Even today, anyone who seeks God with a sincere heart and consecrate themselves to Him will also have his help. God will never forsake him and will always be his sustainer and Savior.

Optional Questions:

I. The announcement of the impending trial (Joel 1- 2:11)

- What is the role that the ministers had to fulfill during these difficult circumstances according to Joel 1:13?

- What is the role of the ministers today, understanding that " we are a chosen people, a royal priesthood"? (1 Peter 2:9)

- What does the phrase "the day of the Lord" mean?

II. The call to repentance (Joel 2)

- What does repentance mean in the Bible?

- What is the result of genuine repentance? Mention examples.

III. The blessings of repentance (Joel 3:1-21)

- What blessings would come upon Judah because of their repentance?

- Why should God's children not take vengeance in our own hands?

- What image does Joel use to talk about God's protection?

Conclusion

Repentance is a genuine expression of remembrance and sincere will to order our actions according to God's purpose. Even if we have sinned, if we change our attitude we can count on his mercy and forgiveness.

God's Judgments and blessings

Francisco Borralles (Mexico)

> **Memory verse:** "This is what the Lord says to Israel: 'Seek me and live'" (Amos 5:4).
>
> **Lesson Aim:** To understand that just as God in his sovereignty has all the power and authority to bring the nations and us to judgment; in His infinite love He seeks to restore us and take us back to His ways.

Introduction

The name Amos means "to be carried, strong, brave." He was the first of the great prophets of Israel. He came from Tekoa, a garrisoned fortress in Judah, 16 km south of Jerusalem. He was a shepherd (Amos 1:1) and collected the fruit of the wild figs that grew in the lower parts of that desert region (Amos 7:14).

He was not a professional prophet (7:14), but seeing the blindness of the nation of Israel to depressing internal conditions, he felt the call of God and moved north, where he began his ministry. At that time, Uzziah was king of Judah and Jeroboam II of Israel. Amos preached in the cities of Samaria and Bethel, and after some time, the priest Amaziah confronted him, alarmed by the severity of his message against the king and the nation (Amos 7:10-17).

I. The judgment of God against the nations (Amos chapt. 1 & 2)

Justice is an attribute of God consistent with His own character. As a just God, He must punish the sins of those who oppose Him. When we try to be independent and live without Him in sin, God reveals His righteousness and exhaustive judgment. God is the only perfect judge who has the right to issue sentence on sinful behavior. We see this judgment prophesied in the words of Amos, who spoke on behalf of the living God (Amos 1:1-2).

Amos announced God's word and judgment to the nations surrounding Israel and Judah. Of course, God has the authority to pass judgment on every nation, and indeed on the whole earth (Psalm 9:8, 96:10). The mentioned proclamations of judgment are directed against: Syria, represented by Damascus, its capital; the Philistines, represented by Gaza; as well as Tire, Edom, Ammon, Moab, Judah and Israel.

A. The sins of the neighboring nations

The Syrians (Damascus) "threshed Gilead with sledges having iron teeth" (1:3). Here we can see cruelty and suffering. The philistines (Gaza) "took captive whole communities and sold them to Edom" (1:6). Here they are being accused of selling entire communities as slaves. Tire, "Because she sold whole communities of captives to Edom, disregarding a treaty of brotherhood" (1:9). Once again selling people into slavery but also breaking alliances. Edom, whose founder was Esau, "Because he pursued his brother with a sword and slaughtered the women of the land, because his anger raged continually and his fury flamed unchecked" (1:11). Edom is accused of violence, femicide continual animosity. Ammon, "ripped open the pregnant women of Gilead in order to extend his borders" (1:13). This is the serious crime of murdering unborn children and their mothers. Moab "burned to ashes the bones of Edom's king" (2:1), showing disrespect for the dead. God judged these nations because they were cruel and did not respect each other's rights.

B. The sins of Judah and Israel

While the neighboring nations were judged for crimes like destroying other peoples, practicing slavery, stealing, waging war, ambition, etc., the two nations who were part of the people of God were judged according to how they had kept, or not kept, God's law.

God judged Judah because "they had rejected the law of the Lord and had not kept his decrees" (2:4). In the alliance that God had made with His people, He had established that if they obeyed his voice, kept and put into practice every commandment, He too would exalt them above all nations, and that great blessings would come upon them (Deut. 28:1-2).

On the contrary, if they neglected the law of God, ceasing to fear God's name, then increasingly, all kinds of plagues and diseases would come upon them and their offspring (Deuteronomy 28:59).

After pronouncing judgements against the neighboring states and Judah, the prophet turns his attention to Israel, the northern kingdom. God had called him specifically to bring His message to Israel.

God accuses them of many crimes where they had broken His law They had forgotten compassion and love for their neighbor, which must be a characteristic of every child of God (Leviticus 25:39-42). They were selling "the innocent for silver, and the needy for a pair of sandals' (2:6): they were trampling "on the heads of the poor as on the dust of the ground" denying "justice to the oppressed" (v.7).

They were practicing sexual immorality (2:7). In the law of God, all types of sexual immorality are explicitly prohibited, and the one mentioned in which a father and his son share the same woman is a situation expressly forbidden (Lev. 20:11, I Cor. 5:1).

C. For three sins … even for four, I will not relent.

The phrase "for three sins … and even for four" is a literary expression. In other words, it was a way of saying that the cup of their wickedness was full and nothing could stop the punishment of God from falling on the land.

This is also a significant wake-up call for the times in which we are living, where the sins mentioned and analyzed in the previous paragraphs are also common now in our own nations; among people who do not have a relationship with God, and do not profess the Christian faith. Every day, the world around us gets more and more contaminated in worldly matters, practicing many forms of sin without considering the will of Almighty God.

The church, like Judah and Israel, as God's own people must remember and act bearing in mind that God has established principles of love and mercy for all of us and for those around us. Remember that "the law of the Lord is perfect" (Psalm 19:7-10).

II. The message for the people of God (Amos chapters 3-6)

A. Amos' first speech (Amos 3:1-12)

Through the prophet, God spoke directly against the children of Israel, to all those he brought up from Egypt, saying that he alone had known them as a family and warns that he will punish them for all their evils (3:1).

Amos 3:1-12 describes a lesson based on the law of cause and effect. There is no effect without cause, or cause without effect. The people of Israel had enjoyed the privileges, therefore their responsibility before God was greater. The same can be said of the church of Christ in our day. We have received liberation from sin and a new life in Christ; that makes us responsible to give God our lives, as well as the honor and glory that He alone deserves (Romans 2:12-13).

Everything the Lord does with His people and with His church will be revealed by His servants. If the Lord speaks to us, we should treasure that word in our hearts, reflect on it in our own lives and proclaim the Word of God to others (Amos 3:7-8). Let us always keep in mind that in the same way that God will bring His righteous judgment upon His people, He will also deliver the righteous and the needy (v.12).

B. Amos' second speech (Amos 4:1-13)

Here the prophet presents an unpleasant and unfavorable comparison. He compares rich women to cows from the wealthy region of Bashan. The complaint against them was that they oppressed the needy, exploiting them, dedicating themselves to enjoying carnal pleasures along with their husbands. He declares the ruin of these women and their descendents.

Amos 4:4-13 shows that the people of God, had sinned (trespassed, rebelled). The prophet mocks them for being hypocrites. They still carried out religious duties, taking the tithes and performing the established sacrifices making sure that everyone praised them for their religiosity. But they were not genuine; they did not have a true relationship of love and obedience to Him.

God sent them difficult situations to make them react: hunger (v:6), lack of rain (v:7), blight, mildew and locusts (v:9), plagues and war (v.10). These were warnings from God that they had to change and come back to Him. It is a dangerous thing to play with God: "Therefore this is what I will do to you, Israel, and because I will do this to you, Israel, prepare to meet your God. He who forms the mountains, who creates the wind, and who reveals his thoughts to mankind, who turns dawn to darkness, and treads on the heights of the earth — the Lord God Almighty is his name" (Amos 4:12-13).

The church too must pay heed to these warnings. Therefore, let us prepare to present ourselves before the LORD of hosts.

C. Amos' third speech (Amos 5:1-27)

God calls His people to repentance in this third discourse. In the midst of the warning voices, we can hear the loving voice of the Father saying, "Seek Me, and live" (v.4). The call is to come to God before He lashes out His judgment. God says through His prophet, if they do not repent, "He will sweep through the tribes of Joseph like a fire" (v.6).

God is the Creator of the universe who orders our times. He is the one who has dominion over all nature and of course over every human being. He invites us to seek for what is good and not for what is bad. God promises to be with us (Amos 5:4, 6, 8-9, 14).

But those who ignore and despise God's warnings will suffer the consequences of their sins. For them, the Day of the Lord will be full of darkness (Amos 5:10, 12, 16-27). It is not enough just to be religious, we need to have a true commitment to Jesus. The prophet spoke out against those who were living solely to carry out religious rituals, without having a true relationship with God. Amos warned them that if they did nor repent of their multitude of sins and darkened understanding, in the Day of their judgement, it would be too late, God would not answer them.

D. Woe to the Complacent (Amos 6:1-14)

Amos grieved for the "notable men" who were complacent, who would receive the consequences of having ignored God in order to pursue their own delights. They trusted in themselves, in their social position or their social relationships, rather than in God (v.1). Verse 7 states that they "will be among the first to go into exile" their "feasting and lounging will end."

The people of God had to be willing to examine their lives and determine whether a calamity or misfortune suffered was a rebuke from God because of having relied on their own strength. God has the authority and power to use the circumstances of life to rebuke and correct us (vv.11-14).

III. Three of Amos' visions (Amos 7)

The prophet Amos was the first prophet to have apocalyptic visions; that is, visual revelations constituting various symbolic elements, about the timely and coming intervention of God in history. Amos' visions are found in the last part of the book that bears his name. There are five in total, we will analyze three of them:

The vision of the locusts (7:1). The description is the threat of a plague of locusts before the harvest was done. Amos saw the plague as unbearable for Israel, so he prayed to God and He revoked the plague.

The vision of fire (7:4-6). God was going to destroy Israel by fire, but through the intercession of Amos, He did not do it. From these stories, we can point out that God is willing to listen to the intercession of his prophets, of the leaders of the church, of His people in general. He will respond to this intercession with love and mercy.

The vision of the plumb line (7:7-9). A plumb line is used to check the verticality of a wall or column in construction. In this case, the Lord sets the plumb line in the midst of His people. He is determining their fidelity. But they have strayed too far. The final phrase of verse 8 expresses: "I will spare them no longer.

IV. Restoration (Amos 9:11-15)

Amos' prophecy ends on a positive note, God is going to bless his people (Amos 9:11-15). After God's judgment comes restoration. "I will restore David's fallen shelter" (9:11) implying renewed fellowship with them. The blessing will be such that "The reaper will be overtaken by the plowman" (9:13). In other words, the harvest will be done immediately after preparing the land for sowing.

He promised to "bring" His "people Israel back from exile" (9:14). They will be rescued from captivity. They will never be uprooted from their country again. For us today, God is announcing freedom over sin and the wonderful promise that nothing can separate us from the love of God in Jesus Christ.

Optional Questions:

I. The judgment of God against the nations (Amos chapters 1 y 2)
   - What would be our reaction to a lay person, rather than a pastor, warning us today about God's judgement?
   - Which of the sins of the nations can be seen today?
   - What should we do as a church about this?

II. The message for the people of God (Amos chapters 3-6)
   - What are some of the blessings we enjoy as children of God?
   - What would be the consequences of ignoring God's invitation "Seek me and you will live." (Amos 5:4)?
   - What do we have to do if we want to listen to this loving call?

III. Three of Amos' visions (Amos 7)
   - Amos interceded for the people. Mention some aspects that should be a reason for intercession today.

IV. Restoration (Amos 9:11-15)
   - What did God promise the people if they learned their lesson?
   - What does this tell us about God?

Conclusion

We must always keep in mind that our God is sovereign, and that nothing is beyond His control. We can be sure of God's love for us, but we must also be aware that He can rebuke us and correct us when we are going wrong, for we are the His sheep, He is our pastor. To keep on his paths we must turn away from our own selfish ways.

Dealing with stuff now while we can

Hernán Massacesi (Argentina)

Memory verse: "The day of the Lord is near for all nations. As you have done, it will be done to you; your deeds will return upon your own head" (Obadiah 1:15).

Lesson Aim: To analyze in depth the current state of our hearts, understanding that present actions and decisions will affect, for better or for worse, our future and that of our children.

Introduction

Have we ever been tempted not to complete an important job? Have we calculated how far a mistake can lead to consequences? Is this something that often happens? Are we aware that if we do not finish a job, there will be repercussions in other dimensions of our lives? Can we think of some issues we have had because we did not finish on time and complete something important and urgent? Have we learned the lesson? We must not forget that the deviation of a centimeter from the same point of departure, with distance, becomes a much greater and even exponential error. How far are we aware that our decisions today will affect our children and future generations? What are we projecting with our actions, words, comments, reactions, patterns, behaviors or silences?

I. Who was Edom?

Geography and history play important roles in this prophecy of Obadiah. There were sharp evident hostilities between Israel's neighbor to the southeast, Edom. These bad feelings had deep roots. Esau, Isaac's eldest son and grandson of Abraham, felt cheated by Jacob, his younger brother to whom he lost his privileges as an elder son (Gen. 25:27-34; 27:1-19, see v. 41). Although according to the writer of Hebrews, Esau himself was the one who did wrong, "See that no one is sexually immoral, or is godless like Esau, who for a single meal sold his inheritance rights as the oldest son" (Heb. 12:16). During their lives, both brothers received other names; Esau was also known as 'Edom' (Gen. 36:1,9) and Jacob as 'Israel' (Gen. 32:22-32).

Those names were adopted by the nations of which the two men were ancestors. The principle of this animosity between these two brothers continued also between the two nations: "But how Esau will be ransacked, his hidden treasures pillaged!" (Obadiah 1:6). Literal but also allegorical language. Obadiah placed God's microscope on Esau, and we can see that the nation of Edom had grown and numbered 250 thousand people. Obadiah inflated Esau like a tire to find the puncture. What was at the beginning a small wound under the skin was now a violent cancer. What was once small in Esau was now expanded 100 thousand times in Edom.

How can affairs, attitudes, improper states deteriorate if they are not properly treated in time and in depth? In at least two erroneous aspects, Esau did not work hard on his life, and that led to serious consequences in his offspring. The prophecy of Obadiah reveals to us what these two aspects were and their corresponding consequences.

II. Esau despised God

A. Esau despised his birthright

Esau's arrogance had its main cause in his contempt of God (Gen. 25:29-34): "Esau despised the birthright." He rejected the blessing of God and the favor of God. For Esau, God was not important. He was strong as a great hunter, self-reliant and trusted completely in his own abilities. Esau represents those who are confident in themselves, who 'despise' God's request to be their center and not just another accessory in their lives.

This explains why God discarded Esau. He knew what was in his heart, that he would not appreciate his blessing or his spiritual inheritance, that Esau was not willing to place God at the center of his life. Hungry, he traded his birthright for a plate of food. Deep down his heart was not right. He underestimated the importance of his father's blessing. Jacob on the other hand, became Israel, 'Prince of God.' Esau represents the flesh and Jacob represents the spirit.

B. Esau did not have an encounter with God

There are no records that Esau had a deep and definitive encounter with God. Esau continued his life trusting in his own strengths, criteria and endeavors. He even distanced himself more from God by living among peoples and cultures that did not have a belief in God (Genesis 36:1-2). This attitude was projected onto his descendants.

C. The magnitude of his contempt for God

Genesis 36 tells us that "Esau took his wives and sons and daughters and all the members of his household, as well as his livestock and all his other animals and all the goods he had acquired in Canaan and moved to a land some distance from his brother Jacob. Their possessions were too great for them to remain together; the land where they were staying could not support them both because of their livestock. So, Esau (that is, Edom) settled in the hill country of Seir (vv.3-8).

He made military alliances: "All your allies will force you to the border; your friends will deceive and overpower you; those who eat your bread will set a trap for you, but you will not detect it" (Obadiah 1:7). Esau's pride was founded on his own wisdom and prudence: "In that day," declares the Lord, "will I not destroy the wise men of Edom, those of understanding in the mountains of Esau?" (V.8). God says we must "Trust in the Lord with all your heart and lean not on your own understanding; in all your ways submit to him, and he will make your paths straight. Do not be wise in your own eyes; fear the Lord and shun evil. This will bring health to your body and nourishment to your bones" (Proverbs 3:5-8).

Edom's pride was founded on their own courage and strength (v.9): "Your warriors, Teman, will be terrified, and everyone in Esau's mountains will be cut down in the slaughter." "Some trust in chariots and some in horses, but we trust in the name of the Lord our God" (Psalm 20:7). "Woe to those who go down to Egypt for help, who rely on horses, who trust in the multitude of their chariots and in the great strength of their horsemen, but do not look to the Holy One of Israel or seek help from the Lord" (Isaiah 31:1).

That deceitful pride had to be firmly dealt with by God. He was going to tear them down from the safest place: "'Though you soar like the eagle and make your nest among the stars, from there I will bring you down,' declares the Lord" (Obadiah 1:4). On the other hand, their allies were going to betray them: "All your allies will force you to the border; your friends will deceive and overpower you; those who eat your bread will set a trap for you, but you will not detect it" (v.7). No doubt the wise men would perish. "'In that day', declares the Lord, 'will I not destroy the wise men of Edom, those of understanding in the mountains of Esau?'" (V.8). Finally, the brave men were going to be cut off and defeated. "Your warriors, Teman, will be terrified, and everyone in Esau's mountains will be cut down in the slaughter"(v.9).

III. Bitterness of heart

Esau had forgiven his brother by word (Genesis 33:8-9) but in his heart there were glimpses of bitterness that were projected on his children and his children's children for several generations (vv.10ff). The bitterness was projected in abuse and violence without limits.

The list of "you should not ..." (vv.12-14) reveal what was in the heart of Edom: insensitivity, delight in the pain of others, boasting of their strength: "You should not gloat over your brother in the day of his misfortune, nor rejoice over the people of Judah in the day of their destruction, nor boast so much in the day of their trouble " (v.12). The escalation of hatred was increasing: from seeing without intervening ... to the passage of dispossession ... and ending with murder (vv.13-14).

A. The root of bitterness

Always a root of bitterness not treated thoroughly, and in time, will bring great pain and affliction. "See to it that no one falls short of the grace of God and that no bitter root grows up to cause trouble and defile many" (Hebrews 12:15). The root of bitterness in our hearts causes us to stop reaching out for God's grace, hindering us in everything we undertake, and for that reason many people can be affected and damaged.

Resentment, arrogance and tradition led over time to the emergence of consequences for a conflict that was not completely over. Esau did not thoroughly deal with his conflict with God who he had despised. Also, he did not fully deal with the conflict with Jacob and kept bitterness in his heart.

Surely Esau did not want this unfortunate and undesirable outcome to affect his family, but it came because he had not fully surrendered to God and because he had not thoroughly dealt with his bitterness with his brother. This can be applied for all sins. Sin is cheating, deceit, treachery, subtle and mortal in many of its aspects and manifestations: anger (Cain's case), sexual lust (Solomon and David), and vanity and flirting (Samson), etc.

The enemy thinks and plots in the long term. His aspirations for destruction point to people and are projected to subsequent generations. That is why we must not forget that what we live today is the result of what we have done or failed to do in the past. "The day of the Lord is near for all nations. As you have done, it will be done to you; your deeds will return upon your own head" (Obadiah 1:15). This tells us that the decisions we make today can bring terrible consequences to our inheritance in the future.

B. End of the root of bitterness

Let's deal with our sin thoroughly. Let's watch over our children. Let's completely deactivate the bomb that threatens our lives and families: "Get rid of all bitterness, rage and anger, brawling and slander, along with every form of malice. Be kind and compassionate to one another, forgiving each other, just as in Christ God forgave you" (Ephesians 4:31-32). Let us not give place to the enemy, and defeat him today in the name of Christ.

Let's go with the scalpel all the way into the cavities of our hearts, remembering that what is not well treated and dealt with in time will eventually bring serious consequences. That is why we should treat bitterness as soon as we discover it, in a complete way. If there is any remnant of bitterness, rancor or hatred, the tendency is that it will always return again, and will become an even bigger problem affecting everything and damaging our relationship with God.

Let us avoid today an unfortunate present, and a worse future full of grudges, arrogance and betrayals: "See to it that no one falls short of the grace of God and that no bitter root grows up to cause trouble and defile many" (Hebrews 12:15).

Let us place the microscope of God on our lives: "Whoever conceals their sins does not prosper, but the one who confesses and renounces them finds mercy" (Prov. 28:13). Let us confess everything to God who has mercy on everyone: "Israel, put your hope in the Lord, for with the Lord is unfailing love and with him is full redemption. He himself will redeem Israel from all their sins" (Psalm 130:7-8). Let us leave at the foot of the cross everything that has scared us or continues to hurt us, everything that brings us bitterness, and let us begin to live a life of victory in Christ: "But now that you have been set free from sin and have become slaves of God, the benefit you reap leads to holiness, and the result is eternal life" (Rom. 6:22).

Optional Questions:

I. Who was Edom?

- What was the background of Edom? (Hebrews 12:16)
- What can happen in the future if issues in our lives are not properly treated in time and in depth?

II. Esau despised God

- In what way did Esau despise God? (Genesis 25:29-34)
- How can we belittle God today?

III. Bitterness of heart

- What is the root of bitterness?
- How or when can we acquire a root of bitterness?
- What consequences does it bring?
- What should we do so that the root of bitterness does not affect us and the lives of those around us?

Conclusion

We must make an intentional decision. Let us remember that our decisions today affect not only our own future, but will reach our children and future generations. Let's devote ourselves to establishing the culture of forgiveness and love for the family and also in the church.

Power of fasting and prayer

Hernán Massacesi (Argentina)

Memory verse: "The Ninevites believed God. A fast was proclaimed, and all of them, from the greatest to the least, put on sackcloth" (Jonah 3:5).

Lesson Aim: To learn how to incorporate the practice of prayer and fasting into our lives as a powerful tool to transform the life of a nation.

Introduction

When we act properly, we get the desired result.

For example:

• When we work correctly, we receive the agreed salary and we even get promotions.

• When we study conscientiously, we grow as people, overcome our limits, constantly rise to new levels of development and obtain achievements.

• When we seriously diet, we lose weight, improve our figure and improve our health.

• When men treat women as they should, they reach their hearts and conquer them with their love.

The same happens in the spiritual world. The difficulty becomes accessible when we act properly. Many times, we do not reach God's purposes and benefits because we do not proceed properly. Who eats a meal they like at least once a week? And who fasts at least once a week? Let us note the difference: We are more dedicated to the passing and superficial than to what actually has the power to transform the most difficult realities.

The Bible tells us that there are situations that do not happen if we do not fast and pray. When the disciples could not exorcise a demon from a young man, Jesus told them: "This kind can come out only by prayer" (Mark 9:29).

The fast of Nineveh, the capital of the Assyrian empire, was an emblematic case in which more than 120,000 people and many animals were saved from destruction and extermination (Jonah 4:11). From this great story we can learn how a fast can reverse destinies and bring complete salvation.

I. Believing in God

It is interesting that only eight words from the prophet Jonah were sufficient for this rebellious people to believe: "Jonah began by going a day's journey into the city, proclaiming, "Forty more days and Nineveh will be overthrown" (Jonah 3:4). The message in Hebrew has an ambiguity we do not perceive in other languages. In Hebrew, 'overthrown' can also be understood as transformed. An intentional ambiguity to cherish hopes in people, who lived far from God.

Finally, the prophecy of Jonah was fulfilled because the city was transformed. The people of Nineveh believed God and proclaimed the fast: "The Ninevites believed God. A fast was proclaimed, and all of them, from the greatest to the least, put on sackcloth" (Jonah 3:5).

In the case of Jonah, it was not even necessary for him to insist on his message. Only one day's journey was enough for the people to believe and begin a process of repentance.

What promptness! In our days, many do not act swiftly to God's call to salvation. We must respond to the call as it says in 2 Chronicles 7:14: "If my people, who are called by my name, will humble themselves and pray and seek my face and turn from their wicked ways, then I will hear from heaven, and I will forgive their sin and will heal their land." Similarly, with just a few words, Paul and Silas brought hope and salvation to the Philippian jailer: "Believe in the Lord Jesus, and you will be saved—you and your household" (Acts 16:31).

II. Refraining from food

Removing food from our routine allows us to focus on what is most urgent, what is most necessary: "This is the proclamation the king of Assyria issued in Nineveh: 'By the decree of the king and his nobles: 'Do not let people or animals, herds or flocks, taste anything; do not let them eat or drink. But let people and animals be covered with sackcloth. Let everyone call urgently on God. Let them give up their evil ways and their violence''' (Jonah 3:7-8). It is interesting to note and highlight the responsibility assumed by the king of Nineveh to the point of declaring fasting from the greatest to the least of them, considering also the animals, oxen and sheep.

The purpose of this time of fasting was to look meticulously inside themselves, searching their hearts and confronting the light of God. The important thing about this initiative is that it began with the highest leader, the king of the nation, who was an example and influence for the rest of the people who followed him. This action shows that we must be exemplary and thus influence those around us. Fasting should involve looking at ourselves, but also looking out for others.

But what is fasting? Fasting is a time set aside for prayer and meditation, without the normal provision of food. How much time should we fast? The time that is necessary, whatever God guides us to do. The Bible talks about fasts of three, seven, twenty-one and even forty days. The time of fasting is that which is proposed intimately, in the presence of God.

Fasting is a spiritual exercise, a voluntary restriction of not eating food for the purpose of seeking God. Fasting is voluntarily giving up the need to consume food. It is an action contrary to the first sinful act of humanity, that of eating the fruit of the tree of the knowledge of good and evil. In contrast, fasting involves voluntarily refusing to eat what is allowed. Fasting is a practice that is frequently used in the Bible. When accompanied by prayer, it is a sign of an intense desire regarding a desperate, urgent, relevant or important need.

Fasting in our life today implies also searching our hearts, allowing ourselves rest for our exhausted, overwhelmed or afflicted souls. It includes repentance, meditation, prayer and communion with God. Although the desires of our flesh struggle against our soul, and the cares and needs of this world, when we fast we seek to silence our senses and submit our body voluntarily to God. The apostle Paul said, "I don't know about you, but I'm running hard for the finish line. I'm giving it everything I've got. No sloppy living for me! I'm staying alert and in top condition. I'm not going to get caught napping, telling everyone else all about it and then missing out myself" (1 Corinthians 9:27, The Message).

Fasting is a way to make prayer more effective. When we fast, we must forget about the food. Remember that Esau sold his inheritance for a bowl of lentils. Also, Noah's generation lived to the full the pleasures of this world, ate and drank, while the flood was coming upon them. In a fast, we distance ourselves from the earthly to go to a spiritual ground, to victory. This search for spiritual realities must cause us to leave the provision of material goods in God's hands. Jesus identified himself as the true bread from heaven, and promised the victory to those who feed on this hidden manna. He said, "It is written: 'Man shall not live on bread alone, but on every word that comes from the mouth of God'" (Matthew 4:4).

III. Urgently crying out to God

Extreme situations demand extreme actions. For this reason the people were asked to pray with urgency: "But let people and animals be covered with sackcloth. Let everyone call urgently on God. Let them give up their evil ways and their violence" (Jonah 3:8). All, absolutely everyone (including the animals) had to experience the sense of generalized urgency of the nation. All living beings had to feel the need to abstain from what until then was considered the most important. Figuratively, they all had to cry out to God.

They cried out to God from a deep need to change, abandoning sin. As David exclaimed: "Have mercy on me, O God, according to your unfailing love; according to your great compassion blot out my transgressions. Wash away all my iniquity and cleanse me from my sin. For I know my transgressions, and my sin is always before me. Against you, you only, have I sinned and done what is evil in your sight; so, you are right in your verdict and justified when you judge" (Psalm 51:1-4). They realized that their lives were not right in God's sight.

Their prayer and fast was a community effort. When he was desperate for his nation, Nehemiah prayed: "Lord, the God of heaven, the great and awesome God, who keeps his covenant of love with those who love him and keep his commandments, let your ear be attentive and your eyes open to hear the prayer your servant is praying before you day and night for your servants, the people of Israel. I confess the sins we Israelites, including myself and my father's family, have committed against you" (Nehemiah 1:5-6).

IV. Repenting of wrong doing

The great sin of the Ninevites involved violent actions: "Let everyone call urgently on God. Let them give up their evil ways and their violence" (Jonah 3:8). Nineveh was famous for the violent way they treated their enemies, plundering their cities and treasures. They were also known for the bad treatment they gave to the vanquished, enslaving them. In addition, they violated and exploited their own people. Paradoxically, 'rapine' (violence, mistreatment, abuse, looting, exploitation) is today one of the most common social sins of which our nations must repent.

God listened with mercy to the Ninevites' cry because they showed sincere repentance and turned from their evil ways. "When God saw what they did and how they turned from their evil ways, he relented and did not bring on them the destruction he had threatened" (Jonah 3:10).

Fasting caused a nation to be saved from total destruction. They fasted with crying and repentance, and were able to connect with the compassionate heart of God, who desires that none should be lost, but that all proceed to repentance. The fast of Nineveh was an urgent cry for the salvation of an entire nation. There are lives, families and cities that today urgently need salvation because their wickedness has reached extreme levels. Let's not act like Jonah, who instead of assuming his task, fled from the presence of God (Jonah 1:3).

Let us set our hearts to pray and fast with intense crying out, as the king of Nineveh did, to turn our people from their wicked ways, so that many may be saved because we have cried out on their behalf. "The weapons we fight with are not the weapons of the world. On the contrary, they have divine power to demolish strongholds. We demolish arguments and every pretension that sets itself up against the knowledge of God, and we take captive every thought to make it obedient to Christ" (2 Corinthians 10:4-5).

When we fast, the only thing that is important is the painful cause of our fast. Do we have anguish? Is there an urgency in our soul? Are we afflicted? Is there a crisis in our life? Let us not wait any longer, let us turn to God in fasting, repentance and clamor. Let us give up for a moment the attention we give to our body, to pour out our soul before the Lord.

If we are in communion with Him, hope will never leave us, no matter the magnitude of the crisis. Even in the most extreme circumstances, we can turn our hearts to the Lord and in fasting, prayer and sincere repentance, find help and salvation.

Optional Questions:

I. Believing in God

- Do we believe that God can answer prayers?
- What were the words mentioned in Jonah 3:4 that led Nineveh to seek God?
- What words can we use today?

II. Refraining from food

- What happens when we fast?
- How many days should we fast?
- What is the significance of fasting in my life?

III. Urgently Crying out to God

- Why do you think God sent everyone to fast?
- Does God ask us to fast today?

IV. Repenting of wrong doing

- Is there an urgency in our soul?
- Is there a crisis or affliction in your life?
- Can fasting be a way out of difficult situations?

Conclusion

Repentance with hope and faith always attracts God's attention. The Ninevites turned away from their evil ways and God turned away from the punishment that was in store for them. Let us pray and fast to change from our evil ways and to bring vital transformation to others (Jonah 1:1-2).

An encounter with Micah

Marco Rocha (Argentina)

Memory verse: "But you, Bethlehem Ephrathah, though you are small among the clans of Judah, out of you will come for me one who will be ruler over Israel, whose origins are from of old, from ancient times" (Micah 5:2).

Lesson Aim: To discover the distinctive features of the ministry of the prophet Micah and delve into the study of some key passages.

Introduction

In order to get to know more deeply an event or location, we need to have more than one perspective. Ask your students to describe a list of characteristics of life in the city in contrast to life in rural areas. Then conclude the activity explaining that the prophet Micah, who came from the rural area, had a contemporary ministry to the prophet Isaiah, who came from a noble family and had direct access to the king's palace. This is why the contribution of Micah is particularly special and allows us to have a more complete picture of an era and of God's purpose for humanity.

I. The prophet of the people

The prophet Micah was born in the village of Moresheth-Gath or Morasti, about 30 km southwest of Jerusalem. Although his place of ministry was the kingdom of Judah, his prophetic writings predate the fall of the kingdom of Samaria, in 721 BC. Therefore they are addressed to both Israel and Judah.

The great difference with his contemporary Isaiah was that while Isaiah was interested in prophesying about the city and the problems of the nation, Micah addressed the common people and individuals. Also known as 'the prophet of the poor', Micah had no qualms about prophesying against the cruelty of the rich over the most vulnerable of his time. His preaching was mainly directed to people of very religious appearance, but who in their hearts were not pious, who showed signs being inconsistent about the practice of their many religious rites and how they lived way from the temple. Micah knew about the corruption that prevailed in the city. On the other hand, he knew firsthand the economic difficulties that the farmers were going through, who because of their debts, hid their lands from the rich in Samaria and Jerusalem.

Faced with such injustices, the prophet was convinced that the rich oppressors would not have the last word, but God, to fulfil His purpose, would bring the Messiah from the small village of Bethlehem.

Next, we will address two important passages from the book of the prophet Micah. Ask the students: Do you find any similarities between the religious and social problems of Micah's time and our contemporary ones? What can we learn from the prophet about how to face these challenges?

II. The announcement of the Savior

Micah 5:2 says, "But you, Bethlehem Ephrathah, though you are small among the clans of Judah, out of you will come for me one who will be ruler over Israel, whose origins are from of old, from ancient times." This passage is one of the most famous in the Old Testament, since it is here that Micah prophesies that the Messiah would be born in Bethlehem of Judea. This passage was also well known to the Jews in the time of Herod, and he helped wise men from the East who sought the newborn king of the Jews.

Micah, in harmony with his origin and the context in which he ministered, presented the Messiah as a man of the people (to the detriment of the idea that would come from Jerusalem), and whose purpose would be to bring peace and contentment to the afflicted, as he expresses in Micah 4:4: "Everyone will sit under their own vine and under their own fig tree, and no one will make them afraid, for the Lord Almighty has spoken." And in Micah 5:4-5 it says, "He will stand and shepherd his flock in the strength of the Lord, in the majesty of the name of the Lord his God. And they will live securely, for then his greatness will reach to the ends of the earth. And he will be our peace…"

This prophecy helped the people of God to keep hope alive during the centuries when they were waiting for the arrival of the Messiah, and it was literally and spiritually fulfilled with the birth of Jesus. The Jewish leaders of the time of Herod were up to date when they quoted Micah when they were asked about the place where the king of Israel was born, as expressed in Matthew 2:4-6: "When he had called together all the people's chief priests and teachers of the law, he asked them where the Messiah was to be born. 'In Bethlehem in Judea,' they replied, 'for this is what the prophet has written: '"But you, Bethlehem, in the land of Judah, are by no means least among the rulers of Judah; for out of you will come a ruler who will shepherd my people Israel."'

The prophecy also says that the Servant of Jehovah would be of the lineage of King David, although he would not be an earthly man, since he comes from eternity, that is to say that He is God incarnate. Under the rule of Christ, His people will be safe because His kingdom will be of peace. This agrees with his contemporary Isaiah: "Of the greatness of his government and peace there will be no end. He will reign on David's throne and over his kingdom, establishing and upholding it with justice and righteousness from that time on and forever. The zeal of the Lord Almighty will accomplish this" (Isaiah 9:7).

III. What the Lord asks of us

Micah 6:6-8 states, "With what shall I come before the Lord and bow down before the exalted God? Shall I come before him with burnt offerings, with calves a year old? Will the Lord be pleased with thousands of rams, with ten thousand rivers of olive oil? Shall I offer my firstborn for my transgression, the fruit of my body for the sin of my soul? He has shown you, O mortal, what is good. And what does the Lord require of you? To act justly and to love mercy and to walk humbly with your God."

This is one of the most impressive passages of the Old Testament. In chapters 6 and 7, a controversy between God and his people is presented. In the face of the generalized thinking of the people of God who considered him a cruel Lord with difficult demands to fulfill, Micah is responsible for brilliantly summarizing the demands in three ways: considering religion as a good relationship with God and men, justice as the basis of all morality, and loving kindness as a way of life. In short, true religion is only possible when there is communion with God.

The people of Judah sought divine favor by performing external duties, and were even willing to accept any condition that would help them buy forgiveness, but they were not willing to change their lives. They were obsessed with the practice of religious acts, but their hearts were far away from God. In this prophecy, Micah sums up the legal, ethical, and spiritual demands indicated by the contemporary prophets Isaiah, Amos, and Hosea, as indicated in Isaiah 30:15: "This is what the Sovereign Lord, the Holy One of Israel, says, 'In repentance and rest is your salvation, in quietness and trust is your strength, but you would have none of it.'"

Amos 5:24 expresses, "But let justice roll on like a river, righteousness like a never-failing stream!" And Hosea 2:19-20 says, "I will betroth you to me forever; I will betroth you in righteousness and justice, in love and compassion. I will betroth you in faithfulness, and you will acknowledge the Lord." Now the requirements of God exposed by Micah are available to everyone who wants to fulfill them. They are no longer demands that contain something mysterious or complex, but something we can do immediately. The term "O mortal" in Micah 6:8 refers to all mankind, therefore its scope is universal. In this way, God himself through the law and the prophets reveals his essential requirement for those who want to adore him and recognize him as their only God.

In our days, in which we already have the revelation of God in Christ, the words of Micah resonate with greater force, because now we can know His will better. In seeking to do justice, we become honest, trustworthy and sincere people, not only for our own good, but also for God and in our interpersonal relationships.

By loving mercy, we are developing a quality superior to justice, since while the latter implies giving each one what they deserve, mercy implies love, compassion and kindness even for those who are not worthy or cannot give something in return.

This is something practical, which impels us to be interested in the oppressed of society, offering much more than material goods, but offering ourselves to help our neighbors.

James affirms that a trial will be conducted without mercy against those who show no mercy: "because judgment without mercy will be shown to anyone who has not been merciful. Mercy triumphs over judgment" (James 2:13). Therefore, we can expect God's mercy according to the kindness we show to others.

The expression "walk humbly before your God" summarizes the first five commandments, which have to do with our relationship with God. Humiliation is the first step to communion with God, recognizing our need for Him and submitting our lives to His will.

Doing justice, loving mercy and humbling ourselves before our God should not be fragmented. Without mercy, we can fall into an inflexible justice, and in doing mercy without justice we open the door, for example, to donations of dishonest origin. There are also people who say they are Christians, but their acts do not reflect justice and mercy. Therefore, the three demands must be considered as a whole, because they give us a description of true religion, only surpassed by the summary of the law and the prophets given by Jesus in Matthew 22:36-40: "'Teacher, which is the greatest commandment in the Law?' Jesus replied: 'Love the Lord your God with all your heart and with all your soul and with all your mind. This is the first and greatest commandment. And the second is like it: Love your neighbor as yourself. All the Law and the Prophets hang on these two commandments.'"

Acceptable worship does not concentrate solely on the fulfillment of rituals, but implies a life of obedience. Therefore, the demands of God expressed in this passage are both moral and spiritual. Even the ritual that God himself instituted must be accompanied by a heart directed toward God, as Jesus also expressed it: "Yet a time is coming and has now come when the true worshipers will worship the Father in the Spirit and in truth, for they are the kind of worshipers the Father seeks. God is spirit, and his worshipers must worship in the Spirit and in truth" (John 4:23-24).

The prophet Micah in this passage is establishing an order of priorities, realizing that the life of holiness is the best evidence of true religion. The people were given the sacrificial system as a means to publicly express a life of devotion, never as an end in itself.

In our days, we must recognize that the principle for the resolution of social ills is that people turn to God with their whole being, in order to walk daily under the powerful guidance of the Holy Spirit.

Optional Questions:

I. The prophet of the people

- What was the difference between the ministry of the prophet Micah and that of his contemporary Isaiah?
- Why is Micah also known as "the prophet of the poor"?

II. The announcement of the Savior

- Why was Micah 5:2 important for the Jewish people?
- Why is it important for us in our day?

III. What the Lord asks of us

- What are the consequences of participating in rituals of worship with a heart far from God?
- What practical measures can you take to avoid falling into the religiosity without holiness that Micah denounced?

Conclusion

Micah not only describes a historical moment of the people of God, but also provides profound teachings for our Christian journey. Micah teaches us that God uses people from different social and economic contexts to express His will. God is against the rich who oppress the needy and, in His love, offers salvation to all who repent of their sins and believe that Jesus Christ is the Lord. Finally, He teaches us that every act of worship must be accompanied by a life of holiness, sensitive to His will and willing to express His justice, mercy and kindness.

God of love and justice

Lesson 21

Eduardo Velázquez (Argentina)

> **Memory verse:** "The Lord is good, a refuge in times of trouble. He cares for those who trust in him" (Nahum 1:7).
>
> **Lesson Aim:** To understand that God is love but that He is also just, and that His justice is expressed in the punishment of evil and sin.

Introduction

What are the personal qualities we attribute to God when we reflect on Him? Perhaps it is His love that stands out since the whole Bible shows us the divine love towards humanity. We could include several other qualities such as kindness, holiness, mercy, patience, etc. We seldom reflect on God's anger or wrath because it is hard for us to associate those characteristics with the qualities mentioned above. Does God get angry? Is He capable of expressing anger? Can a God of love punish us in anger?

In this brief study of the book of Nahum, we will try to answer these questions. To understand why the prophet Nahum pronounced such a dramatic message, we must understand something about what happened a century after Nineveh (capital of the Assyrian empire), repented after Jonah's preaching (Jonah 3:10). Nineveh returned to idolatry, violence and arrogance (Nahum 3:1-4). Assyria was at the height of her power. After the defeat of the Assyrian king Sennacherib (701 BC) recorded in Isaiah 37:36-38, Assyria extended its borders to Egypt. Esarhaddon, Sennacherib's son, led successful military campaigns conquering Galilea and Samaria by 670 BC. (2 Kings 17:24; Ezra 4:2), leaving Syria and Palestine very weak. But God overthrew Nineveh under the ascendant power of the Babylonian king Nabopolassar and his son, Nebuchadnezzar (612 A.C.) The fall of Assyria took place as God had announced.

What can we learn from the message that God gives through the prophet Nahum?

I. God is kind but hates and punishes evil

A. The goodness and righteousness of God

We see that Nineveh was a city that God loved, and this is what he told the prophet Jonah, although Jonah wanted to see the city destroyed: "And should I not have concern for the great city of Nineveh, in which there are more than a hundred and twenty thousand people who cannot tell their right hand from their left—and also many animals?" (Jonah 4:11). God wanted to forgive the city and its inhabitants, many of whom were children, and, indeed, God had forgiven Nineveh.

God is slow to anger, but when people or societies do unpleasant or sinful things, they will suffer the consequences of their own actions, which reflects divine justice. As we often say, truly 'God loves the sinner but hates sin', but that is only part of the story. The Bible tells us that if we love our sins and cling to them at all costs, rejecting the grace of God, we identify ourselves with sin and ultimately, the wrath of God against sin is also expressed against sinners.

Many do not come to God because they see evil in the world or hypocrisy in the churches. They do not understand that since God is slow to anger, He offers his children time to talk about the reality of His love and offers a change of life for sinners. But divine justice will come (John 5:28-29); God will not leave evil and sin unpunished. When people ask why God does not punish evil immediately, help them understand that if He did, none of us would be left standing. We should all be grateful that God gives us time to repent and turn to Him.

B. The pronouncement of God against sin (Nahum 1)

The magnitude of God's wrath and divine power is revealed through violent images in nature (Nahum 1:1-6). We see in these verses that God's wrath is compared to a whirlwind, drought, earthquakes and other natural phenomena. They are common figures for God (Exodus 19:16, Isaiah 28:2, 29:6, etc.). These images show God in control of nature, which indicates the immensity of His power.

The prophet wishes to communicate that no power of nature can rebel before God's lordship, much less the human power of some empire that can be obliterated by any event of nature such as an earthquake, a hurricane or a flood. The purpose of the message is to emphasize the superiority of God's power over any human power built on the cruelty and the deaths of many, as an expression of evil. The Assyrians were famous for their cruelty continuing their conquering and murderous campaigns, provoking the wrath of God that would now be poured out on them.

II. Punishment is a demonstration of divine justice (Nahum 2)

Nahum vividly described the consequences of God's just vengeance, and historically placed this action on the fall of Nineveh, which was destroyed in 612 BC., defeated by the combined forces of the Medes and Babylonians. Chaos characterized the defeat of Nineveh.

The city suffered a four-year siege (616-612 BC). In these verses, certain events are described that indicate to us that their destruction was terrible. Babylon and its allies were responsible for Assyria's destruction. The empire was destroyed. What had made them famous was now pitted against them. They had to suffer what they had made others suffer. The sarcasm is clear, the destruction is approaching.

For the Christian mentality of today, we might ask: Can a God of love do this? The prophet Nahum answers 'yes.' Why does the wrath of God, so frequently mentioned in the Scriptures, present a problem to believers? It is because we think that God is like us and not that we are like Him, made in His image and likeness.

Our anger is usually not just anger, so we think of anger as something negative. However, according to God's holy character, His anger is impartial and does not involve favoritism or differences between people and is not guided by passion or frustration. God's wrath is retributive and proportional, that is, God never gets angry without cause and we receive exactly and precisely what we deserve due to our own choices. The God of Nahum is the same God today, and it is out of love that He does not tolerate evil, and it is out of love that He will not allow evil to triumph over those who seek Him and turn to Him.

Within the general context of the book and its message, we understand that the retributive action of God on Nineveh also has its motivation in doing justice to the people of Israel, who suffered the cruelty of the Assyrians when conquered and taken captive. God showed His goodness and faithfulness towards His chosen people. It seems ironic that Nahum, whose name means 'consoling' or 'compassionate', should announce a trial for revenge. The prophet perceived that the message of the destruction of the Assyrian enemy would bring comfort to Israel. Nahum rejoiced because the righteousness of God was being vindicated.

This also teaches us believers, that we should not depend on our own strengths, possibilities, abilities or our influences and positions when we suffer some kind of injustice, but we should rest on what God will do on our behalf. This section of the book of Nahum that tells us about the destruction of Nineveh leads us to remember what the apostle Paul wrote in Romans 12:17-19: "Do not repay anyone evil for evil. Be careful to do what is right in the eyes of everyone. If it is possible, as far as it depends on you, live at peace with everyone. Do not take revenge, my dear friends, but leave room for God's wrath, for it is written: "It is mine to avenge; I will repay," says the Lord." Paul tells us in this passage that we should not take revenge into our own hands. On the contrary, we need to let God act justly and in good time in situations and with people who act unjustly toward us.

III. The sad condition of not being on God's side (Nahum 3)

The manifestation of the just punishment of God brings drastic consequences on those who do not believe in Him and do not turn from their sinful ways of life, or who turn away from the good way.

A. Defeat

Nahum raises a lament for the fate of Nineveh, and at the same time, summarizes the character of the bloodthirsty city. Nineveh used its beauty, prestige and power to seduce other nations. As a prostitute, it seduced them into false friendships. Then, when the nations lowered their guard, thinking that Assyria was their friend, it destroyed them and plundered them.

Beautiful and impressive on the outside, Nineveh was immoral and treacherous inside. Sometimes behind beautiful facades lie seduction and death. Do not allow an attractive institution, company, movement or person seduce you in such a way that you lower your principles.

Nahum emphasizes the irreversible attitude of Jehovah's vengeance on Nineveh and the Assyrian empire (v.19). This time there is no remedy, there is no possibility of repentance, everyone will laugh at their downfall, and there will be relief for those who suffered through their wickedness.

Nahum ends by saying that the fall of Nineveh brings a message of hope for those who suffer oppression. The Bible teaches that there will be consequences for our actions: "Do not be deceived: God cannot be mocked. A man reaps what he sows" (Galatians 6:7).

B. Humiliation and shame

The prophet compares Nineveh with Thebes, an Egyptian city of great power because of its strategic position for trade, and before which other people came to ask for help, creating a ruinous dependence for its inhabitants. Considered as more powerful than Nineveh, however it ended in captivity (vv. 9-10).

In the same way Nineveh will end and have an even worse fate, because Nineveh is compared with that of a prostitute (vv.4-7) who based her power on seduction and deceit by offering temporary pleasures, and which she placed before the people. The public will watch and ridicule the burlesque spectacle. There they will realize that Assyria's beauty is fantasy, for which they will be disillusioned and no one will feel sorry. This image shows the weakness of Nineveh, its fragility to such an extent that the dominant and exotic city will hide because of the enemy (v.11).

How sad it is to turn away from God, not only personally, but also as a family or as a society or nation. We have enough examples of this when looking around us or studying the history of our peoples. Let us not let anything or anyone seduce us to interrupt our communion with God, because we could end up being humiliated and ashamed. It is a Christian's imperative to present the whole message as Nahum did responding to the historical demands of his time.

- Although God is good, He does not approve of evil and sin; His holy and righteous character reacts against them, punishing them.

- The punishment of God for human wickedness is just; it is the consequence and fair retribution to our own choices and the rejecting of His salvation and loving direction for our lives.

- The consequences of living a life with our backs to God will leads us, our families and societies to a life of misery, defeat, shame and humiliation.

- God who is holy, exercises His justice in retribution to those who act unjustly and, to those who trust in Him, He shows kindness and protection.

For those who believe that God is just a God of love and never full of wrath, they must learn from Nahum that a God who is never capable of becoming enraged is not capable of loving either. The wrath of God is the result of His love. Precisely because He loves is why He gets angry, and because of His love, He must correct and punish.

What makes us mad? We can get really angry when something or someone we love is threatened or hurt. For example, if someone harms a child, we get angry. If someone is not able to get angry when they hear or see evil and injustice, it shows that they are not capable of loving. The person who cannot be outraged by evil cannot love either. If people, upon learning of stories of atrocities and oppression, drug or narcotics trafficking that destroys body and soul among young people, do not feel moved to a terrible sadness and anger, there is something wrong with our society and we are unable to love.

Optional Questions:

I. God is kind but hates and punishes evil

- Discuss with your peers why it is difficult to understand the angry God who punishes? (Nahum 1)

- How would you explain this anger to someone who tells you that God is love and will finally accept everyone?

II. Punishment is a demonstration of divine justice

- Reflect on whether it would be logical to think of a God who is pleased and happy with the good but overlooks the bad (Nahum 2).

III. The sad condition of not being on God's side

- What will be the end of those who turn away from God and do evil? (Nahum 3)

- How do you think you could help a person who lives far from God to understand the good news about Christ, according to the book of Nahum?

Conclusion

The book of the prophet Nahum helps us see God, who in His very essence is love, as also just. His justice will come to affect those who insist on remaining in sin. May God help us to remain faithful to Him, and to guide others to do the same.

A cry for justice and a prayer of hope

David Balcázar (Peru)

Lesson 22

> **Memory verse:** "See, the enemy is puffed up; his desires are not upright— but the righteous person will live by his faithfulness" (Habakkuk 2:4).
>
> **Lesson Aim:** To understand that although there is injustice, and sometimes those who judge are as guilty as those they judge; the just can live by faith in the God of justice which will be manifested.

Introduction

Reading Habakkuk can cause a big impact in the lives of those who study it. Habakkuk was a prophet from the late seventh century and the beginning of the sixth century BC, who saw the injustice that was taking place against his people, and cried out for justice.

His name Habakkuk means: "He that embraces; a wrestler". He had a mission of comfort to the Israelites who suffered injustices.

Generally, it is held that the book of Habakkuk was written before 605 BC, shortly before the captivity of the Jews at the hands of the Babylonians. In the first chapter, these people are referred to as an instrument of the justice of God.

This book cries out for justice, but it also shows the concern of the prophet because God as judge is going to use the wicked Babylonians to judge His people; however, the book ends by showing that they can trust God, who without hesitation will bring justice to everyone, in due time.

I. A clamor falling on deaf ears

Habakkuk 1:1-4 expresses a claim that seems to coincide with the questions that several non-believers make: "Why does God do nothing about injustices?" The following question seems to have resounded in ears for centuries: "How long, Lord ..." (v.2); and the conclusion seems to repeat itself year after year: "...justice is perverted" (v.4). Are there answers to all these questions?

II. A trial that does not seem to be fair

Those chosen to punish the sinful nation of Israel, in which injustices abound, are ... the Chaldeans! (Habakkuk 1:5-11). These people could not be the best judges and Habakkuk knew it:

* The Babylonians were a people that stole land from other people. "They ... sweep across the whole earth to seize dwellings not their own" (v.6).

* The Babylonians were guided by their own cruel laws that were not God's laws, while the Jews were the people with God's law. "They are a law to themselves and promote their own honor" (v.7).

* They had their own gods, not the true God of Israel. They were "guilty people, whose own strength is their god" (v.11).

Habakkuk's cry was being answered, but it seems that he is now more confused, because the 'instruments of punishment' were not fair either.

III. Habakkuk's new cry

God also acts through human beings. He respects the order He established for himself in this world. Humans are responsible for what happens on the earth. Therefore, to punish a nation, another nation was required. However, that was not fair either; and, to Habakkuk's sorrow, that nation was even more sinful than Israel; so, he expressed again his complaint (Habakkuk 1:12-17). "Your eyes are too pure to look on evil; you cannot tolerate wrongdoing. Why then do you tolerate the treacherous? Why are you silent while the wicked swallow up those more righteous than themselves?" (v.13).

The claim of Habakkuk required action; but this did not seem right either, since those who were going to carry out this action were not fair either. All this reminds us of other biblical passages: "There is no one righteous, not even one;" (Romans 3:10) and "Let any one of you who is without sin be the first to throw a stone at her…. At this, those who heard began to go away one at a time, the older ones first, until only Jesus was left, with the woman still standing there" (John 8:7 y 9). Habakkuk wanted an answer. There was injustice among God's people, but those who were going to punish them were worse. It did not seem fair. (Hebrews 2:1) Why did the Lord allow all this?

IV. The Lord's answer

The response of the Lord is quite clear, and it is very important that we also examine it carefully, (Habakkuk 2). Let's analyze it a little:

- The vision of Jehovah will be fulfilled, sooner or later; In other words, the justice of the Lord will be done in His time (vv. 2-3).

- The just shall live by his faith in the Lord; even in the midst of injustice, and in spite of the apparent lack of response (v. 4). Even when he sees that evil 'apparently triumphs', the righteous person will continue to live by faith. His victory and permanence will be through trusting in the Lord. It is very important to understand this!

- Those who covet unjust gain will receive their due. Those who do harm, taking advantage of others must know that sooner or later, they will be punished; therefore, unfair profit is never a good business (v. 9).

- Those who build the city with iniquity are working in vain. As in the previous paragraph, injustice will not bear good fruit (vv. 12-13).

- The vision will be fulfilled, for the earth will be filled with the knowledge of the glory of the Lord. The day of the fulfillment of the vision will arrive. Only those who live by faith will enjoy the glory of the Lord (v. 14).

- Those who worship other gods live in foolishness. Therefore, it is best to live by faith in the invisible God who will fill the earth (vv. 18-19).

- The true God is the Lord, all the earth should be respectfully humble before Him. God will fulfill His purpose and do His work. All the injustice will be duly punished and the righteous will enjoy the blessing of the Lord, independently of their nationality. On that day, God's justice will be carried out; therefore it is very important to humble ourselves and be attentive to the holy God who dwells in his temple (v. 20).

But not all the earth is attentive to God and will persevere. Now Habakkuk understood that all who live in evil will receive their reward, sooner or later; and that the key is to remain faithful to the Lord, living by faith, in the midst of so much evil.

The justice of God will be fulfilled; that is why it is necessary to be attentive and cry with hope. And although in this land, justice is administered by unjust people, the day will come when all the wicked will be punished by the true just Judge.

V. Habakkuk's final prayer is of hope

Habakkuk 3 ends the prophecy with a prayer of hope. The study of this chapter is worthy of a complete book. However, in this short space, we will highlight important aspects:

A. The work of God has been fulfilled in the past and will be fulfilled in the future.

Habakkuk had heard about the work of God in the past, and was confident that He would manifest Himself again. However, this new manifestation of God's work referred to the complete judgment that the Lord will carry out:

- "His glory covered the heavens and his praise filled the earth" (v.3).

- "Plague went before him; pestilence followed his steps" (v.5). The time of the trial had arrived.

- "He stood, and shook the earth; he looked, and made the nations tremble…" (v.6), referring to God's judgment.

- "Sun and moon stood still in the heavens" (v.11). Order of nature will also change before the powerful judgment of God.

- "In wrath you strode through the earth and in anger you threshed the nations" (v.12).

It is the time of the manifestation of God's wrath. God's judgment will be manifested in His time, and when that happens, the whole earth will know who He is; the impure will be eternally condemned, and the righteous will enjoy eternal bliss. When the judgment of God is manifested, it will be shocking, so Habakkuk exclaims, "in wrath remember mercy" (v.20). Those of us who have lived by faith will need "the mercy of the Lord".

B. On that day, the Lord will deliver his people and give them full justice.

When the day of the judgment of the Lord comes, his people will be delivered, the Lord himself will save them! He will punish those who did them wrong, those who treated them with injustice.

Now, Habakkuk understood that the wicked would receive their due punishment (vv.13-15).

C. Habakkuk's hope was that come what may, he would rejoice in the Lord.

These last verses express the heart of the true Christian in the midst of an unjust world and his trust in eternal joy, knowing that our reward is beyond this earthly world. Even if everything goes wrong and there seems to be no justice (vv.16-19):

- "Yet I will wait patiently for the day of calamity to come on the nation invading us" (v.16c).

- "Though the fig tree does not bud and there are no grapes on the vines" (v.17a).

- "Though the olive crop fails and the fields produce no food" (v. 17b).

- "Though there are no sheep in the pen and no cattle in the stalls" (v17c).

- "Yet I will rejoice in the Lord, I will be joyful in God my Savior" (v. 18).

The message of the book of Habakkuk is powerful. Although justice seems not to be manifested in the present, one day God will carry out full justice to everyone. If we live by faith in Him, we will be delivered on that day and enjoy the blessings of our just God.

Optional Questions:

I. A clamor falling on deaf ears.

- What is the prophet Habakkuk's complaint? (Habakkuk 1:1-4)

II. A trial that does not seem to be fair

- What are the characteristics of the chosen nation to punish Israel? (Habakkuk 1:5-11)

III. Habakkuk's new cry

- What is Habakkuk's new cry? (Habakkuk 1:12-17)

- Do similar things happen today?

IV. The Lord's answer

- What are the most important aspects of the Lord's answer? (Habakkuk 2)

V. Habakkuk's final prayer is of hope

- What is Habakkuk's new request? (Habakkuk 3)

- What is our confidence today?

Conclusion

There are many injustices in this world. Good does not always triumph over evil, and often it seems as though God is not listening. Even when bad people accuse us falsely, those who believe in Jesus, live by faith in Him, must trust that He knows what is happening and be assured that sooner or later the wicked will be punished, while the righteous will enjoy true justice and eternal joy.

Notes :

Zephaniah - God's anger against sin

Leticia Cano (Guatemala)

> **Memory verse:** "Seek the Lord, all you humble of the land, you who do what he commands. Seek righteousness, seek humility; perhaps you will be sheltered on the day of the Lord's anger" (Zephaniah 2:3).
>
> **Lesson Aim:** To learn that we must be committed to raise our voices against sin and injustice, encouraging those who commit theses sins to turn to God and repent.

Introduction

We live in times where paganism, religious syncretism and immorality are common. The principles and values of God's Word are being diluted. However, the authentic prophet of God cannot give in to the groups of power that promote elastic moral standards in society.

I. The sentence of God (Zephaniah 1)

In the first verse of Zephaniah, we see that God himself is going to speak through His servant: "The word of the Lord that came to Zephaniah son of Cushi, the son of Gedaliah, the son of Amariah, the son of Hezekiah, during the reign of Josiah son of Amon king of Judah" (Zephaniah 1:1).

A. Imminent destruction

God's creation has suffered the ravages of judgment due to man's sin, from Adam until our days. We should be deeply concerned when we see that sin proliferates around us, because we can be sure that God's judgment will follow (vv.2-3).

B. Attack on idolatry

The Lord pronounced a radical sentence not only on nature but also on people who were disloyal and decided to ignore Him by following idolatrous paganism, worshiping the sun, the moon and the stars, instead of worshiping the all-powerful God that had created them (vv.3-7).

Although King Manasseh repented at the end and tried to amend his pagan practices, the germ of sin had remained in his son Ammon, who re-established the cult of the Canaanite gods. By the time God spoke to Zephaniah, the young king Josiah had inherited a corrupt kingdom which needed a profound spiritual and social reform. This reform started in the eighteenth year of Josiah's reign.

C. Punishment for the wicked

Although Zephaniah was also of royal lineage, he was not afraid to give his message of judgement (vv.8-9). Rulers were to receive the death sentence as well as their followers for never questioning their leaders' sins and blindly following their bad examples, due to their relaxed morals and personal interests.

The message of the prophets is not only for their contemporaries, but is also relevant for us in our contemporary setting. Zephaniah teaches us that God does not overlook sin. Today we read in the newspapers or see on the TV of leaders of nations who should be praised for righteousness and justice, but are corrupt and mutually cover up injustices. God is calling us to raise our voices in God's name against such practices.

D. Disaster and desolation for sinners

The Word of the Lord says that the wages of sin is death (Rom. 6:23), and although God is merciful, that does not give us freedom to rebel against him. God knows what is in each person's heart. God said, "At that time I will search Jerusalem with lamps and punish those who are complacent, who are like wine left on its dregs, who think, 'The Lord will do nothing, either good or bad'" (Zephaniah 1:12). In Zephaniah's day, they were going to lose everything because of their indifference to God, which is a sin (v. 13).

E. Because of His Grace, God warns them

God does not want anybody to be lost; He wants everyone to repent, but His justice demands that sin be punished (vv.14-18).

II. The prophet calls for repentance (Zephaniah 2)

God, through his servant, denounced their sin and provided an opportunity for repentance. Because of His grace He warns that there will be anguish, hardship, desolation, darkness and great tribulation for those sinners who have challenged His authority. He could have only sent the punishment, but moved by mercy, He warned them of judgment because he loved them and did not want their destruction. "Seek the Lord, all you humble of the land, you who do what he commands. Seek righteousness, seek humility; perhaps you will be sheltered on the day of the Lord's anger" (v.3).

A. God's punishment for rebellion of nations

In 2:4-15, God turns his attention to the sins of the surrounding nations: the Philistines, Moab and Ammon, Cush and Assyria, who instead of honoring Jehovah, worshipped idols made with their own hands. These nations openly defied God with idolatrous, aberrant and immoral practices; being implacable, cruel and bloodthirsty. God is not indifferent to human evil. When men fill their heart with arrogance, they are entitled to the just punishment of God. Speaking of Assyria, God said that she will become: "a lair for wild beasts! All who pass by her scoff and shake their fists" (v. 15b).

B. The remnant in the service of God

God speaks of a remnant, or a small part of His people who He will use to punish Moab remains (Zephaniah 2:9). This remnant of God fearing people although they are a minority will be used by God. Even though many challenge God's authority a small group remains faithful to God's purpose.

We can see this illustrated in the 1960's when there was racial segregation in the United States. Rev. Martin Luther King raised his voice in the name of those who could not. He had to face cruelty and offered his own life to the cause. As a result, unjust laws were abolished because a man of God was willing to act rather than passively accept injustice.

As God's people, we are not only called to pronounce His message against sin and to fight for God's interests, but we also need to take an active part in changing the situation. The social disintegration that we see around us cannot be fought with passivity and indifference. The church must not remain silent when the world with its authorities pass laws that are detrimental to our nations. The people of God need to raise their voices against social ills such as same-sex marriage, abortion, corruption, domestic violence and other such social problems. We cannot be indifferent and not think of the country that our children will inherit. We want it to be better than that which we live in.

III. Crime and punishment for the people of God (Zephaniah 3)

There is no excuse for evil anywhere, because God has revealed Himself to humanity (Romans 1:19-25), and when people ignore God, they will be judged by God.

In chapter 3, God's sentence is against Jerusalem, the city of David, the city of God. How could they turn away from God's will and ignore His laws? How could they betray the God who rescued them from Egyptian slavery, looking after them and giving them a land for which they did not work?

A. The prophet denounces Judah's sin

Rebellion, corruption, oppression were the daily practices in Jerusalem, that rebellious, polluted and oppressive city. Called to be the light of the nations, they had fallen into the same sins as the Canaanite people, and even worse, because they did so even though they had the written revelation of the law of the Lord. Notice the seriousness of the sins of Jerusalem: "She obeys no one, she accepts no correction. She does not trust in the Lord, she does not draw near to her God" (3:2).

How much pain rebellious children bring to their parent's hearts. Members of God's family cause pain and indignation when they dare to ignore God's voice speaking to them.

Often, those who were once Christians and fell into sin and turned away are the worst enemies of Christianity. They become stumbling blocks who hinder non-Christians from accepting Jesus because of their bad testimony.

B. Judah, an incorrigible nation

Corruption and bribery were common practices of the nation's leaders. The rulers were corrupt and did not miss any opportunity to spend their ill-gotten riches (v.3). It is very clear that holiness is not compatible with sin. However, the religious leaders were not the only ones who had been perverted. The prophets too come under condemnation, the Lord accuses them of being unprincipled (v. 4).

It is not necessary that people participate in evil to be sinners. By consenting to evil, they are also guilty. The prophets stopped denouncing evil and did not call for repentance. Today too, some 'prophets' announce financial prosperity, attracting many sympathizers, but they seldom speak of integral prosperity that begins with the prosperity of the soul (3 John 2).

God deplores religious syncretism. The priests also sinned by contaminating the sanctuary of God. According to 2 Kings 21 and 22 and 2 Chronicles 33 and 34, during the reigns of Manasseh and Amon, statues of the idols Baal, Asherah, and others seriously offended the honor and holiness of the Lord, corrupting society and separating the people from God.

Those who have received from God positions of authority in the church have the responsibility to live in holiness and not to cover up sin. But in our churches, the sin of relatives, of influential people or of those who give money is often tolerated, excused or covered up. If God did not overlook the sin of those prophets and priests, He will no doubt also punish the apostles, pastors, evangelists, teachers, and other religious leaders of our day who cover over sin, twist the Scriptures, or accommodate them to their own convenience (like those of Zephaniah's time who falsified the law). With that, they gravely offend the sanctity of our Lord and cause sin to proliferate even more.

IV. God's justice

The people of Jerusalem did not learn from God's judgment of the neighboring nations (Zephaniah 3:6). They believed confidently that God would tolerate their affront. God, on the contrary, trusted that His people would learn and correct their evil ways (v.7). But they hastened to corrupt all their deeds and, in this way, became creditors of God's judgment, anger, and the ardor of His wrath that would consume the earth by the fire of his anger (v.8).

God warns that the wages of sin is death (Romans 6:23). Therefore, it is not sensible to provoke God's wrath by living according to how we want. In our midst exists prostitution, sexual exploitation, drug trafficking, homosexuality, abortions and many other sins that incur God's just and imminent punishment. It is time to raise our voices against so much iniquity instead of justifying it.

Promise of restoration to those who repent (Zephaniah 3:9-20)

God says through His prophet: "Then I will purify the lips of the peoples, that all of them may call on the name of the Lord and serve him shoulder to shoulder" (v.9). We do not have to resign ourselves to our nation being consumed by the fire of God's wrath. If, as the people of God, we sincerely repent and turn away from evil, and act against sin, the Lord will renew our life. Sin and the devil cannot rule or shame the redeemed (v.11).

Genuine repentance generates a change in behavior. The Lord speaks of changed lives, of a people who trust in His name, who no longer practice injustice or tell lies, but who can also live without fear and can even raise a song of joy for the Lord (v.13). God's promise to restore His repentant people included setting aside His judgment, casting out enemies and freeing His people from evil, so that they may live confidently (vv.15-20).

As His People, we need to follow His ways and take refuge in repentance, because like a shepherd who loves His sheep, the Lord promises to save those who limp and picks up those who have gone astray; He promises to give "honor and praise among all the peoples of the earth when I restore your fortune" (v:20).

Optional Questions:

I. The sentence of God

- What were the sins of the people according to Zephaniah 1:3-7, 12-13?
- Do we see similar sins in today's society?

II. The prophet calls for repentance

- What is the theme of the passage in Zephaniah 2:1-3?
- Is there any difference between what happened then and what happens today?
- Does Zephaniah 2:9c offer some hope? If so, to whom?

III. Crime and punishment of the people of God

- How did the political and religious leaders collude with sin, even within congregations, according to Zephaniah 3:1-4?
- Does this happen today? How?

IV. God's justice

- What does Zephaniah 3:9-20 promise?

Conclusion

Instead of just consenting to evils committed in our societies, we must learn from what happened to Judah, and apply the correction to our life, before God's judgment comes. As children of God we have the responsibility to denounce sin, to warn of God's judgement - because the wages of sin is death. We must announce the restoration that God will make in the lives of those who repent and obey His commandments.

All hands on deck

J. Victor Riofrío (U.S.A.)

Memory verse: "… 'Be strong, all you people of the land,' declares the Lord, 'and work. For I am with you,' declares the Lord Almighty" (Haggai 2:4).

Lesson Aim: To understand that God longs for His people to be willing always to work hard for Him.

Introduction

The saying 'All hands on deck' indicates that everyone is needed to do the job. Many Christians serve in the work of the Lord sincerely. But for different situations, they deviate from the initial motivation, assume other interests, and even discontinue what they began with so much enthusiasm.

That was what had happened after the people of Israel had returned from the Babylonian exile. God had acted supernaturally bringing His people back to their land, where they needed to rebuild Jerusalem and the temple. Those who returned in the first group had started with great force what God had entrusted to them, but little by little they became discouraged, thought more of themselves and discontinued the work.

We need to take a brief look at the historical situation to which we have referred to understand the context. The years 587-586 B.C. were times of disaster in Jerusalem. When king Nebuchadnezzar took reprisals against the rebellion of the kings of Judah, the city and the temple were destroyed; the majority of the people (priests, rich people, young people and very capable people) were deported to Babylon and the looting was general.

In 539 B.C., Cyrus II of Persia seized Babylon, and after consolidating his power, made wise decisions about the peoples of his domain. Among other things, he issued an edict (538 B.C.) to rebuild the temple in Jerusalem. In 537, the construction work for the Temple began. But, faced with the opposition of the complex population that had remained in the country during the captivity, the work was delayed.

Cyrus died in battle (in 530). His son Cambyses (a tyrant) taxed the Jews with heavy tributes. In the year 522, Cambyses died and Darius I ascended to the throne (different from the Darius of the book of Daniel). His father was Hystaspes, so Darius I is called Darius Histaspes or Darius the Great. His reign was quite long (522-486 BC). This is when the prophecy of Haggai is located.

Haggai means 'festive', perhaps because he was born during a holiday. An ancient tradition holds that he was born in Jerusalem, and therefore, knew Solomon's temple (Hag. 2:3). If this is true, he would have been about 80 years old when he prophesied. How did the prophet Haggai urge the people of Israel to put their hands to work in the reconstruction of the temple that had been left unfinished? In what way can we start again some work of the Lord which has been initiated and then stopped?

Haggai presents five opportune motivations to always put one's hands to the work of the Lord.

I. Think again and go back to the Lord's work (Haggai 1:1-11)

The book starts stating: "In the second year of King Darius, on the first day of the sixth month, the word of the Lord came through the prophet Haggai to Zerubbabel son of Shealtiel, governor of Judah, and to Joshua son of Jozadak, the high priest" (Haggai 1:1).

It had been 18 years since they had stopped rebuilding the temple. They had devoted themselves to arranging their houses extravagantly, and had neglected the house of the Lord (v.4). The recrimination of God to Israel should be considered by many believers today, whose opulence contrasts with the economic hardship of their church. They were motivated to "... Give careful thought to their ways" (v.5).

Due to Israel's neglect of the house of God, their own work was not being productive (v.6). The list of calamities (vv.7-11) became another reason for the exhortation: "Meditate". Jehovah reminds His people that their way of life was not taking into consideration the divine focus. The people expected favorable conditions, good harvests and a comfortable life. But they were not getting good harvests. It had not occurred to them that God's disciplining hand was behind their calamities.

Haggai gave them God's message: "...my house, which remains a ruin, while each of you is busy with your own house" (v.9b). So, they should not blame the economy or the political conditions or just bad luck. 'Meditate'" is like saying 'think carefully, don't grumble, reflect seriously, get out there and work for the Lord!'

II. Depend on God's Spirit for the work (Haggai 1:12-15).

God is pleased when the people listen to his voice. He woke up the spirit of Zerubbabel and of Joshua. The prophet Haggai told them something like this: 'I urge you to work diligently, with all the people, but always do so depending on the power of the Holy Spirit.' Verse 12 says, "Then Zerubbabel son of Shealtiel, Joshua son of Jozadak, the high priest, and the whole remnant of the people obeyed the voice of the Lord their God and the message of the prophet Haggai, because the Lord their God had sent him. And the people feared the Lord."

The Israelites not only obeyed, but feared or reverenced God. He was going to be with them, His Spirit was going to direct and help (v.13). This promise of the Spirit's personal presence was what would encourage them to resume and finish the work.

Without the light of God provided by his Word and the ministry of the Holy Spirit, we cannot go very far in the work of the Lord.

III. Strive and improve the work of the Lord (Haggai 2:1-9)

Almost a month later, Haggai prophesied again. The enthusiasm had cooled down. The workers were discouraged by what the older people told them about the glories of Solomon's temple. But God encouraged them by reminding them of the good of the past (v.5), and announcing a future full of glory. God's promise: "I will shake all nations, and what is desired by all nations will come, and I will fill this house with glory" (v.7). The desire of the nations seems to point to the Messiah.

The people were encouraged to go ahead and improve their new temple as much as possible, although it probably would not reach the level of Solomon's temple. At the same time, they received the hope that days of glory would come without end, when the Messiah would be revealed.

Today, for us who believe, it is foolish to let the anxiety about material needs dominate us when God has infinite resources. Even if there is a lack of resources, we cannot stop working for the Lord.

IV. Consecration in the service of the Lord (Haggai 2:12-19)

It was the seventh month (Haggai 2:1) and the people continued to delay finishing the reconstruction of the temple, and they were not demonstrating total surrender to God. Therefore, Haggai exhorted them to consecrate themselves first, if they wanted the work of their hands to be blessed by God.

On that occasion, the prophet Haggai changed his methodology. Before, he had confronted the remnant with a direct exhortation; Here he used questions. The first (2:12) is related to the transfer of holiness. "If someone carries consecrated meat in the fold of their garment, and that fold touches some bread or stew, some wine, olive oil or other food, does it become consecrated?" (v:12). The answer is 'no' because the law teaches that there can be no transfer of holiness.

The second question focuses on the opposite of the first: "If a person defiled by contact with a dead body touches one of these things, does it become defiled?" "Yes," the priests replied, "it becomes defiled" (v.13). According to the law, contact with a corpse caused contamination. Such a condition prevented the individual from taking part in the worship, and sometimes he had to leave the camp. Also, if that individual touched another, that one also became unclean.

Haggai specified that the labor in the rebuilding of the temple, even the little that had been achieved up to that date, had been contaminated by their spiritual suffering. It is possible to be quite active in the work of God and even have your hands in sacred matters and still be disobedient. Good work can be contaminated by a disobedient heart and a stubborn spirit. To enjoy the complete blessing of God, we have to make sure to eliminate the contagious contamination of sin; we must be consecrated.

V. God supports those in charge of the work of the Lord (Haggai. 2:20-23).

On the twenty-fourth day of the same month, the foundation stone was laid (v.18). That day the Lord gave a new message to Haggai for His people. This time the message was for the governor, Zerubbabel, who was recognized by the Persian authorities as the political leader of the remnant.

The message to the governor presented God as sovereign, and made a list of the works that demonstrated his complete and total control (vv.21-22). God spoke to the political leader at a time when all but the most faithful felt uncertainty about their future. They were demoralized because of lack of achievement in the rebuilding, as well as drought, and attacks from their enemies. He reminded Zerubbabel that he belonged to the house of David, that God had given promises about the offspring of that famous king, and finally, He compared him to a signet ring. Zerubbabel was a link between David and his greater descendant, the true Messiah (v.23). God has the ability to put His plan into action and had already chosen the agents that He would employ to carry out His designs to the full.

God will always be pleased with those who are obedient to him and know how to be loyal servants. The Temple at last was finished in 515 B.C. (Ezra 6:14-16). Although insignificant compared to Solomon's temple, this reconstruction exercised in its time greater influence than that of Solomon's temple in the life of the Jewish nation. Pilgrims from all over arrived because all the rites and sacrifices were centralized.

Haggai was a man with a true prophetic vocation. In a time of crisis, he was obedient to his call, and with courage and perseverance was able to raise the leaders' and the people's spirits to get going and finish the job of rebuilding the temple.

Optional Questions:

I. Think again and go back to the Lord's work (Haggai 1:1-11)

- Why did Haggai exhort the Jews who returned from exile?
- Are you active in God's work?
- What are you doing for Him?

II. Depend on God's Spirit for the work (Haggai 1:12-15).

- Who did the Spirit help?
- What place do you think the Holy Spirit should occupy in our service in the work of the Lord?
- What has happened in your life when you depended only on your own strength?

III. Strive and improve the work of the Lord (Haggai 2:1-9)

- Why did Haggai encourage them again to try and improve the work of rebuilding the temple?
- Do you strive in the work of the Lord?
- How do you usually improve what you are doing to serve the Lord?

IV. Consecration in the service of the Lord (Haggai 2:12-19)

- Do you think that consecration is key to getting His work done?

V. God supports those in charge of the work of the Lord (Haggai. 2:20-23).

- Who should the people of Israel support in order to finish the work of rebuilding the temple in Jerusalem?
- Do you support your leader in the work of the Lord?

Conclusion

Where are our priorities today? The Word of God gives us enough motivation for us to continue working for the Lord. If we have been discouraged, have stopped working for Him, if our priorities have changed, or our attention has been diverted, it's time to get back to doing His work. God wants all hands on deck!

Lesson 25 — A prophecy for today

Walter Rodríguez (Uruguay)

Memory verse: "'Return to me,' declares the Lord Almighty, 'and I will return to you,' says the Lord Almighty" (Zechariah 1:3b).

Lesson Aim: To know the love, mercy and holiness of God when relating to His people.

Introduction

It is likely that some people in your class are immigrants or have had the experience of living outside their place of origin, whether they have moved from one location to another within the same country or have migrated from one country to another. In our day, there are millions of people who do not live in the place where they were born. Some have moved to study, many others migrated looking for opportunities to live better, others moved for political or social issues, etc.

We also have in the world a huge number of people who have had to flee their homes and countries to save their lives, housed in refugee camps until they can be admitted to other countries as refugees. Among those displaced are those who are victims of the trafficking of persons who are forcibly kidnapped or forced to be slaves, especially women exploited as sex workers. Maybe in your community this problem exists. As Christians, we must approach it under the direction of God, looking for suitable ways to show the love of the Lord in such circumstances.

Ask your students to briefly share some positive and negative experiences of being migrants. Ask them to explain the reason why they may have had to leave their places of birth.

Ask: How was it to leave your home? Could you go back? Did you have to learn another language? Did you have to learn new lifestyles? How were you received? Were you welcome? Were you rejected or discriminated against? If you returned, how was that return?

Zechariah is the penultimate book of the Old Testament. It was written between 520 and 518 B.C. when Zerubbabel was governor of Judah, appointed by the emperor Cyrus of Persia, and was accompanied by the high priest Joshua.

The book is clearly divided into two parts: The first covers chapters 1-8; and the second chapters 9-14, and is the most extensive book of the Minor Prophets. Although there is some controversy about the author, especially in the second part, it is traditionally accepted that Zechariah is the author of the entire book.

I. Beginning of a new day

There are political and military explanations about the events that occurred in the Middle East at the time when the kingdoms of the North (Israel) and the South (Judah) were conquered by foreign powers, as well as the three captivities of the Jewish people. But from the point of view of God's relationship with His people, the biblical account emphasizes the punishment for the disobedience of the people who had broken the covenant they had made with God.

The Jewish rulers ignored what God had told them through the prophets. For this reason, the people were taken into captivity by the emperor Nebuchadnezzar, and Jerusalem and the temple were destroyed. At the time of the prophet Zechariah, God intended to restore His relationship with His people. Thus, Cyrus, Persian emperor in 538 BC, published an edict that freed the Jewish people from a captivity that had lasted more than 70 years.

A group of the captives returned to Jerusalem with the purpose of rebuilding the city and especially God's temple. Cyrus not only gave them authorization, but gave them abundant materials and food to start the work. They began to work with enthusiasm, and managed to lay the foundations of the Temple. After a while, the neighboring towns were governed by the emperor Artaxerxes of Persia, who gave the order to interrupt the construction until a new order was issued. The life of those who returned was difficult, because generally the task of pioneers is not simple and the obstacles made the enthusiasm of those who started the reconstruction work vanish.

A few years later, in 520 B.C. when Darius was the emperor, the prophet Haggai and two months later the prophet and priest Zechariah began to preach to the people. Both were dedicated to encouraging the people to finish rebuilding the temple and the city. "So, the elders of the Jews continued to build and prosper under the preaching of Haggai the prophet and Zechariah, a descendant of Iddo. They finished building the temple according to the command of the God of Israel and the decrees of Cyrus, Darius and Artaxerxes, kings of Persia" (Ezra 6:14).

Zechariah had the same vision as Haggai; it was very important to finish the temple to strengthen the faith of the people. However, there were other very important issues to which they should pay attention, such as the personal relationship as a people with God, who was opening up a new opportunity for them to live in peace and prosperity. Zechariah pointed out that if they were faithful, there was a wonderful and bright future that would have no expiration date.

II. It was necessary to restore the relationship

In the first part (chapters 1-8), Zechariah begins with a call to repentance: "'Return to me,' declares the Lord Almighty, 'and I will return to you,' says the Lord Almighty" (1:3). In this call are contained the elements of the agreement that God offered to the people on repeated occasions, and that He continues to offer to His followers even today, an alliance based on love and fidelity.

It seems to say, 'let us agree, let go of that painful habit you have of being rebellious, of not paying attention to my teachings, so that I can lead you on a much better path.' This loving invitation to serious commitment is repeated throughout the Bible.

In the second part of his message, Zechariah mentions eight visions, probably all presented on the same occasion. The prophet arranged his points in the form of allegories that communicated the message in apocalyptic language, which was very popular in the post-exile era.

The theme of the temple was very important for Zechariah, but in this series of visions, he emphasized external purification (four horns and four craftsmen 1:18-21); there will be obstacles, however God provides the help that the people need to achieve the reconstruction. At the same time, it signals an inner purification (the woman in a basket, 5:5-7).

Returning to the first message of repentance, Zechariah speaks of the need to abandon sin. The construction of the temple will result in: removal of guilt (3:9), peace among all citizens (3:10), peace between two leaders (6:13), fertility of the fields (8:11-12) and many people from different nations will seek God in Jerusalem (8:20-23).

III. Hard work is not everything

"So, he said to me, "This is the word of the Lord to Zerubbabel: 'Not by might nor by power, but by my Spirit,' says the Lord Almighty" (4:6). These words belong to the fifth vision, that of the golden candlestick and the two olives. These famous words enclose another of the themes that are repeated in Zechariah, the absolute trust and dependence on God, together with hard work and perseverance, is the way. When the work began, some lost patience and were discouraged, because at first they did not progress as they had dreamed. Perhaps they thought that they did not have everything they needed or that they did not have enough workers. It is possible that some were not convinced that God was with them, that the work had become a mere human project. However, the word that the prophet receives from God is of encouragement, assuring them that He is present: "Who dares despise the day of small things, since the seven eyes of the Lord that range throughout the earth will rejoice when they see the chosen capstone in the hand of Zerubbabel?" (4:10). Those who have been anointed are the instruments that He is using, that He will use to complete the work: "These are the two who are anointed to serve the Lord of all the earth" (4:14).

Very easily today we forget that we are instruments in the hands of God, and we begin to appropriate the task that He has entrusted to us and the possibility of success is reduced to our abilities and our resources, when it is our Lord and God who provides direction and guides us towards what we need.

It is possible that at some stage, things do not look as we expect, but repeatedly Zechariah encourages us to look beyond the circumstances and see with eyes of faith what He will do if we persevere and do not lose heart.

IV. Prophecy of real hope

The second part of the book of Zechariah (chapters 9-14) is notoriously different than the first 8 chapters. Some commentators think that this last part was written by the prophet at the end of his life, while the first part is clearly identified with Zechariah's youth. This section includes several passages that are easily linked to the earthly ministry of the Lord Jesus Christ. For example, 9:9 mentions how the new king of Zion will come to Jerusalem: "Rejoice greatly, Daughter Zion! Shout, Daughter Jerusalem! See, your king comes to you, righteous and victorious, lowly and riding on a donkey, on a colt, the foal of a donkey."

Other interesting references appear in 12:10: "They will look on me, the one they have pierced, and they will mourn for him as one mourns for an only child, and grieve bitterly for him as one grieves for a firstborn son." And 13:6: "If someone asks, 'What are these wounds on your body?' they will answer, 'The wounds I was given at the house of my friends.'"

The tone of these chapters is of hope and restoration for the people of God. There will come a new time of material prosperity and spiritual renewal. For example, in the first part of Zechariah 12:10, which we already quoted, says, "And I will pour out on the house of David and the inhabitants of Jerusalem a spirit of grace and supplication."

These good times are for all those who recognize and worship Jehovah. The mercy of God, for a rebellious people like this, is beyond our comprehension. Throughout the Bible, God reveals himself to be loving and willing to forgive, although the relationship of love and friendship with his people is conditioned by repentance and a behavior of fidelity. This message appears clearly throughout the Bible: there is hope, the Forgiving Father is hoping that His children will come back repentant, willing to follow His teachings with joy and fidelity.

Although God's blessing comes to good and bad, He has a special and loving relationship with His children. He constantly encourages them to persevere, to trust and continually seek to do what pleases Him. On the other hand, he also teaches us to look beyond the circumstances that we are going through, to see that blessing, peace and enjoyment in life as something tied to our relationship with Him.

In times like these, when we talk so much about 'feeling' in worship, we hear little of what God expects from us. While both salvation and entire sanctification are identified with emotional experiences, we need to speak more about our testimony of conduct in the Christian life. The book closes with an image of triumphant holiness. "On that day 'holy to the Lord' will be inscribed on the bells of the horses, and the cooking pots in the Lord's house will be like the sacred bowls in front of the altar" (14:20). The inscription which had to be on the head piece of the high priest will be everywhere even on horses' bells and pots and pans. Holiness will no longer just be priestly, but will reach all aspects of life, and all people.

Optional Questions:

I. Beginning of a new day
- Why was Jerusalem destroyed? (Note 2 Kings chapters 24 and 25)
- Why Cyrus Emperor of Persia decides to free the Jews? (Note Ezra 1)

II. It was necessary to restore the relationship
- What are the two most important messages of Zechariah relevant to this day?

III. Hard work is not everything
- In what way can the message of Zechariah be applied to your life?

IV. Prophecy of a real hope
- What is the general tone of the second part of this book?
- And, why do you think so?

Conclusion

In the prophecies of Zechariah (addressed first to a people in reconstruction), there are excellent lessons for the life of today's believer. One of them is that we must continually exercise faith and be focused on what God wants. Understanding that the difficulties suffered by those who are doing God's will, are simply elements that the enemy uses to distract and weaken the people of God.

Which side are we on?

José Barrientos (Guatemala)

Memory verse: "Let us not become weary in doing good, for at the proper time we will reap a harvest if we do not give up" (Galatians 6:9).

Lesson Aim: To check up if we are walking with God as He wants us to and learn about the correct way to give our offerings.

Introduction

The people of Israel constitute a model of God's relationship with mankind. When studying the book of Malachi, we see our own life reflected in it. This book has been studied by various biblical commentators. For their analysis, they have divided it in different ways. We will adapt the one that offers an adequate form for the proposed objective, making use of very explicit terms of the book. This small but powerful book offers lessons for us for our walk with Christ.

The characteristics of our daily lives have similarities with what Malachi describes, which confirms the contemporary validity of the book. This book has a clear objective which we share: the redemption of mankind by God.

I. Message to priests (Malachi 2:1-9)

In Numbers 3, God's plan for the tribe of Levi is laid out. They played a very important role because they would replace the firstborn as the property of Jehovah. God had spared the firstborn Jews but firstborn children of the Egyptians had died. God gave them specific responsibilities, which included a commitment to God and to the people. In Numbers 3:7 we read, "They are to perform duties for him and for the whole community at the tent of meeting by doing the work of the tabernacle."

A. What did God expect?

Malachi has an explicit warning message from God to the priests: they needed to listen to Him, turn to Him, and worship Him. He reminds them that the covenant that God made with Levi was one of life and peace. God had blessed them (Malachi 2:1-9). The priests were expected to speak wisely and to guide the people about the Word of God. Unfortunately, none of this was happening.

Therefore, God warned them about the need to change their attitude; if not, they would be punished.

B. Is this message relevant for us today?

After the coming of the Lord Jesus Christ, many of the responsibilities were clarified. Although the role of the priests was delegated, in the case of the evangelical church, to the pastors, the responsibility that we have individually was also clarified.

The priests had the responsibility of attending to the people and fundamentally fulfilling an intercessory function in the sacrificial sacrifices. But the sacrifices of animals were insufficient due to the corruption of the priests themselves (Isaiah 1:11-13). Because of their sinful conduct, they put the people off. The sacrifices, which were only symbolic in the Old Testament, were replaced by the true and only lamb without blemish, the lamb of God, God's son Jesus Christ (John 1:29).

When Jesus gave the mandate to go and make disciples (Matthew 28:19-20), he generated a co-responsibility among those who would substitute the role of priests and disciples in general. Among them initially were the apostles, and from them the new organization responsible for the Great Commission: the church.

It would be very easy to say that this is only the pastors' responsibility, but it includes us all. Joshua assumed this when he said, "But as for me and my household, we will serve the Lord" (Joshua 24:15). Peter makes it very clear: "But you are a chosen people, a royal priesthood, a holy nation, God's special possession, that you may declare the praises of him who called you out of darkness into his wonderful light" (1 Peter 2:9). Paul says we have an equal and shared responsibility: "There is neither Jew nor Gentile, neither slave nor free, nor is there male and female, for you are all one in Christ Jesus" (Galatians 3:28). So, we have to ask ourselves: 'Are we fulfilling our priestly role, in our homes in the first place, and then towards others?

II. Message to the people in general (Malachi 3).

The prophet's message includes the prophecy about 'the great day of the Lord.' When we look carefully at this passage, we can see that it is a prophecy about the first coming of Jesus: "I will send my messenger, who will prepare the way before me. Then suddenly the Lord you are seeking will come to his temple; the messenger of the covenant, whom you desire, will come," says the Lord Almighty. But who can endure the day of his coming? Who can stand when he appears? For he will be like a refiner's fire or a launderer's soap. He will sit as a refiner and purifier of silver; he will purify the Levites and refine them like gold and silver" (Malachi 3:1-3).

Jesus confronted the Priests and Levites on many occasions about their hypocrisy. On several occasions, Jesus declared that He was God. Jesus did go to the temple; the first time as a 12-year-old boy who discussed theology with the religious leaders. On another occasion he turned over the tables of the money changers and other profiteers.

A. What can we learn from this prophecy? (Malachi 3:1-5).

This passage reveals that God will give just punishments to those who neglected His commands. Malachi warns that God says to us all, "I will come to put you on trial. I will be quick to testify against sorcerers, adulterers and perjurers, against those who defraud laborers of their wages, who oppress the widows and the fatherless, and deprive the foreigners among you of justice, but do not fear me" (Malachi 3:5). We live in a world in which these social sins persist. Television, the Internet and other technological advances have multiplied the problem.

B. Withholding the tithe, a harmful practice (Malachi 3:6-10)

Lamentations 3:22 says, "Because of the Lord's great love we are not consumed, for his compassions never fail." This idea is present in verse 6: "I the Lord do not change." This is both a promise and a warning. The prophet points out another problem; the people were unwilling to give tithes. God said through his prophet, "Will a mere mortal rob God? Yet you rob me. But you ask, 'How are we robbing you?' In tithes and offerings. You are under a curse—your whole nation—because you are robbing me" (Malachi 3:8-9). The tithes were to be used to look after the needs of the Levites and people in society that had no resources, such as widows and orphans. This unfortunate reluctance has a two-way effect, because by not receiving tithes from the people, the priests were forced to seek other alternatives for their livelihood, and many needy people were suffering.

How we use our money is a guide as to how we are as people. Sins such as envy and greed lead to other sins such as acts of corruption. We need to give our offerings to support the church, and as in olden times to help those people who are needy; it is part of what it means to be a disciple of Jesus. To withhold our tithes and offerings limits what God can do in our community of faith.

Today in some churches that follow the Prosperity Theology, congregations are ordered to give so that they will be blessed. Although Malachi tells us that God blesses those who give their tithes faithfully (3:10-12), we should not give so that we can receive a blessing, but rather out of joy (2 Corinthians 9:7). How is our priestly commitment as a giver before God?

III. Message to those who fear Jehovah

In Malachi's day, Israel spoke arrogantly against God. They wanted to know what they had done to offend Him. God answered them with these words, "You have said, 'It is futile to serve God. What do we gain by carrying out his requirements and going about like mourners before the Lord Almighty? But now we call the arrogant blessed. Certainly, evildoers prosper, and even when they put God to the test, they get away with it'" (Malachi 3:14-15). The bad people were seen to prosper, so they wandered if serving God was a good idea.

In the history of the church, we can see moments when power corrupted. In much of the Medieval period, the kings and popes fought for power over the people. Today, we see a new group of strong leaders who call themselves apostles, or prophets who wield ecclesiastical power over sections of the evangelical church. Many of this new class of leaders are seen to be prosperous Christians.

A. The message of hope (Malachi 3:16-18)

The bad people who prosper do not have the last word. God talks about a remnant, a segment of the people that despite everything that happens around them, continue to please and obey God. "Then those who feared the Lord talked with each other, and the Lord listened and heard. A scroll of remembrance was written in his presence concerning those who feared the Lord and honored his name" (v.16).

Jesus created the church to continue His work. As His disciples, we must submit to His will and live as He lived in the power of the holy Spirit. The powerful may appear to be gaining the upper hand, but in the long run and from an eternal perspective, they will not win. God's people have often had to suffer for their faith. Peter said, "But even if you should suffer for what is right, you are blessed. Do not fear their threats; do not be frightened." (1 Peter 3:14).

B. How that hope is manifested

God our Creator knows the best way to guide us. Jesus himself faced the intense sacrifice that awaited him. At the moment of His baptism, the Father said, "This is my Son, whom I love; with him I am well pleased" (Matthew 3:17b). Malachi tells us that those who fear God will be remembered. They will be His special treasure. God knows who the faithful are: "On the day when I act," says the Lord Almighty, "they will be my treasured possession. I will spare them, just as a father has compassion and spares his son who serves him. And you will again see the distinction between the righteous and the wicked, between those who serve God and those who do not" (Malachi 3:17-8).

C. The fate of the proud (Malachi 4:1-6).

Malachi 4 describes the fate of the righteous and the proud on the day of judgment. On that day, the arrogant will burn like stubble. Those who have ruled in defiance of God will turn to ashes at the feet of the righteous. God says to the faithful, "But for you who revere my name, the sun of righteousness will rise with healing in its rays. And you will go out and frolic like well-fed calves" (Malachi 4:2).

God tells them how to avoid His judgement: "Remember the law of my servant Moses, the decrees and laws I gave him at Horeb for all Israel" (v. 4). This verse tells us that obedience to what God tells us in the Bible is crucial if we want to receive His blessing. It also offers a pathway for redemption to those who are on the wrong road. They can come back, repent, and learn to walk God's pathway in obedience.

The book of Malachi talks to three groups of people:
a) Leaders who are not doing their job well;
b) The majority who are perverse and greedy, and
c) Those who fear God.

Each of us will be in one or other of these three groups. God offers the world the opportunity to turn to Him, receive His forgiveness, and persevere in obedience. But people who continue in unbridled pride and greed will eventually be judged and punished by God for their actions.

Optional Questions:

I. Message to priests (Malachi 2:1-9)

- What is the message of the prophet Malachi to the priests?
- Why does God send them that message?
- According to 1 Peter 2:19, who assumes the role of priests today?

II. Message to the people in general (Malachi 3).

- How does God define the action of not tithing?
- If we do not tithe, in what ways are we robbing God?
- What is God's message to the arrogant and perverse?

III. Message to those who fear Jehovah

- What is our hope for the future?
- What do we have to do?

Conclusion

Being on God's side is the best option. He has shown us the way of repentance and forgiveness. He calls us to walk with Him in obedience, doing what pleases Him. God also wants us to share what we have with others through our tithes and offerings. We should not get tired of doing good because in time, we will reap if we do not lose heart.

The churches in Biblical times

The first church
The church in the heart of the Roman Empire
Tempestuous church of Corinth
Lessons from Philippi
The Colossian Church
Thessalonians: a consistent church
The Church of Ephesus
Smyrna: a challenge to be faithful
Pergamum: a call to commit to the truth
Thyatira: when sin penetrates the church
A wake-up call to the church at Sardis
The greatness of the church at Philadelphia
Church of Laodicea

The first church

Sara Patetta (U.S.A.)

Memory verse: "How good and pleasant it is when God's people live together in unity!" (Psalm 133:1)

Lesson Aim: To learn about the characteristics that God looks for in believers who want to get involved in His work.

Introduction

Ask your students if any of them have participated in an evangelistic team that planed to open up a new church. In relation to this, ask the following questions: Have you thought about the characteristics that the Lord requires from His collaborators? Have you ever wondered why God would choose the format of the church as a vehicle to spread His message?

Jesus specifically stated that Peter was going to be an important figure in building the church. Peter recognized who He was: "You are the Messiah, the Son of the living God." (Matt. 16:16). After Peter had made this confession, Jesus told him, "And I tell you that you are Peter, and on this rock, I will build my church" (v.18).

Alfred Edersheim (1825-1889), a Jewish convert to Christianity and recognized authority on biblical writings, known especially for his book, The Life and Times of Jesus the Messiah, states: "In the words of this confession, Peter has consciously reached the firm ground of Messianic acknowledgment. All else is implied in this, and would follow from it. It is the first real confession of the Church" (p.1032). He adds: "In Hebrew the use of 'assembly' referred to Israel, not in their national but in their religious unity. As here employed, it would convey the prophecy, that His disciples would in the future be joined together in a religious unity; that this religious unity or 'Church' would be a building of which Christ was the Builder; that it would be founded on 'the Petrine' of heaven-taught faith and confession; (p 1034, http://www.ntslibrary.com/).

Peter had the privilege of being the recipient of that revelation from heaven, as well as opening the door (until that time closed to the Gentiles) when he preached the gospel to them for the first time (Acts 10), and called them to be baptized. Clearly, this church was a future task at the time the Lord made his statement (which only Matthew records) as an answer to Peter's confession. The current model of the church was not feasible at that moment in history; because Jesus was present on earth. Once He left, it would continue to fulfill its mission. Thus, after ascending to the Father and sending the following promise of the Holy Spirit to the believers, it became possible to gather the essential elements to reproduce the complete model of His plan to reach the world: "And I will ask the Father, and he will give you another advocate to help you and be with you forever— the Spirit of truth. The world cannot accept him, because it neither sees him nor knows him. But you know him, for he lives with you and will be in you" (John 14:16-17). This will continue until Jesus comes back again.

Throughout the New Testament, we see that God has not neglected that initial project; He continued to expand it, and to provide the necessary instruction during the first century of church history until today: "In the same way, the gospel is bearing fruit and growing throughout the whole world—just as it has been doing among you since the day you heard it and truly understood God's grace" (Colossians 1:6).

So, the church continues to count on the guidance of the Holy Spirit, and one day Christ will present the church "to himself as a radiant church, without stain or wrinkle or any other blemish, but holy and blameless" (Ephesians 5:27). However, this will be at the end of time when the Lord returns to seek the church to be with Him forever.

God provides the information, the means and everything necessary to enable the church to achieve the task assigned according to his eternal plan and his will. The Bible is full of instructions which are totally adequate to make possible the fulfillment of God's great and loving, never changing mission.

Ask your students if they are willing to accept the challenge of sharing God's message of salvation with their communities. Would they like to be a vital part of the redemptive movement that has been underway over time? Would they like to submit to be trained through Bible study and be used by God?

I. The founder and purpose of the church

We find the beginnings of the church of Jesus Christ in this passage: Acts 2:42-47.

A. The founder

It has been said that the book of the Acts of the Apostles, where we find the description of the birth of the church as an institution, could have been very aptly named the 'Acts of the Holy Spirit.' In this book, the ways that the Holy Spirit inspired and empowered the events of the ministry of the apostles are described. We see ordinary men who were previously exposed to the influence and teachings of Jesus speaking boldly about the good news of salvation.

The church, with Jesus as its head, came into being after they had been filled with the Holy Spirit: "And he is the head of the body, the church; he is the beginning and the firstborn from among the dead, so that in everything he might have the supremacy" (Col. 1:18). As a consequence, it is not surprising that a small community redeemed by the blood of Christ, validated and sustained by the Holy Spirit itself, would soon spread throughout the Roman Empire, and with time, would persist alive and well through the centuries.

B. The purpose of church meetings

1. The people of God, the group of those first believers, met with one main purpose: to praise God (Acts 2:47). Even today, that must be the great purpose that identifies the true church of Jesus Christ. In Scripture itself, we find the reason: "Yet you are enthroned as the Holy One; you are the one Israel praises" (Psalm 22:3). As a result, a group of believers strengthened with the very presence and power of God was soon to affect those people around them.

2. They met too to strengthen each other in the faith. The power of the presence of God and the empowerment of the Holy Spirit produced in the body of the believer perseverance in the doctrine of the apostles. Paul gave specific and clear orders to the young pastor Timothy concerning this crucial issue: he needed to have correct doctrine to train other leaders (1 Timothy 4:16). Thus, the gospel is the common element of all Christian people, the very essence of the message of the church.

C. The characteristics of the church

The communion they shared together was characterized by unity. Paul said to the Philippians, "I will know that you stand firm in the one Spirit, striving together as one for the faith of the gospel" (1:27). This condition of unity, being truly brothers in the faith without distinction by social class, culture or gifts, was achieved only by the common love for the gospel, having the same principles, conduct and vision. Incredibly, in those first congregations, there were Jews, Greeks, Romans, Africans, Asians. These believers were all different, but they were one body in Christ (Romans 12:4-7).

Unity is essential to fight against the enemy that wants to divide. There must be union, both to defend and to evangelize (Ephesians 6:11), and to achieve growth by sharing the gifts (Ephesians 4:15-16).

The people in the early church showed love by meeting each other's needs (Acts 2:44-45). Sometime later, Paul himself advised the Philippian Christians to support others who were going through problems, to help and sustain them in the faith (Phil. 4:3). There was cohesion among the members of the early church; they acted as a community (Acts 2:45-46), putting their goods at the disposal of others, as well as eating together in each other's houses with joy and simplicity of heart.

II. Means used by God to build his church

1. Teaching sound doctrine

Acts 2:42 tells us that, "They devoted themselves to the apostles' teaching and to fellowship, to the breaking of bread and to prayer." Paul wrote to Timothy: "you will be a good minister of Christ Jesus, nourished on the truths of the faith and of the good teaching that you have followed" (1 Tim. 4:6). Timothy had learned that sound doctrine from the apostle Paul (2 Tim. 3:10). He warns Timothy against certain people teach false doctrines (1 Tim. 1:3). The apostle John explained the dire consequences of those who do not persevere in the doctrine of Christ (2 John 9); Hence the importance of studying and meditating on the Word of God.

2. The gifts of the Spirit

We also see the use and exercise of personal gifts for edification of the body (Ephesians 4:16). Without the contribution of each member using their particular gifts, it is difficult to achieve growth. Growth will occur in three dimensions:

Vertical: "faith in Christ" (Colossians 1:4a).

Horizontal: "the love you have for all God's people" (Colossians 1:4b)

Volume: "the gospel is bearing fruit and growing throughout the whole world" (Colossians 1:6). It will happen personally; internally, in the church, and collectively in the world to be evangelized.

3. Prayer (Acts 2:42).

By connecting with the source of power, the group of Christians acquired dynamism and purity of purpose. They also learned to depend on God by practicing obedience.

4. Good testimony

God chose to use ordinary and imperfect people, transformed by the gospel message. Paul wrote to the Colossians: "so that you may live a life worthy of the Lord and please him in every way: bearing fruit in every good work, growing in the knowledge of God" (Colossians 1:10). The person who bears fruit in every good work is possessor of certain key characteristics, due precisely to their knowledge of God. Good testimony was very important; for God would use those who non-believers spoke well of (Acts 16:2a), and also those who imitated the mature in the faith (Philippians 3:17). This was and is necessary today to avoid damaging the message of the transforming power of the Holy Spirit. Paul explains about Christians of bad testimony: "now I tell you again even with tears, many live as enemies of the cross of Christ" (Philippians 3:18).

The example of life is important (Philippians 2:14-15), along with ordered daily life (Philippians 1:27), consistent work (1 Timothy 6:1-2), good family relationships (Ephesians 5:33-6:4).

5. Compassionate actions

Caring for the needs of others, whether in economic, emotional or spiritual terms, is very important;

6. Respect for leaders.

Paul encouraged his readers whenever possible, to maintain respectful behavior before civil and religious authorities, respecting elders, pastors and teachers (Philippians 2:29). The love of God and faith in His power to save are some of the characteristics that people will notice, assigning validity to what the person proclaims.

The example of obedience and respect we show when participating in communion, baptism, church attendance, prayer (personal and congregational) and meditation on the Word is important. Being part of the church by fulfilling the Lord's commands is an important part of the worker's testimony and is essential for his credibility.

III. The results

There was exponential growth in the early church as a result of adhering to these means, especially, when practiced in humility following Christ's example (Philippians 2:5-8,14,15). This initial body of believers "continued to meet together in the temple courts. They broke bread in their homes and ate together with glad and sincere hearts, praising God and enjoying the favor of all the people" (Acts 2:46-46). This could not but produce a radical effect on the community, which God would use to implement the organism that He determined to be the vehicle of His redemptive purpose for the whole world and at all times: "And the Lord added to their number daily those who were being saved" (Acts 2:47).

Optional Questions:

I. The founder and purpose of the church

* Name two of the purposes of the church, according to Acts 2:42-47.
* Write two aspects that characterize the communion between brothers.

II. Means used by God to build his church

* What resources did God use to build his church (Acts 2:42-47)?
* What means did He use to establish His Church?
* With what resources do we have today to build the church?

III. Results

* What results can be expected from the Holy Spirit if we keep His Word? (Acts 2:47)
* Are you involved in spreading the message of Jesus to your neighbors?
* Do you consider that we are often unaware that new people are sent by the Holy Spirit?
* How do we take care of new people who come to our church

Conclusion

With the Apostles' doctrinal instruction and the guidance and power of the Holy Spirit, the early church grew so large that it spread throughout the Roman Empire. What about our cities, towns and neighborhoods? We have available to us the same God, the same message, the same power of the Holy Spirit to enable us to impact and transform our societies for Jesus. The challenge is before us now, are we willing to take part in God's great mission?

The church in the heart of the Roman Empire

Daniel Pesado (Espay)

Verses to Memorize: "For I am not ashamed of the gospel, because it is the power of God that brings salvation to everyone who believes" (Romans 1:16a).

Lesson Aim: To learn how a church can thrive in a spiritually adverse situation by cooperating with God and sharing the true gospel of Jesus Christ.

Introduction

The city of Rome today houses Vatican City, the epicenter of the Roman Catholic church. Many Catholics in the world look to Rome for their leadership. It is where their leader, the Pope, resides. Today, in spite of the Vatican holding a strategic position for a section of Christianity, church growth is occurring outside of Rome. But what was the church in Rome like 2,000 years ago?

Rome, as the capital of the Roman Empire, was a very diverse city which presented many challenges for the birth of the Christian church. Many cultures lived side by side, including people with different religious beliefs, such as Jews, pagans and eastern Mystery religions. The Greek philosophers still influenced people's thinking. In addition, three continents converged in its vicinity: Asia, Africa and Europe, which leaves us with a beautiful example of survival and clarity of purpose.

This church was not founded by Paul. He wrote to Rome because he wanted to go to Spain and visit them on the way (Rom. 15:15). He took the opportunity to explain to them some of the fundamental truths of the gospel. Let's see some characteristics of the true church at Rome at the start of Christianity.

I. Paul's theological presentation of the gospel

The church in Rome received from Paul's pen the most complete explanation of the gospel. Paul taught them where the gospel came from, why it was necessary, its effectiveness and its results. Undoubtedly, the apostle understood that the church in Rome, because of its location and influence, needed a clear exposition of the gospel.

A. The reality of sin in the human race

Undoubtedly, the city of Rome offered tremendous opposition to the spirit of the gospel and to the life of holiness. The ambition stimulated by being the administrative center of a huge empire, the power struggles and intrigues that arose from it, insensitivity regarding emergent evil, and the sensuality that pervaded all social classes in the city demanded from the early Christians a clear understanding of how sin is expressed and the role the church can play to curb its evil influence. Paul stated clearly, "There is no one righteous, not even one" … "There is no fear of God before their eyes" (Romans 3:10b, 18).

B. The effectiveness of the gospel of Jesus Christ

But at the same time, the apostle told them that there is only one effective alternative for the city of Rome: the gospel of Jesus Christ "because it is the power of God that brings salvation to everyone who believes" (Romans 1:16). The church in Rome, a city that was a center for the excellence of the political, economic and military power of that time, needed to understand the true nature of the problem they were facing; but, at the same time, they needed to understand the efficacy and radicality of the solution offered by God. In other words, the power of the empire had to be confronted by the power of the gospel of Jesus Christ.

C. The pre-eminence of faith in Jesus Christ for salvation

Paul presents in this epistle that salvation is through faith in Jesus. Paul proclaims this message right at the beginning of his letter. He greets them, expresses his feelings for the Roman Christians and then in a categorical way, proclaims that he is not ashamed of the gospel, because it is the power of God for salvation; and then announces the way: "For in the gospel the righteousness of God is revealed—a righteousness that is by faith from first to last, just as it is written: The righteous will live by faith" (Rom. 1:17).

To understand the dimension of this announcement, we need to remember what happened when in the sixteenth century, Martin Luther became aware of this truth, and unintentionally divided Christianity at the beginning of the Protestant Reformation. It only remains to insist on the fact that "faith comes from hearing the message, and the message is heard through the word about Christ" (Romans 10:17). There is an important message which needs to be proclaimed.

Paul warned the Romans that every person would face the judgment of God; there would be no escape. For this reason, if the church in Rome failed to receive, assimilate and disseminate the gospel of salvation only by faith in Jesus, there would be no alternatives for their citizens on the day of judgment. For this reason, Roman Christians had the enormous privilege of being a part of God's people through the power of the gospel; but, at the same time, they had to take on the great responsibility of sharing it with their fellow citizens.

II. It was a church which had been set apart for God and His work

The apostle had told them that the grace of God was sufficient; it abounded, and because of this, it was possible to overcome sin. But then, he warned them not to use this abundant and effective gift from God to continue sinning.

A. Set apart through the work of Christ

The apostle explained that we are separated by faith in Jesus Christ. The key to understanding this merciful gesture of God is to believe what He says through the apostle in His Word. The offer is precise and firm: "we are all are justified freely by his grace through the redemption that came by Christ Jesus" (Rom. 3:24). "Therefore," Paul later said, "since we have been justified through faith, we have peace with God through our Lord Jesus Christ" (Rom. 5:1). Even later, Paul confirmed this teaching saying that once we believed, we were "baptized into Christ Jesus" (Rom. 6:3). Paul taught the Romans that it was by faith in Christ that they had been set apart for salvation.

B. Set apart because of God's justice

The apostle began by declaring the following: "There is no one righteous, not even one (Romans 3:10b). And he added that in the law of Moses there is no remedy for sin, since the law only provides knowledge of sin; but does not provide the solution (v.20). Considering this, Paul explained: "This righteousness is given through faith in Jesus Christ to all who believe" (Rom.1:22). God "did it to demonstrate his righteousness at the present time, so as to be just and the one who justifies those who have faith in Jesus" (v.26).

As a consequence of this justice received through faith in Jesus, the believer receives an innumerable amount of additional benefits; among others, peace, the richness of God's grace, hope, strength in tribulation. All this results in what Paul also called "reconciliation" with God (Romans 5:1-11).

C. Set apart to live victorious lives

Chapter 7 of Romans has always been controversial. We will not solve it here and now. The central theme of the chapter is the war to death that is fought inside us. The climax of despair emerges in the form of a heartbreaking cry: "What a wretched man I am! Who will rescue me from this body that is subject to death?" (v.24). People struggle to please God, and we fail over and over. This passage describes clearly the truth that only through Jesus Christ our Lord that we can obtain the final victory (Romans 7:25a, 8:1).

III. Paul taught them to be servants

A. The demand for Christian service

Much of the effectiveness of the gospel depends on how the church expresses or lives it. It is for this reason that as Christians, both faith and motivation to serve in love are inseparable. Gratitude and service are therefore also inseparable. For this reason, Paul encouraged the Roman Christians to keep up their spiritual fervor (Romans 12:11b); to share with the Lord's people who are in need, practice hospitality (v.13), and even to be kind and generous to their enemies (v.20a). They need to do what Jesus himself said to his disciples, "Freely you have received; freely give" (Matthew 10:8b).

B. The supremacy of Christian service

The apostle extended the scope of service beyond those of the family of faith (Galatians 6:10). He also mentioned that they must be able to love each other (Romans 12:10). Taking Jesus' example, the church is responsible for showing their gratitude to God by being compassionate to those who oppose the gospel. Paul was a tireless worker in contexts that ignored or rejected the gospel, so he understood the penetrating value of Christian service. For this reason, he encouraged the church in Rome to be generous to the point of blessing those who persecuted them rather than cursing them (v.14a); and, more concretely, he added, "If your enemy is hungry, feed him; if he is thirsty, give him something to drink... Do not be overcome by evil, but overcome evil with good" (vv. 20-21).

Optional Questions:

I. Paul's theological presentation of the gospel

- Do you think that understanding correct doctrine is important?
- Point out three distinctive doctrinal aspects of Paul's letter to the Romans.

II. It was a church which had been set apart for God and His work

- In what way is the gospel of Jesus powerful?
- Romans 7:25 demonstrates a predicament and Romans 8:1 the solution. Explain.

III. Paul taught them to be servants

- How can Christians serve an ungodly society?
- Why is this important?

Conclusion

What can we learn from the instructions Paul gave to the church in Rome that was in a position of disadvantage because of their location in the center of the Empire? They needed to have a good doctrinal foundation. Paul taught them about the power of the gospel for salvation and reconciliation with a just God. They had to be a church that 'walked the talk', and was compassionate to the needs of others.

Notes :

The tempestuous church of Corinth

Dorothy Bullón (Costa Rica)

> **Memory verse:** "Therefore, if anyone is in Christ, the new creation has come: The old has gone, the new is here!" (2 Corinthians 5:17).
>
> **Lesson Aim:** To discover how Paul dealt with a series of problems that arose in the Corinthian church.

Introduction

Paul's letters to the Corinthians reveal a series of problems and difficulties that this young church, founded by Paul himself, was undergoing. Ask the students: What are the most common problems that churches suffer today? Write a list on the board with the answers given. Then add this question: How could these problems be solved?

I. The city of Corinth

Corinth, with a population of around 600,000 people, was the political and commercial capital of the Roman province of Achaea. It was an important port with a 'dry canal' where the boats were moved over rollers the six kilometers between the Adriatic Sea and the Aegean Sea. Corinth was known both as a center for Greek culture and as a commercial city, and was characterized by a cosmopolitan atmosphere hosting people and customs from different parts of the world. It had a reputation of moral depravity. A huge temple stood on a hill overlooking the city dedicated to Aphrodite, the goddess of love.

A. Paul's visit

According to Acts 18:1-18, Paul came to Corinth when Gallio was proconsul (51-52 AD). As was his practice, the he visited the local synagogue every Saturday, until the Jews became aggressive. Because of the Jewish hostility, the apostle went to the house of Titius Justus, which was next to the synagogue. He taught there every day. After this, many Corinthians believed, including Crispus, the head of the synagogue. Paul and his assistants Silas, Timothy, Priscilla, and Aquila remained in the city for about 18 months.

B. Visits and subsequent letters

Carefully reviewing the text of these epistles, we can observe that there were several letters and visits from Paul. He talks about a previous letter in 1 Cor. 5:9: "I have written to you by letter, that you do not unite with the fornicators." Paul received information from the house of Chloe about the Corinthians (1 Cor. 1:11); and also, from Stephanas, Fortunatus and Achaicus (1 Cor. 16:17). The following verses begin with this phrase: "Now about...." suggesting that they were answers that Paul wanted to offer to the concerns of the Corinthians (1 Cor. 7:25, 8:1, 16:1). Likewise, the apostle sent Timothy to the brothers of the Corinthian church to help them (1 Cor. 4:17, 16:10-11); and Titus also visited them to collect the offering for the brothers in Jerusalem (2 Cor. 8:6).

However, although it is not mentioned in Acts, Paul speaks of a third visit (2 Cor. 13:1-2). This visit is commonly called the 'painful visit' (2 Cor. 2:1). It seems that the second letter is composed of two letters: the so-called 'severe letter that Paul gave Titus to deliver to the Corinthians. Paul's reasoning for writing this letter is found in 2 Cor. 2:3-4, 9, 7:8,12; and the third letter could be 2 Corinthians 10 to 13. Then, the remainder of the second epistle would possibly be a fourth letter.

What stands out in Paul's letters to the Corinthian church is the pastoral heart of this apostle who wants the brothers in Corinth to grow in their faith and witness. He spent time with them so that they could understand the faith correctly and act well.

II. The Corinthian church and its problems

It is difficult to know the size of the Corinthian church at the time of this first letter, but we can imagine approximately between 40 to 150 people. The church included some Jews (1 Cor. 7:18-19), although it was composed largely of Gentile converts (1 Cor. 6:9-11, 8:7, 12:2). The statement of Paul in 1 Cor. 1:26 makes it clear that most of the members of this church were of humble social status; although it also implies that some members were wise, powerful and even of noble birth. 1 Cor. 7:21-23 shows that some were slaves.

A. Divisions in the church

The people who came from the house of Chloe informed Paul that there were serious divisions between different factions within the church (I Cor. 1-4). In I Cor. 1:12, we read the following: "What I mean is this: One of you says, "I follow Paul" another, "I follow Apollos" another, "I follow Cephas", still another, "I follow Christ." Paul is describing separate parties that demand alternate allegiances to Apollos (a Jewish Christian preacher), to Peter (one of Jesus' disciples), or Christ (according to what they understood). It is likely that these parties represented divisions within the leadership of the church that considered themselves spiritual elites. They were proud and presumptuous because of their associations with a particular leader, and looked with disdain towards those who were not in their group.

B. Sins of a sexual nature

The main theme of these chapters refers to sexual behavior (I Cor. 5-7). In chapter 5, Paul draws the church's attention to the case of a man from the congregation who lived in an incestuous relationship with his father's wife (I Cor. 5:1). Incest is universally condemned. However, nobody in the church bothered to rebuke or correct this man. Therefore, they were not practicing ecclesiastical discipline. Likewise, instead of dealing with disputes between believers in the church, they were taking them to the pagan courts (I Cor. 6:1-11), thus giving a bad testimony. The hypocrisy in Corinth was evident.

It seems that the liberal attitudes of this city, in terms of sexuality, had affected the Christians. For this reason, Paul calls their attention not to fall into sexual debauchery (fornication) and prostitution (I Cor. 6:12-20).

In chapter 7, Paul answers questions about marriage, divorce, and staying single through ministry. Ask: What sexual sins could exist in our churches today? How are they cared for?

C. Eating foods offered to idols

The meat sellers sold products from the sacrifices that were made in the pagan temples (I Cor. 8-10). The question was this: Can a Christian buy meat that was offered in to false gods? Would not the meat be affected by contact with paganism? Actually, the church council in Jerusalem had already touched on this issue. One of the few obligations that was imposed on the converting Gentiles was this: "You are to abstain from food sacrificed to idols…" (Acts 15:29a).

It seems that some people criticized the believers who bought meat from butchers who offered products from the sacrifices that were made in the pagan temples. This created discord among the Corinthian Christians. Ask: What things can we do as Christians, and what not? Are there legalistic attitudes in our churches?

D. Immature behavior in the church

In chapters 11 through 14, Paul deals with problems in Corinth that have to do with meetings in the church. In chapter 11, he deals with two themes: the different roles of men and women in the church; and the divisions, abuses and misconduct in the Lord's Supper.

Chapters 12 to 14 focus on the theme of spiritual gifts. Paul teaches that everyone will receive gifts, and just as one body has different parts that work for the good of the whole, so it must be with the gifts in the church. However in the Corinthian church, certain gifts were valued over others; hence the apostle spoke about it.

E. Denying the doctrine of the resurrection

In a Hellenistic world like the one in Corinth, the resurrection seemed illogical (I Corinthians 15). When Paul mentioned the resurrection of Jesus in the Areopagos of Athens, the philosophers made fun of him (Acts 17:32). Ask: Do we confront today the types of philosophy that consider the aspects of Christian doctrine as illogical?

F. Criticism of Paul's ministry

In Paul's second epistle to the Corinthians, we can see how some brothers began to try to destroy Paul's reputation (2 Corinthians). The following are some of those criticisms:

1. Paul was inconstant. This accusation is implicit in the declaration of 2 Cor. 1:17.
2. His bodily presence was too humble (2 Cor. 10:1)
3. He wrote terrifying letters (2 Cor. 10:1, 13:10).
4. He was not a good speaker (2 Cor. 10:10, 13:6).
5. He did not accept financial support. While working in Corinth, he made his living making tents (Acts 18:3).
6. He used others to collect money from the Corinthians. His opponents said that the funds raised by Titus for the poor among the saints in Jerusalem was really Paul's cunning plan to take advantage of the Corinthians' money for himself (2 Corinthians 8:16-24).

7. They said that Paul was out of his mind' (2 Corinthians 5:13).

Ask: Before opening our mouths to criticize a leader, what should we do?

III. Paul's Answers

A. The work of the church belongs to God

God allowed Paul to found the church; then Apollos was used to 'water the seed,' 'but the growth' was given by God (1 Corinthians 3:6-9). The church is the temple of God, and we are all His servants: "whether Paul or Apollos or Cephas or the world or life or death or the present or the future—all are yours, and you are of Christ, and Christ is of God" (1 Corinthians 3:22-23). The love between Christian brothers and sisters should prevent divisions.

B. The church must discipline in love, and live in holiness

It is necessary to call attention to those who fall into sexual sin in the congregation, and we must all recognize that our bodies are the temple of the Holy Spirit (1 Corinthians 6:12-20).

Paul emphasizes an important principle: "'I have the right to do anything,' you say—but not everything is beneficial. 'I have the right to do anything'—but I will not be mastered by anything" (1 Corinthians 6:12).

C. Respect the conscience of others

Paul teaches the church in Corinth how a Christian can sacrifice his liberties or rights for the good of the gospel and for the good of others. In 1 Corinthians 10:23-24, he says, "I have the right to do anything, you say—but not everything is beneficial. I have the right to do anything—but not everything is constructive. No one should seek their own good, but the good of others."

D. Love is the essential ingredient for the church

Instead of having meetings of the Lord's Supper where the poor are despised, Paul takes the opportunity to teach how the meeting should be and how everyone should consider each other (1 Corinthians 11:23-34). Paul gives a valuable teaching about the gifts in the church. In 1 Corinthians 13, he refers to love as a central theme in life. This is key; It is what should govern everything. There is another principle: in church services, "everything should be done in a fitting and orderly way" (1 Cor. 14:40).

E. The doctrine of the resurrection is the pillar of faith

Paul goes to great lengths to prove that the resurrection of Christ was a historical reality. This doctrine cannot be left aside without undermining the whole gospel. This is one of the essential doctrines that we must believe to be saved. Responding to this question, Paul gives us valuable teaching on aspects of the resurrection and eternal life (1 Corinthians 15).

F. Paul defends himself

Because of Paul's love for the church in Corinth, he tries to respond to criticism and reconcile himself with the brothers and sisters of this church. The passage in 2 Corinthians 11:16-33 is a testimony of all that it meant for Paul to follow Jesus. Thus, he dignifies the ministry, since he is not just a mere employee; He is really a minister of the Lord.

Optional Questions:

I. The city of Corinth

- How did Paul's relationship with this church begin according to Acts 18:1-18?

II. The Corinthian church and its problems

- What were the six biggest problems that this congregation suffered?

  ◊ 1 Corinthians 1:11-12

  ◊ 1 Corinthians 5:1

  ◊ 1 Corinthians 6:1-2

  ◊ 1 Corinthians 6:12-20

  ◊ 1 Corinthians 7:1-9

  ◊ 1 Corinthians 7:10-16

- Today, what are the causes of divisions in the churches?

- In what ways do divisions harm a congregation?

III. Paul's answers

- What did Paul mean in 1 Cor. 6:12?

Conclusion

The problems facing Paul and the Corinthian church reflect the conditions and problems of the first century. At the same time, they often offer striking parallels to the problems facing Christian communities today. Thanks to Paul's example in responding to these difficulties, we have guidelines to follow today.

Lessons from Philippi

Annabella de San José (Canada)

Memory verse: "Finally, brothers and sisters, whatever is true, whatever is noble, whatever is right, whatever is pure, whatever is lovely, whatever is admirable—if anything is excellent or praiseworthy—think about such things. Whatever you have learned or received or heard from me, or seen in me—put it into practice. And the God of peace will be with you" (Philippians 4:8-9).

Lesson Aim: To identify the strengths of the Philippian church that we can apply to guide our personal life, to develop our ministries, and to support the healthy development of the contemporary church.

Introduction

The church of Philippi had a special place in Paul's heart. Through the letter that the apostle sent them, and by the special events recorded in Acts 16, we can deduce that he had received much blessing through this church. The letter to the Philippians only has 4 chapters; however, it contains a lot of important data. This letter is called the 'epistle of joy'. In spite of being written from prison by the apostle Paul, the words 'joy' and 'rejoicing' are mentioned several times. The letter was written to encourage the church to continue forward with the principles, values and teachings of Christ, even in the midst of tribulations, problems and enemy attacks.

I. The birth of the Philippian church

The history of the establishment of the church at Philippi is narrated in Acts 16. In a single chapter, the writer gives us an idea of important aspects that we need to know about the beginnings. Founded in the city of Philippi, a Roman colony in Macedonia, this church is the first Christian community in Europe (v.12), where apparently there were not many Jews. There does not appear to have been a synagogue. In the Roman cities, the Jews could establish a synagogue if they had a minimum of 10 male heads of household. In the absence of a building to meet in, some Jews gathered together on the banks of the Gangites river to pray (v.13).

The writer of Acts also tells us about the first converts who were touched by the gospel of Christ in the region: Lydia, a wealthy woman from Thyatira accepted Jesus, was baptized and immediately afterwards showed the fruit of her conversion by offering the hospitality of her home to Paul and his companions (vv.14-15). Likewise, a young slave girl who had a spirit of divination and was being used by her masters to make money, was freed from demons by Paul (vv.16-18). For this reason, the apostle Paul was accused by the girl's owners, and Paul and Silas were imprisoned. However, while they were in jail, an earthquake occurred, and the jailer, thinking that they had escaped, drew his sword and was about to kill himself. But the apostle prevented him, and shared the message of Christ with him, and that jailer was converted.

Like Lydia, this jailer immediately bore fruits of his conversion by taking the wounded disciples and attending to them at his home (vv.18-36). After that, the charges against Paul and the others were dropped, and they were able to continue their travels. Many scholars have concluded that Luke was the one who remained ministering in the church for several years, which explains the maturity and strength of this congregation.

But even in the midst of all that is good and exemplary in the Philippian church, it seems that after a while, some customs of the city were infiltrating the congregation. It is possible that some members were proud. Paul exhorts them to consider others as superior, and to work without strife or murmuring (Philippians 2:3, 14).

II. The Philippian church was an inclusive church

At a time when we are accustomed to many comforts and in which, unfortunately, even our churches are preoccupied with obtaining the ultimate in material things rather than spiritual growth, the example of the Philippian church is invaluable. Searching for God is a spiritual matter, regardless of the environment that surrounds us. Those Jews, most of them women, gathered on the banks of the river (no walls, no roof, and far from the city, since they did not have a synagogue) to seek the presence of God. Because of their perseverance in that search, God came to them using Paul and the other disciples. God blessed these new Christians filling them with His Spirit. This church goes down in history as the founders of the European Christianity. Their perseverance, fellowship in the gospel and consistency to bear good fruits are recognized by Paul, who assures them of his prayers and his joy. When Paul remembers that church, his tribulation becomes less painful (Philippians 1:3-26).

The church of the 21st century has an example to follow, even in the midst of obstacles or difficulties. We too must search for God without reservation, bear fruit, persevere, and bring comfort to the lives of others through evangelism and spiritual growth. Like the church in Philippi, the church of the 21st century lives in the midst of an evil generation, in an environment that can easily drag us away from God.

Paul praised the brothers and sisters of this church by telling them that they shone as stars in the world, and encouraged them to remain blameless, reminding them to look after their salvation with fear and trembling (Philippians 2:12-18).

The church of Christ, nowadays, must also take care and be aware of dangers. Pastors, leaders and members have to be attentive to those customs and doctrines that in a permissive world seem correct, are not, and which slyly enter into our congregations by the back door, infiltrating them.

One of the greatest criticisms that the church of Christ has always faced is that women are not given a place and that women are invisible. Paul himself has been targeted as someone who did not want women to speak in the church. But if we analyze the church in Philippi, we see that it was founded by Paul in the house of the first person converted to Christianity in that area: A woman! And he remembers with joy Euodia and Syntyche, women too, whom he mentions as those who struggled with him to carry the gospel: "Therefore, my brothers and sisters, you whom I love and long for, my joy and crown, stand firm in the Lord in this way, dear friends! I plead with Euodia and I plead with Syntyche to be of the same mind in the Lord.

Yes, and I ask you, my true companion, help these women since they have contended at my side in the cause of the gospel" (Philippians 4:1-3). What a good way to include women by encouraging them to get involved in God's work! God uses women too, so we must not put them to one side; they have an important place in God's plan to save the world.

The church of Philippi was a church that included people of different social classes. It was founded by people of the upper class united with people of middle class, and very humble people like the slave freed from demons who probably joined in after being healed. The converted jailer was a representative of the great majority of city dwellers, the working class, and retired military.

Today we need to learn from their example. The church needs everyone's skills, talents, gifts, etc. The kindness of the members of the church helped Paul to be joyful for them, and he encouraged them to continue showing it to everyone: "Let your gentleness be evident to all. The Lord is near" (Philippians 4:5). Gentle kindness will help us to not discriminate today.

III. The Philippian church was a fruitful church

The church of Philippi is characterized by bearing fruit (from the beginning), both material and spiritual. These fruit bring glory to the Lord, but they needed a reminder from the Apostle Paul to continue growing. The personal and congregational life of the church is dynamic, and requires continued growth.

An important contribution of this church was their generosity, which Paul deeply appreciated. Not only because it would help him personally, but because it would benefit him in the expansion of the gospel. They would be an important part of Paul's ministry. Thanks to their offerings, the church helped the progress of the gospel in Europe.

As Christians, we must generous, see to the needs, give joyfully, and God promises to do the multiplication: "Not that I desire your gifts; what I desire is that more be credited to your account. I have received full payment and have more than enough. I am amply supplied, now that I have received from Epaphroditus the gifts you sent. They are a fragrant offering, an acceptable sacrifice, pleasing to God" (Philippians 4:17-18).

Paul encourages the church to continue the good work and be known in the city for spiritual fruit such as love, joy and peace (Philippians 4:4-7). These would help them face life daily and be prepared for the coming of the Lord. Love would motivate them to have better relationships, joy would encourage them to face tribulations with hope (like the apostle Paul), and peace would help them keep their minds centered on Christ Jesus.

For us today, the fruit of the Spirit has the same effect on our personal lives. The church of Philippi had received, heard and seen first-hand many of Paul's teachings. In Philippians 4:8-9, we find one of the most precious counsels that the apostle gave them regarding how to care for our minds. He told them to think about "whatever is true, whatever is noble, whatever is right, whatever is pure, whatever is lovely, whatever is admirable—if anything is excellent or praiseworthy—think about such things. Whatever you have learned or received or heard from me, or seen in me—put it into practice. And the God of peace will be with you."

In this verse, Paul summarized the most complete lesson for the church, not only for the church of Philippi, but also for the church of today, not only as a community, but for each of the members individually. The things he wanted them to think about would help them remain at peace and live with the joy of the Lord in their lives, even in the midst of tribulations, as he did.

The church of Philippi was the crown and joy of Paul (Philippians 4:1), an inclusive church in which the fruit of the Spirit was manifested. It was a giving church, and it brought blessing to the life of this apostle in the midst of his illness, captivity in prisons, and his moments of sadness.

The apostle Paul gave thanks to God for the members of the church, because they were the only ones who sent him financial help, thus enabling him to continue his travels.

Notes :

Optional Questions:

I. The birth of the church of Philippi

- What are some of the characteristics of the Philippian church according to Acts 16?
    ◊ Acts 16:13
    ◊ Acts 16:14-15
    ◊ Acts 16:16-18
- How can you contribute so that your church has these characteristics?

II. The Philippian church was an inclusive church

- What other characteristics did the church present according to Philippians 2:12-18, 4:1-3?
- Do you believe that Paul could say the same about your church? Why?

III. The Philippian church was a fruitful church

- What other characteristics did the church present according to Philippians 4:15-18?
- Compare the church of Philippi with your personal life, and answer: How could you apply the characteristics of this church to improve your spiritual life and that of the ministries?

Conclusion

The church of Philippi was a church that could well be the example of the ideal church that we need to imitate in the 21st century, whether as a congregation, as leaders, or just as members. If we act like they did and follow Paul's advice, our lives can turn around and we will be able to fulfill the mission that Christ entrusted to us.

The Colossian Church

Ulises Solis (Guatemala)

Memory verse: "For in Christ all the fullness of the Deity lives in bodily form, and in Christ you have been brought to fullness. He is the head over every power and authority" (Colossians 2:9-10).

Lesson Aim: To discover how we can be complete in Jesus Christ.

Introduction

The ancient city of Colossae was built on a major trade route through the Lycus River Valley in the Roman province of Asia Minor. It was located about 100 miles inland from Ephesus. The letter to the church of Colossae was written around 60 A.D. when Paul was imprisoned in Rome for the sake of the gospel. It was founded by Epaphras and others who had converted to the gospel in the missionary journeys of the Apostle Paul.

The problem with this church was that it had been infiltrated by false teachers who promoted a heretical doctrine called Gnosticism, promoting a type of special knowledge and denying that Jesus Christ was real, let alone God and Savior. Paul sought to combat this error by proving the deity of Christ; moreover, that Jesus is God, with all His nature and attributes, in other words - the God Man. In addition to this, the epistle emphasizes true wisdom, and the Kingship of God in the person of Jesus Christ who is supreme, in everything and over everyone. Paul argues, "The Son is the image of the invisible God, the firstborn over all creation" (Col. 1:15). Let's see the characteristics of this church.

I. Characteristics of the Colossian church (Chapter 1)

The Colossian congregation was mostly made up of gentiles. We can see this in the following: "Once you were alienated from God and were enemies in your minds because of your evil behavior... God has chosen to make known among the Gentiles the glorious riches of this mystery, which is Christ in you, the hope of glory" (Col. 1:21,27). Paul uses the terminology of 'enmity' to refer to all those who had been outside the covenant of promise; but God, in His deep love, was now choosing to include them through the blood of Christ shed on the cross.

A. The epistle begins with a greeting and thanksgiving for Colossian believers for whom Paul prays unceasingly for strength, wisdom and presents them with the atoning work of Christ (Colossians 1:9-14). It was obvious that Paul wanted the body of Christ in Colossae to not be deceived by the wrong doctrine taught by false teachers.

B. After this introduction, he expounds a profound doctrinal issue presenting Christ as the image of the invisible God, with absolute supremacy and pre-eminent over all creation (Col. 1:15-23).

C. In structure, this epistle bears a resemblance to the epistle to the Ephesians, though with different emphases. The emphasis of the epistle of Ephesians was Ecclesiological, and this letter sent to the Colossians was more Christological. Paul teaches the Colossians that through Christ's death on the cross, believers can live in holiness, and can be "without blemish and free from accusation" before God (Colossians 1:22).

II. The experience of the Colossian church (Colossians 2:1-7)

It is very likely that Epaphras paid them a visit and then shared their news with the apostle, who was imprisoned in Rome, giving him a detailed report of the spiritual development of the church. Much of the news was good, which is why Paul offers thanksgiving to God on learning of their love and firmness in the Lord (Col. 1:3-8).

But later, Paul shows his deep concern for the doctrinal threat that was infiltrating the church: "I want you to know how hard I am contending for you" (Col. 2:1a). Paul wanted to confront these false teachers face to face, and rescue some who had gone astray, but he could not, because he was in prison. To counteract this heretical influence, Paul prayed for them and wrote this profoundly Christological letter under the guidance of the Holy Spirit.

A. Paul, in his letter to the Colossians, makes a powerful call to the brothers and sisters to be encouraged: "My goal is that they may be encouraged in heart and united in love, so that they may have the full riches of complete understanding, in order that they may know the mystery of God, namely, Christ" (Col. 2:2). The special identity of a healthy church is love for God and his neighbor (John 13:34-35). By this virtue, the world will know the genuine church of the Lord.

B. The church must be equipped with wisdom and firm convictions in Christ; for only in Him are all the treasures of wisdom and knowledge hidden so that no one can deceive them with clever arguments (Col. 2:3-4).

C. This letter teaches that the church must remain faithful to its commitment to faith in Christ. They must walk with Christ who is the immovable foundation. Those who know about construction maintain that a building with a good foundation lasts for a long time. Thus, the church must be founded and built on Christ.

D. The church is called to deepen its roots of knowledge in Christ and in His Word. Only the Lord Jesus is the source of life and strength for the believer in the face of today's erroneous fads and doctrines (Col. 2:6-7).

III. Biblical foundations of sound doctrine (Colossians 2:8-23)

In the following section of the Pauline epistle, we can find the essence of the doctrine Paul wanted them to learn about. This was an important and difficult task that the apostle set out to do because the false teachers wanted to add on extra teaching about Christ. Sound doctrine in this section refers to the orthodox foundations that emanate from biblical truth, which are not watered down or compromised by anything. If you want you can call it dogma; for example: We believe that Jesus is God (John 10:30). However, faced with the threat to sound doctrine, Paul urges them to remain alert: "See to it that no one takes you captive through hollow and deceptive philosophy, which depends on human tradition and the elemental spiritual forces of this world rather than on Christ… Therefore, do not let anyone judge you by what you eat or drink, or with regard to a religious festival, a New Moon celebration or a Sabbath day" (Col. 2:8, 16-23). Apparently, there were some converted Jewish members who liked Gnosticism, which was a kind of religious syncretism that contained some philosophical components but held that the humanity of Christ was not real.

A. In Col. 2:9-10, Paul shows them their solid foundation by telling them that the whole fullness of the deity dwells in Christ, and Christians are complete in Him, who is the head of all principalities and powers.

B. For false teachers, this simple truth of the gospel was not enough. They said that it was necessary for the Colossian brothers and sisters to accept other truths that emanated from philosophy, that is, human knowledge, astrology or Jewish circumcision. Paul refutes this by talking about real circumcision. He says, "In him you were also circumcised with a circumcision not performed by human hands. Your whole self, ruled by the flesh was put off when you were circumcised by Christ, having been buried with him in baptism, in which you were also raised with him through your faith in the working of God, who raised him from the dead" (Col. 2:11-14).

C. There is no doubt that this group of false teachers also included extreme asceticism (Col. 2:16, 21) that included dietary rules about what could or couldn't be eaten, and the invocation of angels (v.18), which was a kind of cult. All of this was mixed with a false humility.

D. The exhortation to this church is that it should cling firmly to Christ, and not depend on angelic mediators or false and pseudo spiritual practices. Paul told the Colossian brothers and sisters not to allow themselves to be enslaved by legalistic attitudes. He taught them that although asceticism taught self-discipline, "such regulations indeed have an appearance of wisdom, with their self-imposed worship, their false humility and their harsh treatment of the body, but they lack any value in restraining sensual indulgence" (Col. 2:20-23). Only Christ and his grace are sufficient in these spiritual aspects.

IV. Ethical and social approach (Colossians chapters 3 & 4)

Paul's letters often start with theology and finish with ethical commands. This letter is no exception. If Christians have risen with Christ, then they will seeks eternal values and have a different lifestyle (Col. 3:1-4). These must be the virtues or characteristics also of today's churches. We must keep our eyes on Christ and persevere in the race of the Christian faith, showing to the world a lifestyle based on Christlike values.

A. The first thing is to take off the old self with its practices which threaten to make us abandon our new life in God (v. 9).

B. The church should clothe itself with "compassion, kindness, humility, gentleness and patience… And over all these virtues put on love, which binds them all together in perfect unity" (vv.12-15). The Bible teaches that love is one of the main characteristics of the church. Since we are a loving community, people should know that we are the disciples of Christ. We live in a world of violence, hatred and wars, as well as hostility towards the values of the Kingdom and towards God. This situation opens a space for the church to take the Word of God seriously, putting into practice what it teaches every day.

C. In Col. 3:18-25, Paul gives instructions for Christian households in very practical ways. As a result of the new life in Christ, social relationships between spouses and other loved ones must be different. Employees must be responsible, respectful and efficient, knowing that the best reward will be received from the Lord who does not favor persons.

D. In Colossians 4:1, Paul teaches that employers must be fair in their dealings with their employees. Then, Paul reminds the church not to neglect the life of prayer, and lets them know that they also must pray for the missionaries, and in their case, that God will open the door for Paul's team to fulfill their roles as missionary-evangelists (vv. 2-5). He exhorts them to always speak gracefully, "seasoned with salt," knowing how to share the gospel with prudence (v. 6).

E. The letter ends with Paul's greetings to all his friends, and especially to Tychicus, his fellow servant who seems to be the bearer of this epistle (Col. 4:7).

The epistle to the Colossians is a letter of hope and peace for everyone who believes in Jesus Christ. We are shown that as believers, each of us becomes heir to His Kingdom. God has reconciled us to Himself through the atoning death of Jesus Christ on the cross (Col. 1:20- 23). He calls us to complete consecration and warns against being deceived by vain and empty philosophies (Col. 2:8). In Christ, our destiny is certain. We need to fill our minds and hearts with God's plans and actions (Col. 3:1-4).

Finally, the apostle asks them to maintain a life of prayer, and to take every opportunity to bear witness to Christ and act wisely toward those who do not yet know God (Col. 4:2-6).

Optional Questions:

I. Characteristics of the Colossian church (Chapter 1)

- How does the epistle begin according to Col. 1:9-14?
- What important teachings does Paul give to the church in Col. 1:15-23?

II. The experience of the Colossian church (Colossians 2:1-7)

- What is the virtue that the believer must exhibit at all times (Col. 1:3-8)?
- What should the church deepen and build according to Col. 2:6-7?

III. Biblical foundations of sound doctrine (Colossians 2:8-23)

- What teaching did Paul give to the church in Col. 2:9-21?

IV. Ethical and social approach (Colossians chapters 3 & 4)

- What should Christians be like according to Col. 3:12-15.
- Do you consider that the gospel of Christ demands a different lifestyle in the various areas of our lives?
- Explain your answer

Conclusion

There will always be those who are confused, as well as false teachers willing to confuse others. Through his letter to the Colossian church, Paul urges us today to live consecrated to God and be sure to understand clearly the message of the true gospel, which through God's grace we have in an accessible form in the Bible. We must be careful not to get confused!

Thessalonians: a consistent church

Débora Acuña (Chili)

> **Memory verse:** "We remember before our God and Father your work produced by faith, your labor prompted by love, and your endurance inspired by hope in our Lord Jesus Christ" (1 Thessalonians 1:3).
>
> **Lesson Aim:** To understand the importance of having a good testimony, which is generated by staying consistent in faith and love.

Introduction

Without a doubt, the apostle Paul was a great missionary. His love for Christ led him to give his whole life to the proclamation of the Lord Jesus Christ as Savior. He understood that 'go' implied a change of location. In his missionary journeys guided by the Holy Spirit, he managed to establish many churches in Europe, which over the years took the message to the whole world.

Thessalonica (now called Thessaloniki) was visited by Paul during his second missionary journey. Its position at the junction of several important roads connecting trade routes to Rome made it a valuable center for the spread of the Gospel. Although today we know who Jesus is, it is important that we place ourselves in the place of the people of that time. It had only been a few decades since Jesus had been crucified by his people (who did not recognize him). Most likely, many would not even have heard his name, since his ministry was short. For some, Jesus was just another prophet, for others, a preacher to crowds. How did the message of Jesus reach the Thessalonians?

I. The beginnings of the Thessalonian church

Paul, along with Silas and Timothy, arrived and went directly to the Jewish synagogue to proclaim the message of Jesus. The Word of God says that Paul stayed there for three days to rest (Acts 17:1-2), debating with them, guided by the Holy Spirit and the Scriptures, declaring who Jesus really was (Acts 17:3). When Paul went on his missionary journeys, he was prepared and organized. Here are some important points:

A. A strategic place:

Biblical truth could be preached anywhere, but the synagogue was a good place to begin, because there, Paul would find a good group of people he could talk with who were used to reading the Old Testament Scriptures and were aware of messianic prophecies.

B. The proclamation

Remember that Jesus had been rejected by his people and crucified. They had not understood that He was the Christ they expected, and that the reign of the Messiah was not a political reign here on earth. They certainly were not expecting their messiah to be someone who would live among the poor and rub shoulders with sinners, or walk about preaching, healing the sick and doing miracles. They were expecting a conquering king ... very different from Jesus' profile.

Paul proclaimed Jesus as the Messiah they had been waiting for. His message was based on the Scriptures. Those that listened to him reveal how prophecy had been fulfilled in Jesus could decide for themselves whether to believe or not. The apostle Paul shared the gospel message, and the Holy Spirit touched hearts, convincing them of the truth.

C. The first fruits in Thessalonica

For the glory of God, those three days had their fruits. The Word of God tells us that some believed. Those who decided to believe were the first members of the Thessalonian church, who were in charge of proclaiming the gospel to others: "Some of the Jews were persuaded and joined Paul and Silas, as did a large number of God-fearing Greeks and quite a few prominent women" (Acts 17:4). But those who did not believe caused trouble; they wanted at all costs to make Paul leave the city. But that did not stop the Word from being preached and believed. It is also necessary to mention that the church suffered persecution (2 Thessalonians 1:5-7).

II. Affirming the church

Paul had to leave Thessalonica quickly because the Jews organized an uproar to harm him. But those who believed were not left on their own (just like the other churches that were planted in previous trips). They were at all times in Paul's heart, and if he could not visit them, he would send some of his traveling companions to affirm the church. In the case of Thessalonica, Timothy visited them: "So, when we could stand it no longer, we thought it best to be left by ourselves in Athens. We sent Timothy, who is our brother and co-worker in God's service in spreading the gospel of Christ, to strengthen and encourage you in your faith, so that no one would be unsettled by these trials. For you know quite well that we are destined for them" (1 Thess. 3:1-3). Paul cared about each church he planted. So, he tried to visit them, send some of his travelling companions, and wrote them letters of encouragement.

A. He reminded them that although he and his collaborators continued to preach the Word of God, they still kept an eye on each church, and were concerned that they would continue in their service to God (1 Thess. 1:2-6).

B. The apostle recognized the strengths and weaknesses of each church, and encouraged them to go forward doing what pleases God (1 Thes. 4:1-12).

C. He also explained the message of the gospel to them, teaching them how they should conduct themselves in holiness and at peace with their neighbor (1 Thess. 5:12-15).

D. The apostle Paul reminded the Thessalonians that Christ will return. They were not to be fooled by anyone. They needed to be prepared for His second coming (1 Thess. 4:13-18). This church suffered persecutions.

III. Extending the Kingdom with their good testimony

The church of Thessalonica, without a doubt, was special. They had a good testimony, were patient under pressure, and this gave external evidence of their inner spiritual values. The apostle Paul urges them to stand firm under the pressures: "We remember before our God and Father your work produced by faith, your labor prompted by love, and your endurance inspired by hope in our Lord Jesus Christ" (1 Thess. 1:3). In this verse, the apostle also uses the three words mentioned in 1 Cor. 13:13 which reads: "And now these three remain: faith, hope and love. But the greatest of these is love."

God's Church has to be a loving church which is also a persevering church in moments of tribulations. We can see too from his letters that Paul loved them the Thessalonians.

A. A joyful church in the midst of the tribulation

God wants his church to learn to worship Him despite their circumstances. Even when we pass through different complicated moments, our joy in Him will always remain. For this, our communion with God is important. The Holy Spirit will guide and nourish our lives constantly: "You became imitators of us and of the Lord, for you welcomed the message in the midst of severe suffering with the joy given by the Holy Spirit" (1 Thess. 1:6).

B. A loving and beloved church

God is love, and wants His church to imitate him. We need to be like Him, feel like He does. Holiness and love go hand in hand. The brothers and sisters in Thessalonica gave their lives to God sincerely and let the Holy Spirit act in them. They were not envious, bitter or filled with doubt. Nothing prevented them from showing others that God is love. They made a great impact on other people: "Now about your love for one another we do not need to write to you, for you yourselves have been taught by God to love each other. And in fact, you do love all of God's family throughout Macedonia. Yet we urge you, brothers and sisters, to do so more and more" (Thess. 4:9-10).

They were characterized by the love that flowed between them and towards others. In fact, the others recognized them by these attributes: "We remember before our God and Father your work produced by faith, your labor prompted by love, and your endurance inspired by hope in our Lord Jesus Christ" (1 Thess. 1:3). That testimony came to Paul even when he was far away: "But Timothy has just now come to us from you and has brought good news about your faith and love. He has told us that you always have pleasant memories of us and that you long to see us, just as we also long to see you" (1 Thess. 3:6).

C. A church that grows in faith and love

The church of God cannot stay the same; it must advance, strengthen and grow through the work of the Holy Spirit. He moves in our lives; He changes us, transforms us, restores us and guides us. As God's church, we have been called to grow constantly. We will have to face difficult situations, which will give us the opportunity to trust in God. These difficult circumstances will teach us to be more united, to love more deeply, and to be stronger in our faith. If we put God first, preaching Christ as a priority and always share the good news about Jesus to people who do not know God, then we can move forward, grow together, and trust more in God. The Thessalonian church grew in faith and love: "We ought always to thank God for you, brothers and sisters, and rightly so, because your faith is growing more and more, and the love all of you have for one another is increasing. Therefore, among God's churches we boast about your perseverance and faith in all the persecutions and trials you are enduring" (2 Thess. 1:3-4).

D. A church of good testimony

It is clear from what we have seen that this church had a good testimony. It did not waste time arguing amongst themselves, or fighting for who was right. Their lives honored and exalted God. Because of their faithful testimony, many believed. The people saw a change in them and wanted to be part of this church. So many other people in Thessalonica met Christ through the good witness of the Thessalonian brothers and sisters.

Today, we are also called to bear witness of love, holiness, faith. Therefore, let's be constantly ordering our priorities so that God's purposes can become real in our lives. Paul told them, "And so you became a model to all the believers in Macedonia and Achaia. The Lord's message rang out from you not only in Macedonia and Achaia—your faith in God has become known everywhere. Therefore, we do not need to say anything about it, for they themselves report what kind of reception you gave us. They tell how you turned to God from idols to serve the living and true God" (1 Thess. 1:7-9).

Today we need to preach the same message. Maybe many years have passed, but the message should not change. We have been called to preach Christ; everyone needs to know that He came to live, die and be resurrected to give us salvation and eternal life. Today it should be easier for us to share the Good News. Many have already heard about Christ. We can learn about him also from Christian films, radio networks, internet sites, the online Bible, and many more opportunities. We have a lot of resources to spread the Word of God, and many ways to make it known. Today, the Word of God is a great reference for many, and almost all the signs of the end-times are being fulfilled. Read the Bible, and prepare to preach Christ, salvation and his second coming. Imitate the Thessalonian church and spread the Kingdom with your good testimony.

The letter to the Thessalonian Christians came to them when they were going through difficult times, but in spite of this, the church was putting down roots and growing. They endured difficulties with joy, preached and extended the Kingdom of God through their testimonies. Besides, they were humble and obedient to the Word, and each time the apostle taught them, they accepted the teaching with love, understanding that it was God who spoke through this servant.

Optional Questions:

I. The beginnings of the Thessalonian church

- How many days was Paul in the synagogue? (Acts 17:1-2)

- What did Paul do during that time? (Acts 17:3)

- Do you think it was easy for Paul to deliver the message of salvation? Why?

- Do you think it is easy to deliver the message of salvation now? Why?

II. Affirming the church

- Was it important for Timothy to visit the church in Thessalonica, according to 1 Thessalonians 3:1-3? Why or why not?

- Do you consider it important that the church be told its strengths and weaknesses; to be taught and corrected about how they should walk (1 Thess. 4:1-12)? Why?

III. Extending the Kingdom with their good testimony

- What are the qualities of the Thessalonica church that you would highlight? Why?

- How could the present church give a good testimony and live in faith, love and constant growth?

Conclusion

The church of God must persevere in faith and love. We have much to learn from this church in Thessalonica. Let us pray to God help us to be humble, obedient, bear good testimony and be constant. Just as the Thessalonian Christians did, let's work together to extend the Kingdom of God.

To end this class, I share these words of E. M. Bounds "Men are God's method. The church is seeking better methods; God is seeking better men!"

The church of Ephesus

Wilson Sánchez (Peru)

Memory verse: "I know your deeds, your hard work and your perseverance. I know that you cannot tolerate wicked people, that you have tested those who claim to be apostles but are not, and have found them false" (Revelation 2:2).

Lesson Aim: To understand that God wants active churches that have not forgotten to have communion with Him, in order to remain spiritual healthy.

Introduction

We often find ourselves working hard for God while at the same forgetting to spend time alone with our Lord. Ask one or two of your students to share briefly what they felt when they first accepted Jesus in their hearts, and how this has changed in their lives. While it is true that the Ephesian church had very good characteristics, they also lacked a very important one, love for God. Its members were heart-sick. Revelation 2:1-7 tells us some things that we should not forget.

I. The Ephesian church had an invisible disease

A. They were working hard

Jesus tells them, "I know your deeds, your hard work and your perseverance" (v.2a). Apparently, the church in Ephesus had no problem - they were serving. They possessed two qualities that are indispensable in every church: 'work and perseverance.' The Ephesian church was an active church. They were not just sitting around with their arms crossed. In verse 3, the Lord tells them that they have: "endured hardships for my name." Jesus tells this church that He knows all the faithful service they have rendered because they were working hard and even suffering.

In addition to their hard work, they were a church that knew how to persevere. This church did not give up in spite of the different difficulties. In verse 3, the lord tells them, "You have persevered... not grown weary." Perseverance is a necessary quality in the Christian life because it assures us of salvation (Matthew 24:13). Perseverance is the key to success when we start a business, school, a job

or the Christian life. Success comes to those who persevere till the end what they have started, try again after an initial failure, pursue their objectives, and stay focused and working on the task. They are not lazy, do not look for easy answers, do not take shortcuts or advantages, do not easily lose interest and do not take 'spiritual vacations.' They are faithful, because God is faithful (1 Cor. 1:9; 2:10).

B. They had sound doctrine

The church in Ephesus was doctrinally strict. Jesus tells them, "I know that you cannot tolerate wicked people, that you have tested those who claim to be apostles but are not, and have found them false" (Rev. 2:2). The brothers and sisters in Ephesus had sufficient theological knowledge to discern the false teaching and unmask the false apostles. They even worried about the bad influence of the Nicolaitans according to verse 6, since the latter practiced immorality. This church had a reputation for being active, faithful and sound in doctrine. They must have felt good after hearing these compliments, and maybe they even felt proud. In short, before the eyes of others, Ephesus was a role model. They seemed healthy from head to toe.

Some churches today feel good about themselves because they are very hard workers. They have activities programmed throughout the year, and believe themselves to be faithful to the doctrine. They are very pleased with themselves and feel that they have reached a level of spirituality and maturity that other churches have not reached. But, if the Lord were to test them, would they pass? If the Lord took an x-ray, would He detect something wrong in those congregations? Paul said, "If anyone thinks they are something when they are not, they deceive themselves. Each one should test their own actions. Then they can take pride in themselves alone, without comparing themselves to someone else, or each one should carry their own load" (Galatians 6:3-5).

He also said, "So, if you think you are standing firm, be careful that you don't fall!" (1 Corinthians 10:12).

II. The diagnosis of the disease

A. Jesus puts His finger on the problem

Jesus, after a thorough examination of the spiritual state of the church, found a problem, a serious problem, a deadly problem. There are many diseases that we cannot see, but, little by little, they prevent the organs from functioning correctly. If these ailments are not detected in time, they can cause death. Jesus knew every heartbeat of the church in Ephesus. The church was still a remarkable church, but it lacked a key element that Jesus seeks in everyone - love. There was something that tarnished this church, the absence of love. Therefore, Jesus says to them, "Yet I hold this against you: You have forsaken the love you had at first" (Revelation 2:4). Jesus, being a specialist in the matter of love, immediately realized the defect of this church. This could spoil all the good that the church was doing. The Ephesian church was so busy working for Christ, and like the story of Martha, did not have time to love Him and be near Him (Luke 10:38-42).

Love cannot be replaced by the work we do for Him. The Lord must always occupy the first place in our hearts. The Ephesians no longer showed the love of Christ they had in the first years as a church. Good works cannot replace relationships! These believers had become obsessed with the works instead of concentrating on Christ, and they had lost the fervor of their love for the Lord. On the outside, they seemed very religious working for Christ, but their hearts had cooled to the one they served.

The Lord recognizes everything we do for Him, but He is more interested in our relationship with Him. Paul said the following: "If I speak in the tongues of men or of angels, but do not have love, I am only a resounding gong or a clanging cymbal. If I have the gift of prophecy and can fathom all mysteries and all knowledge, and if I have a faith that can move mountains, but do not have love, I am nothing. If I give all I possess to the poor and give over my body to hardship that I may boast, but do not have love,

I gain nothing" (1 Corinthians 13:1-3). Love is the secret ingredient we need to have if we want to please God.

B. Jesus tells them that they are responsible

Notice that Jesus said, "You have forsaken..." (Rev. 2:4). He did not say 'you have lost' or that it has been stolen from you. The Ephesian church was guilty of 'forsaking,' or giving up their first love. Here we can notice voluntary negligence. Sometimes, when we start a project, program, or plan, we usually start with a lot of enthusiasm and we really want it. But as time goes by, the weight of commitment becomes heavier. In addition, in the process, challenges, obstacles and stumbling blocks arise. Many times, the energy with which we started at the beginning is fading and, in the face of this, it is possible to fall into the temptation of blaming our lack of love on the pastor, the other brothers and sisters, the circumstances, etc. But the reality is that we ourselves have allowed the flame of love to go dim.

There are churches like Ephesus that meet faithfully, but they do not do it for love anymore. They sing, but they do not do it for love anymore. They pray, but they do not do it for love anymore. They preach, but they do not do it for love anymore. They are sound in doctrine, however they no longer do so out of love. It is not just the responsibility of the pastor, the rest of the congregation or the circumstances, etc.; We have allowed our flame of love to dim or even to blow out.

Today there are churches like the Ephesian church that meet faithfully, sing, pray, are sound in doctrine, serve; but this has become a routine and they do not do it for love anymore. The love of God and the love of the brothers is the supreme characteristic of a true Christian, Jesus said, "Love the Lord your God with all your heart and with all your soul and with all your mind. This is the first and greatest commandment. And the second is like it: Love your neighbor as yourself. All the Law and the Prophets hang on these two commandments" (Matt. 22:37-40).

III. A disease that needs to be treated

After seeing the severity of the disease, the finest medical specialist recommended the church in Ephesus to get into action. There was a treatment to follow if they wanted to continue living.

A. The first step

God told each of the Ephesian brothers and sisters to remember their previous state: "Consider how far you have fallen!" (Revelation 2:5a). It is very important to remember how or where we were before having this disease. To leave the first love is to be fallen. Therefore, we need to remember how we were when we first became Christians. We need to remember our joy when we were baptized, our thrill of going to church each Sunday, our willingness to help others, our desire to evangelize the whole world, and how grateful we were for what the Lord had done for us. The Lord knows that if we remember how we were before, we will want to repeat it.

The prodigal son remembered how he had been in his father's house before, and compared it to his current situation. He realized that he was better before: "When he came to his senses, he said, 'How many of my father's hired servants have food to spare, and here I am starving to death!'" (Luke 15:17). Today we must do the same and compare how we were when we knew the Lord, and how we are now. We may be surprised to discover that we are not even a shadow of what we once were.

B. The second step

We need to repent (Rev. 2:5). After reflecting on how we have led our lives, we must repent of the things we have done wrong. Repentance is recognizing that we are to blame for our own sickness, of lack of love. Repenting will lead us to make changes. This is a call to let God direct our lives; it is a call for a change of priorities. If before our priority was work, now it must be prayer, reading the Bible and loving God and our neighbors. It is a call to break with the present lifestyle to what God wants us to do and be. There can be no transformation without repentance.

C. The third step

It is important to start over, and return to our first works (v.5). Repentance must go hand in hand with the decision to begin again. The Ephesian Christians needed to go back to their 'first works' which emanated from their 'first love.' A church or an individual will be known by their actions. They need to go back to arriving early at the church service with joy, staying after the service talking with the brothers and sisters, inviting people to come to church, showing eagerness to support the activities of the church and studying the Bible regularly. They need to remember how they were in the period of 'first love.'

The spiritual Physician warns the church in Ephesus of death: "If you do not repent, I will come to you and remove your lampstand from its place" (v. 5). Christ warns the church that if it does not return to that first state, it will lose its right to exist as a church. The Lord threatens to remove its candlestick from the place where it is. The candlestick represents the congregation (Revelation 1:20). The church that does not fulfill God's purposes has no right to exist. This admonition is very strong for any church! Yes, there is a cure for this disease, but we have to apply the remedy of Jesus. Do not leave it for later on.

Optional Questions:

I. The Ephesian church had an invisible disease

- What are the two positive characteristics of the Ephesian church? (Revelation 2:2-3)
- What is sound doctrine? (Revelation 2:2)

II. The diagnosis of the disease

- What was the illness that Jesus diagnosed in the church in Ephesus? (Revelation 2:4)
- What does the expression of Revelation 2:4 mean: "Yet I hold this against you: You have forsaken the love you had at first"?

III. A disease that needs to be treated

- What remedy does Jesus give to the church in Ephesus so that it does not die? (Revelation 2:5)
- What is the relevance of the expression of Revelation 2:5 today: "do the things you did at first"?

Conclusion

Heart disease or spiritual disease is a disease that cannot be seen, but once it has been diagnosed, it needs to be attended to. It is not enough to work hard for God. We need to maintain a loving relationship with the owner of the work - God. We must not neglect our communion with Him. We must depend on each day to be filled with His love to do the work he has entrusted to us. Working for God cannot replace loving God.

Smyrna: a challenge to be faithful

Lety Cano (Guatemala)

Memory verse: "Be faithful, even to the point of death, and I will give you life as your victor's crown" (Revelation 2:10b).

Lesson Aim: To learn to decide to be faithful to the call of Christ even in the midst of adversity.

Introduction

"What does it mean to be a Christian in Syria?" is the title of a video that calls for reflection on the price of being a Christian. In our day, the church is persecuted in many countries that do not profess Christianity. To be a Christian in these places means to renounce family, work, freedom and life. Are we willing to suffer for the love of Christ? In the Western Hemisphere, there may be no political persecution, but Christians can suffer other types of persecution such as social rejection.

Are we willing to pay the price of remaining faithful to God until death? That was the message of God to the church in Smyrna (Revelation 2:8-11).

I. The Lord's message to the church in Smyrna

Smyrna was a prosperous port city established on the shores of the Aegean Sea, one of the provinces of the Roman Empire. Smyrna or Izmir as it is called today, was a busy Turkish city. The church in Smyrna was one of the seven churches of Asia Minor to whom the Lord Jesus Christ sent a message of hope (Revelation 2:8).

God establishes churches and sustains them in all kinds of situations, manifesting His attributes through which we find consolation and hope in the midst of trials. When this letter arrived in Smyrna with the Lord's message, they were undergoing a time of severe persecution. It seems that the Judaizers had made false accusations against them to the Roman authorities. This was probably during the government of the cruel emperor Domitian. The Lord gave John a message for the pastor of the Church of Smyrna to give them strength to face adversity with courage.

A. The eternity of Jesus Christ (v.8)

What relevance does the eternity of the Lord have for a church crushed by adversities?

While adversity afflicts us, we must remember that it is temporary and transient. The eternity of Christ inspires confidence, consolation and hope. The Lord of time and space is in control of the suffering we face: "For our light and momentary troubles are achieving for us an eternal glory that far outweighs them all" (2 Corinthians 4:17). The tribulation is temporary; but eternity with Christ is forever.

The message to the pastor was: "These are the words of him who is the First and the Last, who died and came to life again" (Revelation 2:8). The expression "the first and the last" speaks of His eternity ... He will never end. The Lord can be trusted, He is completely reliable. He who is superior to the temporality of human beings sends his Word to affirm their faith and give encouragement to His people who face danger of persecution and death.

B. The Lord of life

"He who died and came to life again" (v.8b) is the one who is sending them the message. The Lord decided to die by his own will: "The reason my Father loves me is that I lay down my life—only to take it up again. No one takes it from me, but I lay it down of my own accord. I have authority to lay it down and authority to take it up again. This command I received from my Father" (John 10:17-18). Christ rose again, and therefore is able to make us victorious; our life is secure in Him. We may physically cease to exist, but we will have eternity in the presence of God if we are faithful to His teachings.

Those who do not know Jesus Christ as Lord and Savior are lost in the midst of a world of problems.

But to the Christian, even when physical existence is taken away from him, eternal life awaits him with the risen Lord, who has power over life and death.

The church of Smyrna received encouragement to know that the eternal and victorious God was watching over them, as He does for His children who love Him unconditionally. No wonder the biblical writer said, "If God is for us, who is against us?" (Romans 8:31b). The hope that the church of Smyrna found in God is the same that we find in the eternal and victorious Lord Jesus Christ. He can renew our strength when we feel weak. In the midst of the trials, we need to know this: "If we endure, we will also reign with him. If we disown him, he will also disown us" (2 Timothy 2:12).

II. The Lord knows what is happening to the church

The divine omniscience is the exclusive attribute of God; He knows absolutely everything. Nothing is hidden, nothing goes unnoticed by Him: "I know your afflictions and your poverty—yet you are rich! I know about the slander of those who say they are Jews and are not, but are a synagogue of Satan" (Revelation 2:9).

A. The Lord knows what we do

The church of Smyrna had served God despite living in the midst of a society dominated by idolatry, vices and persecution. These circumstances had not been an impediment for the church to carry out the Work of God (Revelation 2:9a).

The church always faces adversity. In some cases, there is political and religious persecution against Christians, while in other situations, the enemy attacks the church with entertainment, excessive work and other distractions, so that many Christians claim to have no time to serve God. Even so, there is a remnant that serves the Lord despite their occupations, and that does not go unnoticed. God knows who serves him and who does not want to.

Regardless of the circumstances, those who work for the Kingdom of God must be aware that God is noticing what we do: "I know your afflictions and your poverty…" (Rev. 2:9). What better incentive than this to encourage us to work hard for the Lord!

B. The Lord knows our troubles

Any unfavorable situation we face can discourage us. The congregation in Smyrna suffered unjustly. It was there where, years later, the 85-year-old Polycarp offered his life and gave an example of fidelity in times of persecution. The church suffered because of the Jews who saw Christianity as an abominable sect, and because the Romans were polytheists and felt threatened by a religion with a single God (v.9b). Even so, the church was not alone, God was aware of their afflictions. It was a true test of who were truly Christians.

If today we suffer afflictions as the Church of Christ, we are not alone either. God does not ignore our suffering, and that gives us hope. The Lord said, "I have told you these things, so that in me you may have peace. In this world you will have trouble. But take heart! I have overcome the world" (John 16:33).

C. The Lord knows our needs

During the imperial persecutions, Christians were stripped of their property, suffering shortages and many limitations. The Christians of Smyrna suffered poverty (Revelation 2:9b). They had no way of satisfying their basic needs. When there is a shortage, we suffer anguish, especially if there are loved ones who suffer through insufficient resources. Obedience to God can often represent material poverty, but it is also an opportunity to foster faith and experience the miraculous provision of God.

The existence of material goods must not condition our fidelity to God. As the prophet Habakkuk affirmed: "Though the fig tree does not bud and there are no grapes on the vines…yet I will rejoice in the Lord, I will be joyful in God my Savior. The Sovereign Lord is my strength; he makes my feet like the feet of a deer, he enables me to tread on the heights" (Habakkuk 3:17-19).

But the Lord who knows the intimacies of our hearts also praised the congregation of Smyrna for their spiritual wealth: "yet you are rich!" (v. 9). Surely, communion with God had endowed them with strength and faith to receive this recognition from the omniscient and almighty God! On the contrary, many who are rich in temporal goods, suffer through their own decision terrible spiritual poverty that weakens when they have to face and overcome trials.

If we are suffering from poverty, it is better for us to be rich in the spiritual things because in that way, God himself will satisfy all our needs according to His riches in glory. But let us remember that the material provision should not condition our fidelity to the Lord who gave His life to save ours.

D. The Lord knows our enemies

The lord said in His message, "I know about the slander of those who say they are Jews and are not, but are a synagogue of Satan" (Revelation 2:9). The Jews were the chosen people of God, but they had become the worst enemies of the church. Although they were Jews and technically God's people who pretended to defend God's interests, in reality they were in opposition.

The religious who attack the church of Christ will have to face our God who is love, but who is also a consuming fire. How could those who knew the law and the prophets attack Christians with such hatred? Jeremiah reminds us, "But the Lord is with me like a mighty warrior; so, my persecutors will stumble and not prevail. They will fail and be thoroughly disgraced; their dishonor will never be forgotten" (Jeremiah 20:11).

Christians should have no enemies, but there are many who are enemies of Christians, although they appear to be merciful and religious. God will fight against them. The Lord also reveals what they really are: "... synagogue of Satan." They were serving the purposes of the enemy of the Lord and His church as many do today.

III. The Lord offers hope for His church

A. "Do not be afraid"

The Church in Smyrna was afraid. On one hand they had the Jews against them, and on the other, the superstitious and ignorant Roman society. As if that were not enough, there was also the implacable and jealous Roman Emperor and His idolatry! However, considering all of this, the Redeemer says encouraging words to the church in Smyrna: "Do not be afraid of what you are about to suffer. I tell you, the devil will put some of you in prison to test you, and you will suffer persecution for ten days…" (Rev. 2:10a). Surely, this warning would scare anyone because the message revealed that the Christians of Smyrna awaited prison, trial and tribulation. It was natural to be frightened in the midst of so many difficulties, but the victorious Lord gave them encouragement, comfort, confidence and security, as He does today if we are faithful like this church. We read, "Be faithful, even to the point of death and I will give you life as your victor's crown" (v.10c).

The prisons of that time were no better than ours today. The conditions were cruel and inhuman, and the servants of the devil would do everything possible to send many Christians there, not only to be locked up, but also to kill them. However, all the enemies together could not stop the Lord's church, because according to Tertullian, the 'blood of the martyrs is the seed of Christianity.'

B. "I will give you life as your victor's crown."

Fidelity can lead to death: "For whoever wants to save their life will lose it, but whoever loses their life for me will find it" (Matthew 16:25). In addition, the Lord promised His church that they would not suffer the harm of the second death, that is, the eternal separation from God. Fidelity to God will be rewarded, but the victors' crown is only for those who reach the end (v.10c).

Optional Questions:

I. The Lord's message to the church in Smyrna

- Describe how Jesus presented Himself to the suffering church of Smyrna (v:8).
- How do we present Christ today?
- Do you think that we put enough emphasis on Christ His attributes, or what He gives us?
- How should we present Him?

II. The Lord knows what is happening to the church

- What kind of suffering did the church face (v.9)?
- What kind of suffering does the church face today?

III. The Lord offers hope for His church

- What incentives did the church receive from the Lord?
- Are we today worthy of those incentives?

Conclusion

The church of Smyrna was challenged by the Lord to be faithful, even at the cost of losing their lives. He gave them hope and the promise of eternal life in His presence. Perhaps right now, we are going through trials and tribulation, and this message is also relevant for us now. We need to remain faithful to God in the face of all adverse circumstances, and afterwards, we will enjoy eternity with Christ.

Pergamum: a call to commit to the truth

Lesson 35

Sharon Víquez (Costa Rica)

Memory verse: "Repent therefore! Otherwise, I will soon come to you and will fight against them with the sword of my mouth" (Revelation 2:16).

Lesson Aim: To understand that God wants his church to avoid false teachings and combat errors with the truth of his Word.

Introduction

Every action has either positive or negative consequences. The church in Pergamum (Revelation 2:12-17) needed to come to terms with this truth. Throughout this lesson, we will see that the Word of God, the sword of truth, is the only thing that can help us discern what is truth from lies in order to be free from false teachings.

I. Historical context of Pergamum

Pergamum was an ancient Greek city situated 16 miles from the Aegean Sea on a lofty isolated hill on the northern side of the broad valley of the Caicus River. The site is occupied by the modern Turkish town of Bergma in the province of İzmir. Pergamum was a famous for its large library home to 200,000 volumes.

According to witnesses of that time, Pergamum was devoted to idolatry more than all the rest of Asia. It was the most important religious center of the Roman Empire. There they had centers for four sects that worshiped the gods Zeus, Dionysus, Asclepius (the god of healing) and Athena. The Lord refers to Pergamos as the place "where Satan has his throne."

A. A church committed to its faith

In the midst of this socio-cultural situation, the Pergamum Christians received the Lord's recognition for being a church that maintained their faith in Jesus and did not deny their faith (Rev. 2:13-14). The passage gives the example of Antipas, referring to him as a 'faithful witness'. The term 'witness, in the New Testament, refers to a proclamation in words, deeds or suffering. Rev. 1:5 mentions this same term for Jesus Christ when he says, "and from Jesus Christ, who is the faithful witness, the firstborn from the dead, and the ruler of the kings of the earth."

Being a witness to Christ in Pergamum was not an easy task, especially since this city was the center of the imperial cult, which threatened the annihilation of the very existence of the church. Refusing to take part in imperial cult constituted high treason to the Roman state.

B. But they had adapted their morals

As in all the letters to the churches, we find that after highlighting a positive quality, reference is also made to a weakness. In the case of the church of Pergamum, we find two specific situations:

i) "There are some among you who hold to the teaching of Balaam, who taught Balak to entice the Israelites to sin…" (Revelation 2:14) and,

ii) "Likewise, you also have those who hold to the teaching of the Nicolaitans" (v.15).

The common term between both assertions is the word 'hold to', or tolerate. There is a place for respecting other people's religious points of view, but in this case, they were being affected by erroneous teachings and adapting to a life of 'libertinism' instead of true freedom.

II. The Pergamum church was losing their way

A. Balaam made a bad decision

In studying the story of Balaam in Numbers 22, we can see that Balaam was a prophet of the Lord who at the request of Balak, king of the Moabites received an order form the Lord: "Go back to your own country, for the Lord has refused to let me go with you" (Numbers 22:13b). The second time he was asked to curse Israel in exchange for riches, Balaam again stands firm in his position. Balaam answered them: "Even if Balak gave me all the silver and gold in his palace, I could not do anything great or small to go beyond the command of the Lord my God" (Numbers 22:18).

However, God gives the order to Balaam to accompany the envoys of King Balac. On the way, something happened to Balaam's heart that does not allow him to recognize God's presence. "The angel of the Lord asked him, Why have you beaten your donkey these three times? I have come here to oppose you because your path is a reckless one before me" (Numbers 22:32).

After that divine warning, the biblical story tells us about the three attempts made by Balak for Balaam to curse Israel; but in all cases, he could only utter a word of blessing against them, and therefore, he made him return to his people. But certainly, evil already existed in Balaam's heart. This is evident in Numbers 31:16 which states: "They were the ones who followed Balaam's advice and enticed the Israelites to be unfaithful to the Lord in the Peor incident, so that a plague struck the Lord's people."

B. The Nicolaitans: making an agreement with pagans

Acts 6:5 says, "This proposal pleased the whole group. They chose Stephen, a man full of faith and of the Holy Spirit; also, Philip, Procorus, Nicanor, Timon, Parmenas, and Nicolas from Antioch, a convert to Judaism." In this verse, Nicholas of Antioch is mentioned. He is supposed to have given his name to a group in the early church that sought to reach an agreement with paganism. The idea was that Christians could take part without problems in some of the social and religious activities of the society in which they found themselves. The historical reference of Irenaeus, Clement and Tertullian suggest that this group became a Gnostic sect.

The figure of the Nicolaitans, in the way they acted, is related to that of Balaam. They were teaching a message which had not come from God, a deviation from true doctrine. Seduced by their own personal ambitions and desires, they had become tolerant of the practices of other pagan peoples.

III. The divine call is 'to repent'

God calls all those who had allowed their faith to deviate from the truth to repent. Rev. 2:16 says, "Repent therefore! Otherwise, I will soon come to you and will fight against them with the sword of my mouth." The sword of the Spirit is the only one that separates the truth from falsehood. Only the Word of God can deactivate our dependence on sin and induce us to repentance, helping us to realize who is the only one who can have mercy on us and forgive us.

Both problems censored by God in the letter to Pergamum are related to a departure from the truth. In the same way, when the church today abandons its daily encounter with the Word of God, it begins to give ground to the enemy, allowing him to destroy the church from within.

A. The contemporary church is also at a crossroads

When we have to go through trials, God's people have only two paths to follow: the example of Antipas, who remained faithful and did not deny his faith; or the example of Balaam, who when things got difficult, could not resist the temptation and gave in to it.

We live in the midst of a society that every day becomes more hostile to divine counsel. God continually exhorts us to remain obedient to His teaching, and to conduct ourselves according to His counsel. But He does not make us to do it. The crossroads we face are not different from the ones described in the letter to the church in Pergamum. We are asked to live according to the counsel of the Word of God, in spite of whatever the consequences might be, and not to conform ourselves or adapt our faith to this world's culture. The Bible reminds us that the believer must not conform to the culture of this world but rather renew our understanding (Romans 12:1-2).

This renewal only occurs in those who make the Word of God their manual for life, and allow it to transform them from within (convictions) as well on the outside (practices): "For the Word of God is alive and active. Sharper than any double-edged sword, it penetrates even to dividing soul and spirit, joints and marrow; it judges the thoughts and attitudes of the heart" (Hebrews 4:12).

The Lord himself indicates to the Pergamum Christians that "He will fight with the sword of his mouth." The Word of God will show us clearly the sins which we must renounce and the lack of character we must correct. His Word transforms us: "All Scripture is God-breathed and is useful for teaching, rebuking, correcting and training in righteousness" (2 Timothy 3:16).

B. The promised reward

False teachers have always been present in the history of the church: "There were also false prophets among the people, just as there will be false teachers among you. They will secretly introduce destructive heresies, even denying the sovereign Lord who bought them—bringing swift destruction on themselves" (2 Peter 2:1). Every generation has had Christians like Antipas, faithful witnesses of the Lord. To them the Lord gives them a promise: "Whoever has ears, let them hear what the Spirit says to the churches. To the one who is victorious, I will give some of the hidden manna. I will also give that person a white stone with a new name written on it, known only to the one who receives it" (Rev. 2:17).

The phrase 'the one who is victorious' refers to the one who remains firm to the end (Matthew 24:4-14). In other words, Christians who do not let themselves be seduced by false teachings, because they know what is true. Jesus said, "I am the true vine, and my Father is the gardener. He cuts off every branch in me that bears no fruit, while every branch that does bear fruit he prunes so that it will be even more fruitful" (John 15:1-2).

C. One of the rewards is already in our hands

'Manna' typifies a type of bread received by the Israelites during the exodus. Jesus also describes himself as the bread of life in John 6:25-35. We have received our salvation through the merits of Christ, who gave himself for us to give us life. We must be faithful to this divine gift. Our task in this world is to stand firm to what we believe to be true biblical basis for our convictions as Christians. Jesus is the bread of life that He has given that gave and continues to give life to the world.

D. Eternal reward

Rev. 2:17 mentions the following expression: "I will also give that person a white stone with a new name written on it, known only to the one who receives it." This expression refers to the gift of eternal life. In ancient times, white stones were used as awards, and a stone with the engraved name could be used

as an invitation to an event. This is the invitation to the best of events: "Then the angel said to me, write this: Blessed are those who are invited to the wedding supper of the Lamb! And he added, these are the true words of God" (Rev. 19:9).

We are called to care for the salvation that has been granted to us by grace, to be faithful to the divine demands of a life of holiness (Heb. 12:14), to keep in our hearts the counsel of God's Word and not separate ourselves from it (Psalm 119:1-5, 10-12, 33-35). And we are also called to share this truth with others who need to hear this good news (2 Tim. 4:2).

Optional Questions:

I. Historical context of Pergamum

- What is the recognition that the church of Pergamum receives in Revelation 2:13?
- What is the weakness that the church of Pergamum had in Revelation 2:14-15?
- What are the strengths and weaknesses of our church today?

II. The Pergamum church was losing their way

- What false teachings are around now?
- How can we combat them?

III. The divine call is 'to repent'

- What is the call mentioned in Rev. 2:16?
- What is the promise that is mentioned in Revelation 2:17?
- How much time do we dedicate to seeking God and studying the Word as an antidote to falling into false doctrines?

Conclusion

When we hear the voice of God, are we faithful to His demands? Does our life inspire others to stand firm in their faith, or are we stumbling blocks which cause others to fall? Gratitude for the gift of salvation that we have received from His hand, and the blessed counsel of His Word, will cause us to be like Antipas. We too will become recommended by the Lord gladly as one of His "faithful witnesses."

Thyatira: When sin penetrates the church

Lesson 36

Daniel Pesado (Spain)

Memory verse: "Then all the churches will know that I am he who searches hearts and minds, and I will repay each of you according to your deeds" (Revelation 2:23b).

Lesson Aim: To understand that, until Christ returns, we must live lives free of contamination, and go on with perseverance and excellence.

Introduction

Founded by the Greek ruler, Seleucus I Nicator approximately three centuries before the time of Christ, the small city became a commercial center for the economy of the area. Thyatira was famous for its dyeing facilities, and was a center of the purple cloth trade, an expensive commodity. It's now part of Turkey. Lydia, whom Paul met in Philippi, came from Thyatira: "One of those listening was a woman from the city of Thyatira named Lydia, a dealer in purple cloth. She was a worshiper of God. The Lord opened her heart to respond to Paul's message" (Acts 16:14).

The risen Lord sent a message to this church (Revelation 2:18-29), addressed "to the angel of the church in Thyatira." Probably this angel was none other than the pastor, God's messenger there. When God entrusts angels with some task, they are important messages. God uses his most qualified 'manpower'.

The excellence of the task entrusted to the church requires that those who cooperate with God must understand what He is asking them to do, and also how He is asking them to behave. Our lives must reflect our Maker. As the world looks at us, they need to see the image of the one whom the church represents.

We can be assured that the whole message of the Bible tells us that God never conceals His true intentions towards the world, which he loves unconditionally. He reveals His will to His servants (prophets, kings, apostles, among others). His desire is that we will participate with Him by taking His salvation to the ends of the Earth. The prophet Amos says, "Surely the Sovereign Lord does nothing without revealing his plan to his servants the prophets" (Amos 3:7). The message is as important as the messenger.

The apostle John, whom most scholars consider to be the author of Revelations, probably wrote this book towards the end of the reign of the Emperor Domitian (who reigned from 81-96 AD). He had seen many changes in the church since it was founded around 33 A.D. In his writings, he expressed with great subtlety the necessary concordance between the holy nature of the Father, of the Son, (who establishes the church) and of the Spirit, (who was guiding the writer), himself as the author, of the messengers (who were to carry the letters) and of the Thyatiran church itself as the addressee.

I. What the church at Thyatira was doing right

The letter to Thyatira begins in Revelation 2:18 describing Jesus as: "The Son of God, whose eyes are like blazing fire." These eyes penetrate far beyond the mere appearance or exterior image. God never acts on what the church shows outwardly or pretends to be. With his intense and scrutinizing gaze, he reaches the very heart of the church, and looks at the intentions and motivations that move it. In other words, God is interested not only in what we do, but also how we do it and why. "Nothing in all creation is hidden from God's sight. Everything is uncovered and laid bare before the eyes of him to whom we must give account" (Hebrews 4:13).

A. "I know your deeds" (v.19a).

The church in Thyatira received a word of approval or praise in the first place for their deeds. It may be difficult for some Christians to understand that God is interested in what the church members are doing. Before the Protestant Reformation, the Roman Catholic Church put a lot of emphasis on salvation by works. Today there is a tendency for the pendulum to swing totally the other way disdaining or

115

devaluating all kinds of good deeds. Neither extreme is correct. Paul clearly describes the relationship between saving faith and works in Ephesians, saying, "For it is by grace you have been saved, through faith—and this is not from yourselves, it is the gift of God— not by works, so that no one can boast" (Ephesians 2:8-9). But immediately he adds: "For we are God's handiwork, created in Christ Jesus to do good works, which God prepared in advance for us to do" (Ephesians 2:10a). Although we will not be saved by doing good deeds, these must come as a result of a new life in Christ.

B. "I know…your love and faith, your service and perseverance" (v.19b).

The Lord explained a little more about the characteristics of this church.

1. **Love** (gr. Agape). It was love that moved God to send His Son into the world, and therefore, love must be what motivates and sustains the church's task. Jesus said it clearly, "By this everyone will know that you are my disciples, if you love one another" (John 13:35). The apostle John himself in his writings continually emphasizes love as the factor that unites us to God; brothers and sisters in the Lord must love each other.

2. **Faith.** Faith activates the power of God. Through faith, God in His grace applies His blessings to the church, and through it to the world (Hebrews 11:6).

3. **Service.** Service is the lifestyle that the Lord expects the church to express: "For even the Son of Man did not come to be served, but to serve, and to give his life as a ransom for many" (Mark 10:45).

4. **Perseverance.** We must persevere. Love produces patience, and this helps us not to give up when non-Christians resist the message. Patience makes it possible to create new opportunities (Luke 21:19).

C. "I know…that you are now doing more than you did at first" (v.19c).

Surely, the period between Pentecost and the time of writing Revelation allowed John to see how the church had grown in size and influence. The church had multiplied its ministries and demonstrated a practical gospel, not only in words, but also good deeds bringing relief to the needy. Undoubtedly with the right motivation (love, faith, service, perseverance), service in the name of the Lord has unlimited possibilities. The emphasis on service and the increase of kindly deeds must challenge us to not allow ourselves to stagnate, but continue expressing our faith through what we do, especially in contexts where there are a lot of needy people.

II. "Nevertheless, I have this against you" (v. 20a).

The Lord shows great wisdom. First, he praised them for the good things they were doing. However, immediately afterwards He had to give them a terrible warning.

A. "You tolerate that woman Jezebel" (v. 20a)

They were tolerating sin in the congregation and that was dangerous. Jezebel refers to the pagan and terrible wife of King Ahab, who led the king to practice idolatry, greed, murder and persecute the prophets of God to unimaginable extremes (1 Kings 16:29-34, 18:1-19, 21; 2 Kings 9:30-37). She, and her name, is a prototype of evil or sin.

In the congregation of Thyatira, there was a false prophetess who had been teaching false doctrines. She promoted participation in banquets, probably organized by the guilds in which the bronze workers, the textile industry and some groups of artisans were grouped, where they ate the food that had been sacrificed to idols. They got drunk and carried out unbridled sexual practices. Today in many churches, the love and mercy which sinners need are confused with tolerance for their sinful lifestyles. This distorts and renders the gospel of Jesus Christ ineffective.

B. The consequence of sin (vv. 20-23).

The announced consequence allows us to understand the gravity of the sin committed. Being thrown on a bed of suffering expresses the painful consequences, suffering and agony produced by their sin. The tribulation is a sign of the confusion and disorientation in which those who oppose God will fall. The result will even lead to death of those who are dragged down by the false teaching.

C. The remedy for sin

God always gives us an opportunity. This prophetess was invited to repent (v. 21). She refused to take this medicine, and those like her who refuse to repent are putting a great obstacle between themselves and God. We must repent in humility, recognizing the wrong we are doing. This remedy is hugely efficient; repentance stops the judgment and consequent destruction.

III. The Lord gives them a final word of encouragement

There is a great difference between those who honor God and those who do not, between those who live a life that glorifies him and those who only seek to satisfy their tireless search for pleasure. Verse 24 says, "Now I say to the rest of you in Thyatira, to you who do not hold to her teaching and have not learned Satan's so-called deep secrets, 'I will not impose any other burden on you, except to hold on to what you have until I come.'" We will all be judged one day.

1. The Judge.

The one who determines the difference is the judge who announces his authority in an unmistakable way: "I am he who searches hearts and minds" (v.23b). And Jesus himself affirms it: "For judgment I have come into this world" (John 9:39a). This judge cannot be deceived or cheated. Paul also warns us: "Do not be deceived: God cannot be mocked. A man reaps what he sows" (Galatians 6:7).

2. The trial

This judgment will be according to God's justice. God is a fair Judge (Acts 17:31). Jesus said, "But if I do judge, my decisions are true, because I am not alone. I stand with the Father, who sent me" (John 8:16). The day when all human beings will be judged, the trial will be unappealable. We can pretend to ignore, forget, mock, and deceive ourselves about the existence of this judgment, but we will not be able to avoid it.

3. The outcome

Those who do not follow the permissive, corrupt and immoral lifestyle are assured: "I will not impose any other burden on you, except to hold on to what you have until I come" (Revelation 2:24c). They needed to hold out against the rebellion and contempt shown by the followers of the false priestess who, for some time, enjoyed favoritism and prosperity.

4. The prize

To those who are victorious (v.26) God will "give authority over the nations" (v.26b). This is a reference to Psalm 2 that ensures us that one day God will govern the nations with justice and the faithful will reign with Him. And in addition, they will receive the "morning star" (2:28). This appears to be a reference to the presence of Jesus, the greatest prize that every human being can aspire to (Revelation 22:6).

The last words of the letter to the church in Thyatira are a demonstration of the permanent need to listen and be guided by "what the Spirit says to the churches. The Spirit is that divine agent by which we are taught, exhorted, warned and motivated not to lower our guard. The message is not just for Thyatira, it is for all churches, including us, today.

Optional Questions:

I. What the church at Thyatira was doing right

- Read Revelation 2:19 and make a list of reasons why God might give a word of approval or praise to your church.
- Is your church active in working among the needy in the community?
- Specifically, what are they doing?

II. "Nevertheless, I have this against you" (v. 20a).

- How is the "Jezebel spirit" manifested in churches today? Mention some examples that you know.
- How should the church fight against those who seek to seduce and contaminate the Work of God? Give some concrete examples.
- What is the terrible warning of Rev. 2:21-23?

III. The Lord gives them a final word of encouragement

- How can we be continually renewing our minds (Romans 12:2)?
- How can we do even more to help those in need around us (Revelations 2:19)

Conclusion

The book of Revelations contains sections that are a bit hard to understand yet this letter to the church at Thyatira contains a very clear message: God does not admit sin; and if we do not repent, the implacable judgment of God will fall upon our churches also today. Yet the whole message is one of hope. God, through the Spirit, does everything possible to warn us and help us remain faithful until his return. There were and there are, in the history of Christianity, men and women who established churches, gave their lives in missionary work, fought for the rights of the most destitute, and were martyrs.

A wake-up call to the church at Sardis

J. Víctor Riofrío (U.S.A.)

Memory verse: "The one who is victorious will, like them, be dressed in white. I will never blot out the name of that person from the book of life, but will acknowledge that name before my Father and his angels" (Revelation 3:5).

Lesson Aim: To understand that it is possible to revive a dead church.

Introduction

A young pastor was asked to take charge of a dying church. He prayed for wisdom to know how to avoid the death of this congregation. One morning, he came up with an idea. He went to the offices of the village newspaper and published in the local newspaper in the obituary section a funeral notice that read: "Next Sunday, in the facilities of the evangelical church of our city, we will perform the funeral service to dismiss the mortal remains of our beloved and traditional church, which lamentably passed away a while ago. We invite all friends and family to lay her to rest." Of course, this aroused the interest and curiosity of everyone. In the city, everyone was talking about it. The members looked forward to Sunday.

When the Church doors opened, there was a large crowd waiting outside. One by one, the people came in and quietly occupied a place in the pews. At the front behind the pulpit, the young pastor waited. In front of the platform was a lustrous coffin which rested on its pedestals, surrounded by some wreaths and flowers.

After greeting those present, the pastor began the service. He spoke about the goodness of the beloved local evangelical church, how it had begun, its achievements and its moments of glory. Then, he said, "Unfortunately, today we have met to say goodbye, and I want to invite you to go one at a time to give the church a last goodbye before we bury her."

There was a queue of people waiting to go to the coffin. Neatly placed at the bottom of the coffin was a large mirror. Everyone who looked inside saw themselves. Many tears began to run down those faces. It was a moment of deep reflection. The young pastor began with great success the restoration of that congregation which soon experimented a revival and continued to grow.

The Lord Jesus Christ commanded the apostle John to record this letter to the first century church of Sardis. He sent this message, precisely with the same purpose as the young pastor of the story recounted above. He wanted the church, which was unfortunately dead, to revive and be saved.

The city of Sardis was a typical example of the contrast between a splendid past and a present in ruins. Sardis was a degraded city. 700 years before this letter was written, Sardis had been one of the largest cities in the world. But by this time, it was a city without life and without spirit. In that depressing atmosphere, the Christian church too had lost its vitality and was a dead body rather than a living church.

We can still listen to what the Holy Spirit has to say to the churches, because these messages of Christ are just as relevant for us now as they were in the first century. Churches are people, and human nature has not changed. So as we continue our study, we should not look at these letters as ancient relics. On the contrary, they are mirrors in which we must see ourselves! The message to Sardis, recorded in Revelation 3:1-6, is a warning to all those churches that live in past glory.

But there is hope, because Christ is the head of the church and He can give new life. What should the church of Sardis do to revive? How to wake up a church that is already considered to be dead? In the message of Christ to the church of Sardis, we find four firm steps that we must take to revive a dead church.

I. First step: Recognize the decadent reality

Sardis was the largest city of the Greeks ... a city recognized for its strength and magnitude. It had high walls and was located on top of a hill. They aimed at being safe and invincible. But on two occasions, they had been conquered because they were complacent, and the inhabitants did not recognize their faults. This town always lived in the past, when everyone recognized that Sardis was strong and active. Both the city and the church had once been great but had gone into decline.

Unfortunately, the church was not what it had once been. Christ spoke to them very clearly, telling them: "I know your deeds; you have a reputation of being alive, but you are dead" (v.1b). That church was like Samson, who did not realize that the Spirit had abandoned him. People can continue doing the same things, but if the power is no longer there, everything they do is in vain.

The first step for a church to wake up is to recognize that it is a dying church, which has been abandoned by the life-giving Spirit and is living only on 'past glories.' They must admit that there is a serious problem. They need to look in the mirror, the first step towards their restoration.

II. Second step: Follow the divine guidelines for recovery

If the church of Sardis could admit that it was spiritually dead, she would then be ready to attend carefully the guidelines that Jesus would give her to follow, counsels which would help her to take firm steps to become a living church again. Christ was very precise in his guidelines, pointing out five key actions to follow: **"Wake up, strengthen** what remains and is about to die… **Remember,** therefore, what you have received and heard; **hold it fast,** and **repent"** (vv. 2-3).

They needed to wake-up! Just as the city had been taken by surprise for not being awake, so the church of Sardis was at the mercy of Satan because of a general lack of vigilance. The call was to not rest on their laurels. The Lord said to them: *"what remains and is about to die…"* (v.2b). What remained, forms and structures, people and organized institutions, orthodoxy itself, were on the verge of dying for lack of having the Spirit with them. The Lord expresses the motive: *"for I have found your deeds unfinished in the sight of my God"* (v.2b). Yes, there were 'deeds', but they were empty of interior content (faith, love, service, hope, etc.). They were a shallow church. They had not been working for the Lord correctly,

just appearing to do well in the eyes of the people. But the people noticed and nothing is hidden from the eyes of God.

The Lord said to them, *"Remember, therefore, what you have received and heard"* (v.3). They had been well taught, they had seen God work, and now Jesus is asking them to remember. They had received the message of salvation, with its promises, its privileges and also with the demand of true discipleship. Their love had grown cold; they had become inactive. They had forgotten the true meaning of the gospel. Over and over, Christians must go back to the cross and remember what God has done for them in Jesus Christ.

"Hold fast, and repent" (v.3). To hold on to something is to grasp it and not to let go. This church needed to go back to the essential truths of the gospel, obey and stay awake to fulfill the will of God. Repent indicates the urgency of the change of mentality, it had to be once and for all.

If we do not pay serious attention to the Word of the Lord, there will be consequences: *"But if you do not wake up, I will come like a thief, and you will not know at what time I will come to you"* (v.3). If the church does not wake up and stay vigilant, the Lord will come suddenly, as it had happened to the city on the occasions when it was taken by the enemy.

III. Third step: Value the example of the few faithful

Although a majority of the members of the Sardis church had fallen into disobedience to the Lord, a minority had remained faithful: "Yet you have a few people in Sardis who have not soiled their clothes" (v.4a). Sardis was famous for its textile industry. Those who stained their clothes were removed from the public list of citizenship. These few faithful who did not stain their lives, conforming and surrendering as others did, receive a promise from the Lord: "They will walk with me, dressed in white, for they are worthy" (v.4). Walking with Christ symbolizes salvation and fellowship with Him. White robes symbolize God's justice, victory and glory. The white color is attributed to Christ (Revelation 1:14), to his angels (Revelation 15:6), and to his elect (Rev. 19:14). In the case of Sardis, a city recognized by its dyers, the figure of the white garments communicated with great impact and marked beauty the blessing of the faithful to be for eternity in the company of their Lord and Almighty Savior. This verse shows also that not all faithful Christians were martyrs, but like those who experienced martyrdom, they are also worthy.

The Lord considers the remnant. For this reason, if we are part of Him, we must not be discouraged or throw in the towel. We are called to remain faithful in the hope of injecting vitality into the rest.

IV. Fourth step: Persist until you reach the eternal promise

Once they become a living church again, Jesus commends Sardis to continue faithfully until they reach the eternal promise. Everyone will know that they were once a dead church that has come to life again. Those who win are given a triple promise that also relates to the white garment. The three promises mean in essence the same thing, namely eternal life.

1. "He who overcomes will be clothed in white garments": (v.5a). Like faithful believers who will receive white garments from the Lord Jesus Christ, whoever wins living among the dissolute pagan society will be clothed in white garments. White garments were promised to the victorious. This is the appropriate attire for heaven.

2. "I will never blot out the name of that person from the book of life" (v.5b). This is what the words of Jesus in Matthew 10:22 mean: "the one who stands firm to the end will be saved." This is, eternally. Not only is their name safe in the heavenly record, but it will not run the risk of being erased. The condition for the name to remain in the book of life is to be victorious.

3. Jesus said he would "acknowledge that name before my Father and his angels" (v.5c). Christ will not be ashamed to recognize His own. Here the language echoes Matthew 10:32 which says, "Whoever acknowledges me before others, I will also acknowledge before my Father in heaven." We have the wonderful promise that Christ will present us before the heavenly Father at the end of time.

Revelation 3:6 has a recurring phrase that emphasizes our responsibility to listen: "Whoever has ears, let them hear what the Spirit says to the churches." These letters were to be read aloud in the churches. The church of Sardis was guilty because of its spiritual dryness. They had abandoned the responsibility of testifying for Christ. It is probable that the majority of the members professed to be Christians, but they were dead spiritually, far from the will of God and in constant disobedience. However, there was a small remnant faithful to the Lord.

Today's churches and Christians as individuals must heed the message of the Lord to the church of Sardis. We must sincerely acknowledge if we have fallen so low that we are about to die. Churches need to be vigilant; they need to defend the good that still remains, not forget the original meaning of the true gospel, take care of the progress achieved, and repent from the heart of having given place to spiritual decay. The churches of today need to strengthen the essentials of following Christ, faithfully obey and stand firm until the day comes to meet with our Savior, Jesus Christ.

Optional Questions:

I. First step: Recognize the decadent reality

- What did it mean and what does it mean to be a 'dead church'? (Revelation 3:1b)
- What was the reality that the church of Sardis had to recognize?

II. Second step: Follow the divine guidelines for recovery

- What are the five actions (guidelines) that the church of Sardis needed to follow to become a living church? (Revelation 3:2-3)
- Do we need to take any of those actions in our church, understanding that each of us is an important part of it?

III. Third step: Value the example of the few faithful

- What does what Revelation 3:4 mean?
- What other characteristics can you observe in those who are faithful to the Lord in your congregation?

IV. Fourth step: Persist until you reach the eternal promise

- What is the challenge that each of us must meet today so that our names are not blotted out of the book of life?

Conclusion

We need to notice that it is not enough to have our names written in the church membership here on earth. The truly important thing is to be certain that, by faith in the person of the Lord Jesus Christ, our name has been inscribed in the book of life. Yes, it is possible to be a worthy Christian today, because our name is inscribed in the book of life!

The greatness of the church at Philadelphia

Litzy Vidaurre (Spain)

Memory verse: "That is why, for Christ's sake, I delight in weaknesses, in insults, in hardships, in persecutions, in difficulties. For when I am weak, then I am strong" (2 Corinthians 12:10).

Lesson Aim: To learn that God sees things differently from the world by looking at the example of this small church in Philadelphia. God is not so interested in us being big and strong, but rather that we are faithful to His Word.

Introduction

Although the Philadelphian church was the smallest of the seven churches, it was one of the two churches, with Smyrna, which received more praise and less condemnation. This church was small and weak: "I know that you have little strength" (Revelation 3:8b). But it had a quality that made it bigger than the others; faithfulness in the midst of hard trials.

Ask students to share in the class which qualities would make a church 'great' today. For example, would it be the church with the best worship group, or a large church with a large budget, etc. In this lesson, we will appreciate how God measures greatness differently according to Revelation 3:7-12.

I. The city of Philadelphia

A. Its geographic location

The ancient city of Philadelphia, was situated near the Cogamus River, some 27 miles from Sardis and 48 miles from Laodicea. Philadelphia was known for its variety of temples and worship centers. The city was built on the slope of Mount Tmolus overlooking a fertile valley.

Philadelphia stood at the place where the borders of Mysia, Lydia, and Phrygia met. It was characteristically a border town. It was in the middle of the imperial route from Rome to Troas, making it the gateway to the East.

Its geographical location also gave it a big disadvantage since it was in an area constantly hit by earthquakes. It was destroyed in 17 A.D. along with Sardis and other cities of the Lydia Valley. It was the smallest city in terms of population, because out of fear of the constant tremors, the inhabitants chose to live on the outskirts of the city. In addition, it was the youngest city compared to the other churches mentioned in Revelation. Therefore, the city of Philadelphia, as well as the church, were both small and young.

B. Philadelphia's history

Philadelphia, which means 'one who loves his brother', was founded by Attalus II (who reigned from 159 to 138 B.C. According to historians, Philadelphia was founded with the mission of spreading Greek customs, culture and language in the eastern part of Lydia and Phrygia. They succeeded in making Greek the only language in the region of Lydia. This aspect of dissemination of the culture and language of the city meant that the Philadelphia church also had an 'open door' to spread the message of salvation through Jesus Christ. For this reason, the Philadelphia church was also considered a missionary church. Its modern name is "Alashehir".

In Revelation 3:8, we see that Jesus had "placed before" them "an open door that no one can shut." It is the Lord Himself who provides this church with the opportunity to preach and spread the gospel to other nations.

C. The religious background in Philadelphia

The city of Philadelphia was known to house the temples of Artemis, Helios, Zeus, Dionysus and Aphrodite, and have many religious festivities. The main pagan worship was for the god Dionysus, although the main opposition of the Philadelphia church came from the 'synagogue of Satan' which, according to Revelation 3:9, "claim to be Jews though they are not, but are liars."

These false Jews caused even more opposition than the pagans because of their hatred and zeal towards the Christians of the time. Mainly, they opposed and persecuted the Christians who had converted from Judaism. These false Jews were Jews by race and religion who professed to be descendants of Abraham, but they were not.

Jesus identifies himself as "holy and true" (v.7). Holiness is a proper attribute of God in the Old Testament. The Holy One of Israel and Christ are one, and they are authentic in contrast to those of 'the synagogue of Satan.' Christ is the true God, distinct from false gods who claim to be what they are not.

II. The great virtue of this small church

A. Obedient to the Word

Revelation 3:8 says, "I know your deeds...I know that you have little strength, yet you have kept my Word and have not denied my name." Although the church in Philadelphia was small and weak, we see that it was praised for being obedient to God's Word. Of course, the little strength of this little church does not refer to its spiritual strength, but it was a small church in number and resources. Even so, out of their smallness came the source of their power in Christ; they had remained faithful to the Word. This quality is the first that the Lord highlights. They had remained obedient to the Word even in the midst of persecution and after passing through hard trials. Although its members formed a weak and unimportant church in the eyes of men, in the eyes of God they were a large and strong church.

This little church is an example of obedience in the midst of adverse circumstances. In the midst of opposition, this church remained obedient to the Word of truth. The promises Jesus gave them strengthen them more. Remember that our 'smallness' or insignificance in the eyes of people is our source of spiritual strength in Christ when we learn to keep His Word.

B. They were faithful to Christ

The second reason for praise of this small church is that they had not denied the name of Christ. Although the church had gone through a time of trial, it remained faithful to Christ. We are not sure what it meant to follow Christ at that time, but it is clear that staying true to Christ was a quality worthy of mention and praise. Surely, it would have been easier for them to deny their faith and live in 'peace' with everyone, but this church preferred life in Christ rather than yield to human pressures.

The Word is what allows us to know the truth of Jesus; it guides us in our communion with Him, and strengthens us to not deny His name in times of trouble and trials. Therefore, our lives should reflect His name at all times, in times of peace or in times of difficulty. The Lord is aware of our weaknesses, but these should not be an excuse or reason to not stay faithful.

C. They were beloved by Christ

In Revelation 3:9, we see how the Lord promises them victory over their enemies and persecutors: "I will make those who are of the synagogue of Satan, who claim to be Jews though they are not, but are liars—I will make them come and fall down at your feet and acknowledge that I have loved you." The Lord Himself will cause these persecutors to honor the church, and above that, they will recognize that the small and weak church has the approval and love of the Lord. She is the beloved of the Lord. This is the greatest honor and happiness that any church can have, to enjoy the love and favor of Christ. And this love would be evident to everyone, even their enemies would see it and they would have no choice but to recognize it.

What a great privilege for this persecuted church, who had been mistreated by its enemies, but loved by Christ! These are words of comfort and encouragement for a church that had received nothing but rejection. The church that had been excluded by society would be exalted over those who rejected it, and everyone would see that Jesus was with them.

III. The reward for those who overcome

The Lord promised to stay close to this church that had been faithful in the midst of difficult times. All those who were victorious were to receive a reward in three aspects: they were going to be able to prevail over their enemies' falsehoods, they were going to prevail in trails, and they were going to pass the test and become an immovable column in God's temple.

A. Prevailing over their enemies' falsehoods

Verse 9 tells us: "I will make those who are of the synagogue of Satan, who claim to be Jews though they are not, but are liars—I will make them come and fall down at your feet and acknowledge that I have loved you." Christ would make their enemies realize their errors. Christ would have these false Jews come and kneel at the feet of the church in Philadelphia, and they would have to acknowledge that they had been wrong. Of course, this does not imply that they would worship the church itself, but rather some Jews would even be converted to Christianity.

In other words, Christ promises them public recognition of their authenticity. In reality they were the church representing the holy and true God.

B. Prevailing in trials

In Revelation 3:10, we find the following promise: "Since you have kept my command to endure patiently, I will also keep you from the hour of trial that is going to come on the whole world to test the inhabitants of the earth." Since the Philadelphia church had patiently waited on Christ and remained faithful preaching the gospel, Christ promised to help them persevere in difficult times. This, however, does not mean that Christ will exempt them from the trials but that He would guard and protect them in the midst of trials and tribulations.

This wonderful promise is also for us. We too who preach the gospel and remain faithful to Christ are better able to face any trial that befalls us. It is the same Lord who gives us this strength and security in times of difficulty. We will still be able to prevail before the final test "that is going to come on the whole world to test the inhabitants of the earth" (v.10). Only Christ can give us this assurance of salvation and eternal life.

C. To be an immovable column in God's temple

Finally, the Lord declares the following: "The one who is victorious I will make a pillar in the temple of my God" (Revelation 3:12a). This image guarantees the victorious ones a place within the temple of God. That is to say that they will be an immovable column in complete communion with God and with the firmness that will make it impossible for them to fall.

This promise does not stop there, but this column will have a triple inscription: "I will write on them the name of my God and the name of the city of my God, the new Jerusalem, which is coming down out of heaven from my God; and I will also write on them my new name" (v.12b). It will be, then, a firm and stable column, the absolute property of God (the name of my God); belonging to a new citizenship (the name of the city of my God, the new Jerusalem) and full recognition of the character and identity of Christ (my new name).

What else is left for this small church to do? The Lord says one last thing: "Hold on to what you have, so that no one will take your crown" (Revelation 3:11). Along with the blessing and the promises, they must remain faithful to God, and take care of what they have achieved with so much effort.

Optional Questions:

I. The city of Philadelphia

- Write at least one significant aspect about the city of Philadelphia in relation to the church that was there.

  ◊ Its geographical location:

  ◊ Its historical background:

  ◊ Its religious background:

II. The great virtue of this small church

- What are the three qualities of the Philadelphia church (Revelation 3:8)?

III. The reward for those who overcome

- What does it mean that they will prevail over false ones (Revelation 3:9)?

- If Christ promises to keep us from trials, does this mean that He exempts us from them?

- What three inscriptions will the immovable column carry?

Conclusion

The little church in Philadelphia, though weak and poor in the eyes of people, knew how to remain faithful to the Lord in the midst of hard trials. They were worthy of praise in the eyes of God. Is your life worthy of the Christ's praise?

The church of Laodicea

Ela González (Guatemala)

Memory verse: "Here I am! I stand at the door and knock. If anyone hears my voice and opens the door, I will come in and eat with that person, and they with me" (Revelation 3:20).

Lesson Aim: To learn that God knows the sins of the churches, but through His great mercy He is ready to forgive, forget and restore.

Introduction

The church of Laodicea is the last of the seven churches of Asia Minor: Ephesus, Smyrna, Pergamum, Thyatira, Sardis, Philadelphia and Laodicea. The Lord wrote to each of them telling them that He knew what they were doing. In each case, the Lord recognized their good deeds and situations. However, there were reasons to call their attention because many of them had sinned and gone astray. The Laodicean church was the only one for which the Lord had no good words, only condemnation. To the six previous churches, the Lord had said to them: "I know your deeds ... But I have this against you." But the Lord said to them:, "So, because you are lukewarm—neither hot nor cold—I am about to spit you out of my mouth" (3:16).

I. Geographic location and history

A. Geographical location of Laodicea

Laodicea, located at the crossroads of important trade routes between Colossae and Philadelphia, was situated on a hill between fertile valleys irrigated by the waters of the Lycus River.

B. Brief history of Laodicea

Laodicea was a prosperous city, famous for its black wool industry extracted from black sheep that were bred for that purpose, and with which they manufactured clothing and carpets. It was an important commercial and administrative center with an established banking system. They had a medical school in this city, where medicines were produced, mainly eye drops made with dust from rocks in the area. However, there was a lack of water there because the Lycus river dried up in the summer and they had to transport water from hot water springs; but because of the long journey, it arrived lukewarm, cloudy and unfit for human consumption. The city was destroyed in the year 62 A.D. by an earthquake. But since it was a city of economically well-off inhabitants, it was rebuilt in a very short time by themselves, without the help of the State. Of all the churches mentioned in the book of Revelation, Laodicea was the richest church.

II. Recipients and Sender of the letter

A. The recipient - the angel

In the Greek language, "aggelos" could imply either a human or celestial messenger or envoy. In the case of this letter, John receives the order to write to the angels of the seven churches. Commentators suggest several possible meanings. It could have referred to the senior pastor, a bishop, an elder, or the leader. Church tradition names Archippus, (mentioned in Philemon v.2, Colossians 4:17) as the leader of the Laodicean church. The 'angel' could also be the church itself.

B. Sender of the letter

Although John was the author, he only received the message through the Lord. He was the intermediary between the church of Laodicea and the Lord. Revelation 3:14 says, *To the angel of the church in Laodicea write: These are the words of the Amen, the faithful and true witness, the ruler of God's creation.*

III. Accusations and condemnations of the church

A. Neither one thing or the other

Revelation 3:15 says, "I know your deeds, that you are neither cold nor hot. I wish you were either one or the other!" The Laodiceans knew what it meant to have lukewarm water; the water they often received was not only warm, but murky. Warm water is not pleasant to drink, unless we are sick. Water is good to drink cold, at room temperature, or refrigerated according to each person's taste; but it's not nice warm. God, in this case, points out that the lukewarm state of this church caused him disgust. It nauseated Him; he could not stand it. And for that reason he said, "I will spit you out of my mouth" (v.16).

B. Arrogance, pride and self-sufficiency

The Lord said to them, "You say, 'I am rich; I have acquired wealth and do not need a thing'" (v.17a). They were an arrogant, proud and self-sufficient church. Why did God reject this church? We saw previously that Laodicea was a wealthy place of much commerce, possibly the largest of all the surrounding cities. This church declared that it was rich and this had come by their own merits. The phrase: "I am rich" is an indicator that this church had achieved it by its work, by its astuteness in administration and business, but without considering God in their prosperity. Therefore, the Lord continued: "But you do not realize that you are wretched, pitiful, poor, blind and naked" (v.17b).

In our day, many churches have fallen or are falling into the sin of ambition for power; they are proud that they are better than others. To maintain this, they have unnecessary expenses, build luxurious churches with the justification that God deserves the best, which we do not deny. However, when someone told Jesus that they would follow Him wherever He went, thinking that following Jesus would raise their social and economic status, Jesus replied, "Foxes have dens and birds have nests, but the Son of Man has no place to lay his head" (Luke 9:58). Many of Jesus' followers followed him because He fed them and He spoke of riches in heaven. However, God wants us to have inner richness, spiritual wealth, grateful hearts, content with what we have. As the apostle Paul said in Philippians 4:11b: "I have learned to be content whatever the circumstances."

When we seek first the Kingdom of God, not material riches, God promises to supply our needs. It is not a sin to be rich. In fact, many of the characters mentioned in the Bible were, but they always feared God, they put Him first and were faithful not only with tithes and offerings, but also by giving their time. They remembered those who had needs, and God fulfilled His promises to them, and He continues to do so today.

C. Who did they think they were?

The Laodicean church, in saying, "I have acquired wealth and do not need a thing" (v.17a), was declaring that they did not need God. Having wealth and material blessing is not enough. Jesus told his disciples and the crowd in Mark 8:35-37, "For whoever wants to save their life will lose it, but whoever loses their life for me and for the gospel will save it. What good is it for someone to gain the whole world, yet forfeit their soul? Or what can anyone give in exchange for their soul?"

God does not need us. Rather it is us humans who need Him at all times and in all conditions: in joy, in sorrow, in abundance, and in scarcity. Let those words spoken by the Laodiceans never leave our mouths.

IV. The advice, warning and promise of God

A. The advice

In response to the attitude of the Laodiceans, God, in His anger, ironically told this church in Revelation 3:18, *"I counsel you to buy from me gold refined in the fire, so you can become rich; and white clothes to wear, so you can cover your shameful nakedness; and salve to put on your eyes, so you can see."*

Laodicea was a city that handled a lot of money, it had a lot of wealth. They could, therefore, buy what they wanted. The main trade product in that city was the manufacture of garments made from the wool of black sheep. The Lord spoke to them of white garments. They also had a medical school, where they made medicine for the eyes; and He advised them to anoint their eyes with eye salve, but these were spiritual eye drops so that their spiritual blindness could be healed. This could be an application of what Jesus said about reward: *"Give away your life; you'll find life given back, but not merely given back—given back with bonus and blessing. Giving, not getting, is the way. Generosity begets generosity"* (Luke 6:38b The Message Tr.).

B. The warning

In Revelation 3:19, the Lord said to them, *"Those whom I love I rebuke and discipline So be earnest and* repent." Without repentance and confession, there is no forgiveness. We too must ask ourselves if we have said or done things that displease God. Have we allowed the fires of the Holy Spirit to go out in our lives? Are we neither warm nor cold just lukewarm. If so we are in danger of being "spat out of God's mouth."

C. The promise

In Revelation 3:20-21, there is a promise: "Here I am! I stand at the door and knock. If anyone hears my voice and opens the door, I will come in and eat with that person, and they with me. To the one who is victorious, I will give the right to sit with me on my throne, just as I was victorious and sat down with my Father on his throne."

The mercy and love of God are so great that despite the evil committed by many, He has great and precious promises for His children, for those who allow Him to enter their lives and who hear His voice. But for this to happen, we must submit our wills to maintain a victorious life that is pleasing to Him. Jesus overcame sin and death. Therefore, He asked the Laodiceans to be victorious, to put their pride to one side ... to realize that spiritual riches cannot not be bought with money.

His message to all seven churches was: "Whoever has ears, let them hear what the Spirit says to the churches" (3:22). To the first three, He told them this before the promise, while the remaining four were told at the end. Although this commandment was given to the seven churches, it is a message that our contemporary church, wherever it is the world, must pay attention to. In the letters to the seven churches, the Lord is talking about 'spiritual ears.'

Paul explains about this in 1 Corinthians 2:10-14: "The Spirit searches all things, even the deep things of God. For who knows a person's thoughts except their own spirit within them? In the same way no one knows the thoughts of God except the Spirit of God. What we have received is not the spirit of the world, but the Spirit who is from God, so that we may understand what God has freely given us. This is what we speak, not in words taught us by human wisdom but in words taught by the Spirit, explaining spiritual realities with Spirit-taught words. The person without the Spirit does not accept the things that come from the Spirit of God but considers them foolishness, and cannot understand them because they are discerned only through the Spirit."

Notice in that passage that there are our spirits (written with a small 's') and the Spirit of God, (written with a capital 'S'). We need to open our hearts so that the Spirit of God can help us to clearly hear God's voice. May this lesson inspire us to do good deeds while maintaining our faith, because as the Bible says, "without faith it is impossible to please God" (Hebrews 11:6a)..

Optional Questions:

I. Geographic location and history

- What were the important activities of the Laodiceans?

II. Recipients and Sender and of the letter

- To whom was the letter addressed (Revelation 3:14)?
- Who was the sender, and what was John's role in the letter?

III. Accusations and condemnations of the church

- What are the accusations with which the letter begins (Revelation 3:15)?
- What reasons did the Lord have to point to the church of Laodicea (Revelation 3:17)?
- Are these characteristic of our churches today?

IV. The advice, warning and promise of God

- What was God's warning to the Laodicean church (Revelation 3:19)?
- What was God's promise to the Laodicean church (Revelation 3:20-21)?
- What did you learn from this lesson today for your life?

Conclusion

We need to open our heart up so that God's Spirit might dwell in us, enabling us to hear what He wants to say to each one of us. May this lesson inspire us to humbly keeping our faith in Jesus, and recognize that everything we have comes from God ,and therefore, we must do good deeds.

What lessons can we learn from them?

Sin is serious

The consequences of making bad decisions

Successes and failures of King Jehoshaphat

The importance of listening to good advice

The three believers

Caleb's positive attitude

The return of the slave Onesimus

Steps in the training of John Mark

A Miracle with purpose

A disciple like Christ

The correct petition

Nehemiah's huge request

Married couple that served God together

Sin is serious

Daniel Pesado (Spain)

Memory verse: "How is it that Satan has so filled your heart that you have lied to the Holy Spirit? (Acts 5:3)

Lesson Aim: To recognize that lying goes against God's will, and brings bad consequences.

Introduction

Throughout the Bible, we find events that show us a God, who from a human perspective, may seem too severe to us. We find he judged characters like Nadab and Abihu (Leviticus 10:1-2); Hophni and Phinehas sons of Eli (1 Samuel 2, 4); Uzzah, who touched the ark of God; Jezebel; etc. And in the New Testament, we have Herod Agrippa, Hymenaeus, Alexander, among others, who suffered sudden and terrible deaths or were put aside.

This lesson focuses on the tragic story of Ananias and Saphira recorded in Acts 5:1-11. Thinking about these cases, ask your students:

- Could such sad events have been avoided?

- Did these people have knowledge of the consequences that their decisions would bring?

- To what extent is it possible to harmonize the destiny of these people with the mercy of God?

- In the case of Ananias and Saphira, did that part of the offering given to the church have any value?

- If we had to decide, what would we have done with that offering?

- Who caused the death of Ananias and Saphira?

- What was the sin of Ananias and Sapphira?

Probably, the simplest question to answer is the last one; for the passage itself declares that they were punished for trying to deceive God: "You have not lied just to human beings but to God" (Acts 5:4b).

But although direct, this response is not sufficient to help us understand the severity of the punishment received. It is important that we broaden our perspective and thus capture the true dimension of this sad event. The Jerusalem church reacted: "Great fear seized the whole church and all who heard about these events" (5:11).

I. The context of deception

The strength of Ananias and Sapphira's punishment was relative to the historic moment that this new church was experimenting.

A. The context of revival

This was the very time when the church was beginning, and this inauguration was accompanied by a powerful down pouring of the Holy Spirit (Acts 2:4, 43b, 46-47). The Holy Spirit had always been active in the Old Testament, but mostly empowering certain individuals for specific tasks. But in the Upper Room on the day of Pentecost, something new happened. The Holy Spirit filled all 120 disciples. From that moment on, the young church, with the twelve apostles up front, began to preach, and the response to the message of the gospel was immediate and wonderful. About 3,000 people were added to the church (Acts 2:41). At the same time, a continuous process of evangelism and conversion began (Acts 2:47b, 4:4,5:14). An enormous number of people converted to Jesus, and as a result, there was such a real, vibrant and profound communion expressed in great unity (Acts 1:14,2:1,46, 4:24, 5:12).

B. A context of abundance of grace

Everything that happened was the result of the real presence of Jesus, through the Holy Spirit, among the believers (Acts 4:33). The grace of God manifested itself in many ways in the life of the young congregation. Acts 2:46 says, "Every day they continued to meet together in the temple courts. They broke bread in their homes and ate together with glad and sincere hearts."

Many miracles occurred" (Acts 3:1-10, 5:12,14). In addition, they were bold, strong in their faith and had courage to testify. God greatly supported the church.

C. A context of reverence

Acts 2:43 says, "Everyone was filled with awe at the many wonders and signs performed by the apostles." Some people poked fun at what was happening (2:13); others were afraid of the disciples (Acts 5:13); others felt jealousy (v.17); still others were enraged (v.33); others "were greatly disturbed" (Acts 4:2). But at the same time, some were "utterly amazed" (Acts 2:7). Many were "cut to the heart" (v.37), and many believed in Jesus (2:41, 4:4). Just mentioning the name of Jesus aroused faith and admiration in people (Acts 3:6, 16).

The first Christians knew where this unique blessing had come from. The non-believers ignored it although, perhaps, many suspected it. But everything arose from the undeniable presence of Jesus in the midst of His people. "Great fear seized the whole church and all who heard about these events" (5:12). This was the result of being aware of being in the presence of someone with an important, great, holy and unfathomable power. The presence of Jesus produced reverence.

II. The content of the deception

A. Ananias and Sapphira **tried to deceive the apostles**

The apostles, the leaders at that time, were the visible face of the church. They were the ones who were consulted and who made the main decisions. Paying attention to the context (Acts 1-8) allows us to understand that activity in the church was frenetic. The brothers and sisters met daily, they shared meals, ministered to the sick, preached, taught or discipled thousands of converts, looked after widows and orphans and, all this in a situation of overt threat and persecution.

It is probable that this couple - Ananias and Sapphira - thought it opportune to use their access to the busy apostles to obtain some credibility. But if there is anyone we should respect in this world, it is

Christians who have a genuine and intense prayer life. The psalmist says, "would not God have discovered it, since he knows the secrets of the heart?" (Psalm 44:21b); and the prophet Amos adds: "Surely the Sovereign Lord does nothing without revealing his plan to his servants the prophets" (Amos 3:7). Also, the light of God, through the Holy Spirit, reveals deceit and evil, "the fruitless works of darkness" (Ephesians 5:11-13).

B. Ananias and Sapphira **tried to deceive God**

The Bible is full of warnings about the futility of trying to deceive God, His people or His servants. Kings, false prophets, fortune-tellers and even some followers of the apostles tried to deceive God. In the case of Ananias and Sapphira, the terrible sin committed is not so obvious. In Acts 5:3, Peter tells them, "Ananias, how is it that Satan has so filled your heart that you have lied to the Holy Spirit and have kept for yourself some of the money you received for the land?" Did Satan force them to sin? The truth is that they allowed Satan to fill their hearts.

Sin begins a process by which it numbs, dulls or obscures our spirit and mind, and we deceive ourselves by ignoring that God cannot be mocked. "Don't be misled: No one makes a fool of God. What a person plants, he will harvest" (Galatians 6:7 The Message). Ananias and Sapphira had forgotten this. Jesus told the crowd by the Sea of Galilee that "For whatever is hidden is meant to be disclosed, and whatever is concealed is meant to be brought out into the open" (Mark 4:22).

C. Ananias and Sapphira **deceived themselves**

Undoubtedly, the pride of the heart must have deceived Ananias and Sapphira (Obadiah 3), for Jeremiah tells us, "I the Lord search the heart and examine the mind, to reward each person according to their conduct, according to what their deeds deserve" (Jeremiah 17:10, cf. Revelation 2:23). Also, James assures us that hearing the Word and not obeying it leads us to deceit (Santiago 1:22).

It is hard to believe that this couple, living in a cultural context so religious and knowledgeable of the law of Moses, had intended such a deception and had not considered the personal consequences. We know that they lived with real fanatics like the Pharisees (who believed they had the correct interpretation of the law), the Sadducees (who, although opposed to the Pharisees, considered themselves purists in relation to the law), the Essenes (mostly ascetics), and even more, the Zealots (the radical wing of the Pharisees). Even so, it seems that they did not understand the consequences of their decision, and they tried to deceive the apostles. However, they were simply deceiving themselves.

III. The consequence of deception

It is easy to deduce from this fact that God wanted to give a key lesson for the rest of the life of the church. The seriousness of the sin had to be demonstrated - the ineffectiveness of deception, and the inexorable consequences of sin.

A. The price of the property

Was it worth it? Knowing the end of the story, we now know that it was not. But even so, we are seduced innumerable times to try to sin and believe that we can get away with it, pretending that there will be no consequences. The truly sad fact is that even though we know the damage that sin can cause, we continue doing it.

B. The price of deception

Their deception did not consist in subtracting part of the price of the property sold. They could have retained the full price because the property was theirs. What they wanted was recognition, in other words, 'spiritual credit', glory that did not belong to them, because they were not willing to pay the real price for it.

What second intention could they have had when trying to benefit from a false credibility, from a false commitment? Through this carnal attitude totally opposed to the true spirit of renunciation, surrender, and sacrifice modeled to perfection by Jesus, they undoubtedly sought to acquire a status that did not correspond to them within the nascent church. If this had been achieved, it would have caused much greater damage to the credibility of Christianity. The price paid by them was, to some extent, representative of the risk to which they exposed the church in its beginnings.

C. The price of sin

Paul says in Romans 6:23, *"For the wages of sin is death, but the gift of God is eternal life in Christ Jesus our Lord."* Dr. Louie Bustle always said, *"Sin always pays, and pays badly."* In other words, we are free,

and therefore we can choose to sin, but we will not be free to choose the consequences of our sin.

Optional Questions:

I. The context of deception

*   Are people today tempted in the same way as Ananias and Saphira (Acts 5:1-10)?

*   Can you remember a similar recent story? If so, please share it.

II. The content of the deception

*   Can you explain in your own words what was Ananias and Saphira's sin, according to Acts 5:1-4?

*   Knowing the risks that they run, what powerful reasons can 'push' people to try to manipulate, falsify, maneuver with cunning, or in short, pretend to deceive the Holy Spirit?

III. The consequence of deception

*   What would we say to someone who claimed that God was too severe or strict in His punishment of Ananias and Saphira?

*   How could we harmonize and explain the biblical statements that God is love and, at the same time, condemns sin harshly?

*   Do you consider in a negative or positive way the conclusion of Acts 5:11 which says, "Great fear seized the whole church and all who heard about these events?" Why?

Conclusion

There are many lessons we can get from this tragic story. Among others, that everything we do has consequences. Also, that the church is in God's hands, so nothing can impede the advancement of His Kingdom. What we do is seen by God. The most important is that sin is a matter of extreme gravity. We are free to choose to sin, but we cannot choose or control the results. Also, we must understand that many times the consequences of sin are irreversible.

The consequences of making bad decisions

Leticia Cano (Guatemala)

Memory verse: "Do not be deceived: God cannot be mocked. A man reaps what he sows" (Galatians 6:7).

Lesson Aim: To learn to ask for God's direction before making decisions, in order to avoid unpleasant consequences.

Introduction

There is no bad luck or good luck, only consequences. Frequently, we want to explore and experience unknown areas, and many times we do it without asking for advice. We will see in Genesis 34 that the consequences are not long in coming, and many times, they are not pleasant.

I. The scope of security

The story that occupies us in this lesson is centered on Dinah, a young and beautiful girl, the only daughter of patriarch Jacob and Leah. The family was in the territory belonging to the Hivites. Jacob had bought some land where he placed his tent for his family.

A. Father's camp

The camp of the patriarch Jacob offered his family provision, shelter and security. Just before this passage, he refused to be escorted by the people of Esau to protect those who were weak. Jacob's men went out to graze the cattle, while the women and children stayed in the camp to take care of one another. Jacob also stayed with them. The distribution of roles and responsibilities was necessary for the well-being of the large family.

Our Heavenly Father also offers us security, respect, direction and provisions. Outside of Him, there is danger we cannot survive, because the Scripture warns us: "Be alert and of sober mind. Your enemy the devil prowls around like a roaring lion looking for someone to devour" (1 Peter 5:8b).

B. Hazards outside the camp

In her father's camp, Dinah did not need anything. However, one day she was curious. As the patriarch's only daughter, she enjoyed care, respect and consideration, and maybe for that reason, she would have believed that their neighbors would treat her in the same way.

Curiosity and ingenuity won out over prudence, and Dinah went out to meet the Canaanite girls (Genesis 34:1). But someone with bad intentions was watching her. Young people today too dare to go out with worldly people or non-believers, go to parties where drugs are shared, people are having sex as well as other types of evil. Although it seems fun to do these things, the results can be dire. The devil disguises himself as an angel of light to deceive and destroy. Those who have been in the church from childhood are often tempted to leave the secure environment of the gospel and their family to get to know what people in the world do. Maybe they think they can go and return without anything bad happening, but this is not the case.

John, a 19-year-old boy whose life is currently hanging between life and death, was severely beaten and found almost dead early one morning. From his childhood, John had a free reign to do and go where he wanted. No one set any limits for him. Ask your students: What other dangers do we encounter outside of Christ? (Here we suggest that you brainstorm with the students to get them to participate).

II. Unrestrained passions

A. Shechem's immorality

By rubbing shoulders with the Canaanite people, Dinah met Shechem, a prince of that place (v.2). He was a Hivite, a Canaanite tribe. God once said about them that they were people who practiced abominable customs (Leviticus 18:24-30). The Canaanites were the descendants of Cam, who in the course of time abandoned the God of their ancestor Noah, and exchanged the true God for corruptible images. The ethics of these people allowed them all kinds of immorality. So Shechem, an abusive youth moved by his disordered passions, took Dina by force and raped her. The different biblical versions agree that it was a violent and forced act.

Can we make excuses for the abuser, such as: 'she provoked him', or 'she was after him' or 'she shouldn't have been walking out alone' etc.? No, there is certainly no justification for sexual abuse. The abuser is one hundred percent guilty, not only of sin, but also of a crime.

Here we are touching a topic we don't like to talk about, but it is a frightening reality in many families. Rape is almost never reported, and when the victim's story is heard, she is not believed, or accused of having provoked the abuser. As a result, the abuser can continue to destroy other innocent people. The church has the responsibility to denounce and guide the culprit to restoration, as well as help the victim overcome, with the grace of God, that stigma, which if not for the Lord, will lacerate their heart the rest of their life.

Returning to the biblical story of Genesis 34, for the capricious Canaanite prince, there was nothing wrong with that, since he was accustomed to take whatever he pleased. This pagan did not have the knowledge of the God of Abraham, as Jacob and his family did. However, that was not an excuse either, because God makes himself known to all men. Within each human being there is a voice that has been given the name of 'conscience', which warns us when we are going to do something which is wrong.

B. Love does not do anything wrong

After the rape, Shechem became infatuated and wanted to marry Dinah on the grounds that he was in love with her. The correct thing is to ask, and then take. But Shechem had acted the other way around, taking and then asking. Therefore, that man only had a whim and not love, because love can and must wait (vv.3-4). In addition, Shechem retained Dina in his house, and we do not find in the passage an apology for the offense, but only the request to take her as his wife.

Society has become corrupted to such an extent that institutions increasingly report not only women, but also girls who are pregnant as a result of being raped. This crime has often been committed by a close relative of the victims. We need to be aware of this evil and assume the responsibility of respecting and protecting our children from predators.

III. The end does not justify the means

That Hebrew family was not acting correctly (vv.6-18). A daughter who left her safety boundaries, a father who got angry about the abuse but did not do anything, an invisible mother who did not exert herself, and brothers who assume (as their father did not) the role of avengers. How many families have collapsed because their parents are passive and do not assume their functions as providers and protectors!

The descendants of Abraham should not have associated with the Canaanites, and Jacob and his family knew it. God called them to be a holy nation, but Jacob's family did not consult God to ask for guidance as to what to do in that tragedy.

A. Deadly trap

In response to the request of Shechem's father Hamor to ask for Dinah's hand in marriage, it was her brothers who took the lead in the conversation, while Jacob remained quiet. Jacob's sons said that if all the men were circumcised, then Dinah could marry Shechem. Their plan was that if Hamor and his people agreed, they would be vulnerable. (vv.14,15, 20-22).

Later in the genealogies of the Bible, we find some people of other nationalities who converted to the Hebrew faith, but the people of Shechem were not challenged to accept the only true God in their hearts, but only to practice an external rite.

Some may take this biblical event as justification for acting incorrectly. However, we need to mention that the need for justice does not excuse us in making use of improper means that conflict with ethics and morality. Shechem's sin did not justify theirs. Crises bring out the best or the worst in people. The imperious need to punish the abuse of Shechem was justifiable, but certainly the means used were unjustifiable.

B. Lying, murder and theft

After Dinah's dishonor, a whirlwind of ills was unleashed. Dinah's imprudence, Shechem's immorality and abuse, and the violence of Jacob's sons all led to a very complicated situation. Dinah's brothers lied. They had no intention of treating those people well, and used deception as a strategy to destroy them (vv. 25-28). The Bible says that the men of Shechem were circumcised, obeying their leaders. But the day when the pain was most intense, they were attacked and killed. Watch out! Evil is a destructive avalanche. Jacob's family could not justify lying, murder, robbery and kidnapping because of the rape of their sister. The plundering went beyond avenging dishonor.

Neither the lie, nor the murder, nor the theft are justified. They were making a law to themselves. The law that God gave to Moses years later to regulate human coexistence would be necessary. How could those descendants of the father of faith act with such evil? And the answer is, because unlike Grandpa Abraham, those sons of Jacob did not have a personal relationship with God.

IV. Collateral damage

A. The crying of the innocent

Men, children and women paid for Shechem's sin (v.29). The whim of a willing prince ended with the honor of a woman and the life of her people. This situation is repeated in our societies, since many live irrationally, doing what they want, believing that nothing will happen to them. But the truth is that their sinful acts destroy them, and those around them. It is the destructive nature of sin. Vicious or unfaithful men are the cause of their family's misfortune. Capricious young people, rebel and cause pain and sadness for their parents. Indolent women abandon their family causing abandonment, loneliness and much sadness to themselves and others. Indifferent and hardened hearts of sin offend God and challenge His authority, drawing judgment upon their own lives.

B. Discredit of a family chosen by God

How difficult it is to convince someone to be a Christian when there are so many who set a bad example around them! Jacob was heir to the promise that God had made to Abraham to make of him and his offspring a great nation distinct from the Chaldeans and Canaanites. Therefore, they had to distinguish themselves by acting differently from those who did not know the true God (v.30, 31). However, their attitudes did not bring light, but darkness to the neighboring towns.

Jacob was a weak father in the face of his children's impulsiveness. He as patriarch had the supreme authority to make decisions and act, but he did not. Does this seem familiar to us? When parents succumb to their children by failing to correct them and allowing them to take over the household, they are throwing away the authority received from God, and will one day have to account to the Lord for the negligent way they have brought up their children.

There are few redeeming attitudes in this tragic event. These attitudes are the following: The first thing is that the sons of Jacob did not accept the gifts of Shechem, and the second is that they did not accept that their sister was treated like an impudent woman.

Simeon and Levi were the ones who perpetrated the killing, but when the other brothers arrived (vv.27-29), they also participated in the plunder and captivity of women and children who had nothing to do with the offense of their ruler. In the end, all of Dinah's brothers participated in that evil. No wonder, years later, the Lord said that he had come to save the vile and despised of the world. This situation is not different from our own life. We too were evil before the eyes of God, and only His mercy rescued us from the path of eternal damnation.

Jacob and his family could no longer continue their peaceful stay in that land (v.30), so they had to leave. Fleeing was another consequence of the impulsive and irrational decisions of this family.

Conclusion

To remain within the scope of the safety of the heavenly Father is indispensable to avoid exposing ourselves to the destructive danger of sin. The end does not justify the means. Even when we are victims of injustice, we must act within the parameters of justice. Sin is a cause of sadness, pain and death for the one who sins and for those around him. In the midst of the crisis, we need to go to God in search of advice to make wise decisions.

Optional Questions:

I. The scope of security

- What were the causes that gave rise to this story, according to Genesis 34:1-2?
- Can you remember a similar situation in which imprudence has started a tragedy?

II. Unrestrained passions

- What was Shechem and Hamor's attitude in this situation? (Genesis 34:3-4)
- What do you think could have been a better solution?
- After reading the complete story of Genesis 34, let's analyze the situation together by completing the following chart:

Positive aspects of the story	Negative aspects of the story	Interesting aspects of the story

Successes and failures of King Jehoshaphat

Dorothy Bullón (Costa Rica)

Memory verse: "There is, however, some good in you, for you have rid the land of the Asherah poles and have set your heart on seeking God" (2 Chronicles 19:3).

Lesson Aim: To discover and learn King Jehoshaphat's good deeds as well as his errors.

Introduction

Jehoshaphat was one of the best kings of Judah. He reigned for 25 years in the ninth century B.C. His name Jehoshaphat means 'the Lord is Judge.' 2 Chronicles 17:3-4 says that "The Lord was with Jehoshaphat because he followed the ways of his father David before him. He did not consult the Baals but sought the God of his father and followed his commands rather than the practices of Israel." Ahab, who had given so many headaches to the prophets Elijah and Elisha, was the king of Israel in the North.

I. King Jehoshaphat's successes

Jehoshaphat had a good relationship with God and did many praiseworthy things, even better than many of the kings who followed him (2 Chronicles 17:1-6).

A. He protected his territory

Many times in our countries we worry about security. In the news every day we hear incidents of robberies and assaults. According to 2 Chronicles 17:2, Jehoshaphat began his reign with defensive measures against Israel. He put an army in all the fortified cities of Judah, and he placed garrisons in the land of Judah and in the cities. It seems he had a great permanent army, including cavalry (1 Kings 22:4; Chronicles 17:14). Jehoshaphat's leadership was so effective, and the blessing of God so rich, resulting in internal peace and military security. Even the Philistines, former adversaries, became vassals paying tribute to Judah (2 Chronicles 17:11).

Ask: As parents, what can we do to ensure that all members of our family are always safe?

B. He taught his people to believe only in God

The reign of Jehoshaphat seems to have been one of unusual religious activity. This is demonstrated by the following verse: "The Lord was with Jehoshaphat because he followed the ways of his father David before him. He did not consult the Baals but sought the God of his father and followed his commands rather than the practices of Israel" (2 Chronicles 17:3-4). He also tried to remove false gods such as Baal and Asherah from the high places (v.6). Because of his zeal for God, Jehoshaphat was rewarded with power and "he had great wealth and honor" (2 Chronicles 17:5).

Also, Jehoshaphat established an itinerant school, open to the public, a rare innovation in its time. For this, he appointed 16 men who traveled the country teaching the law of God to the people of the cities of Judah (2 Chronicles 17:7-9). Since the temple was in Jerusalem and many only came in the capital on feast days to worship God, these schools were an inspiring and precursor idea of the synagogues that began formally in exile centuries later.

Ask: What actions can we take so that all members of our family understand deeply about God and His work?

C. Appointed judges

Jehoshaphat visited the people, although he lived in Jerusalem, and "he went out again among the people from Beersheba to the hill country of Ephraim and turned them back to the Lord, the God of their ancestors" (2 Chronicles 19:4b). He also appointed judges to preside in the courts of common pleas he established in all the fortified cities of Judah (vv.5-7).

The judges had to act with rectitude, with respect of persons, and without bribery (v.7). In addition to these local courts, he established two courts of appeal in Jerusalem (vv.8-11): An ecclesiastical court headed by the priest Amariah, and a civil court led by "Zebadiah son of Ishmael, the leader of the tribe of Judah, will be over you in any matter concerning the king" (v.11). The judges had to proceed "faithfully and wholeheartedly in the fear of the Lord" (v.9).

Ask: Is there anything that your church can do in your neighborhood or city so there is less injustice? What should be the prophetic role of the church?

D. He prayed to the Lord and God gave him the victory

The passage in 2 Chronicles 20:1-18 begins with bad news; "for after this, the Moabites and Ammonites with some of the Meunites came to wage war against Jehoshaphat. Some people came and told Jehoshaphat, 'A vast army is coming against you from Edom, from the other side of the Dead Sea. It is already in Hazezon Tamar'" (v.1).

Jehoshaphat's reaction reveals his attitude: "Alarmed, Jehoshaphat resolved to inquire of the Lord, and he proclaimed a fast for all Judah. The people of Judah came together to seek help from the Lord; indeed, they came from every town in Judah to seek him" (vv. 3-4).

Jehoshaphat went to the only person who could help him: God! Later, we read Jehoshaphat's prayer and we can notice that it is steeped in references to the past (2 Chronicles 20:6-12). He recites the attributes of God, not to inform God, who is omniscient, but to review the greatness of the Lord in his own mind and in the minds of the people.

The prophet Jahaziel declared, "Do not be afraid or discouraged because of this vast army. For the battle is not yours, but God's" (v.15b). Believing is one thing, but acting is another. The plan did not seem logical ... marching like a great choir singing praises to God towards an enemy that is armed to the teeth! These singers were betting their lives on the truth of that Word from God. When they left for this apparently mad mission, Jehoshaphat encouraged the people saying: "Listen to me, Judah and people of Jerusalem! Have faith in the Lord our God and you will be upheld; have faith in his prophets and you will be successful" (v.20b). The evidence of this king's confidence is seen in the fact that they continued marching, and God gave them victory. This chapter began with the note of fear (v.3), and ends saying, "The fear of God came on all the surrounding kingdoms when they heard how the Lord had fought against the enemies of Israel" (v.29).

Discuss in class: What is the role of true worship of God in the life of the believer and the church?

E. King Jehoshaphat's epitaph

Jehoshaphat was a leader who visited and protected his people. Obviously he was a good administrator because he knew how to delegate tasks to the right people. Also, he had a close relationship with the Lord and respected the law of God, and listened to the voice of God given by the prophets (2 Chronicles 20:32-34).

Jehoshaphat was faithful to the Lord "doing what is right in the eyes of the Lord." However, and despite his efforts, "The high places, however, were not removed, and the people still had not set their hearts on the God of their ancestors" (v.33).

Suggest to the students the following: Write on a piece of paper the phrase or sentence they would like to appear on their epitaph. If they want, they can share what they wrote.

II. King Jehoshaphat's misdeeds

Jehoshaphat had a great weakness, and that is that he did not discern with whom he should make alliances. Therefore, "Jehu the seer, the son of Hanani, went out to meet him and said to the king, 'Should you help the wicked and love those who hate the Lord? Because of this, the wrath of the Lord is on you'" (2 Chronicles 19:2).

A. His alliance with the house of Ahab

Although he was a good king, Jehoshaphat had a character flaw: He made alliances with the ungodly Ahab (2 Chronicles 18:1-34). In contrast to the ancient kings of Judah, Jehoshaphat saw greater benefit in an alliance with Israel rather than in a civil war, so he made peace with Israel. The verse of 2 Chronicles 18:1 says the following: "Now Jehoshaphat had great wealth and honor, and he allied himself with Ahab by marriage."

The political union seems to have been based on the marriage of Joram, son of Jehoshaphat, with Athalia, daughter of Ahab and Jezebel. This was

135

certainly against God's wishes, because God forbids marriages (and indeed all alliances) between His people and the people committed to evil. Later, Athalia, would be the most cruel and pagan queen of Judah.

Shortly after the marriage, Jehoshaphat joined Ahab in a campaign against Syria (v. 3). The good king wanted confirmation that he was doing the right thing, so he asked for God's counsel through the prophetic voice. The pagan Ahab consulted 400 of his prophets who spoke only of victory. Not convinced, Jehoshaphat asked for the opinion of a prophet of God. Micaiah, the prophet, said they would not win the battle. The prophecy was fulfilled and Ahab lost his life.

The New Testament is clear: "Do not be yoked together with unbelievers. For what do righteousness and wickedness have in common? Or what fellowship can light have with darkness? What harmony is there between Christ and Belial? Or what does a believer have in common with an unbeliever?" (2 Corinthians 6:14-15).

Surely, Jehoshaphat knew the story of the reign of Ahab and Jezebel, and how Jezebel had tried to turn Israel into a people who served false gods. It was a terrible mistake to marry his son to Athaliah, and also to go to war with Ahab. A Hebrew proverb reads, "But associate with a godly person whom you know to be a keeper of the commandments, who is like-minded with yourself, and who will grieve with you if you fail" (Sirach 37:12).

Ask: What are the wrong alliances we can make? What can be the consequences of these decisions?

B. His alliance with Ahaziah

Proverbs 26:11 says, "As a dog returns to its vomit, so fools repeat their folly." Returning to the story that is being studied, the Bible says, "Later, Jehoshaphat king of Judah made an alliance with Ahaziah, king of Israel, whose ways were wicked" (2 Chronicles 20:35). This alliance with Ahaziah, the son of Ahab, had a purpose of maritime commerce with Tarshish. Let's read what the Word says, "Eliezer son of Dodavahu of Mareshah prophesied against Jehoshaphat, saying, 'Because you have made an alliance with Ahaziah, the Lord will destroy what you have made. The ships were wrecked and were not able to set sail to trade'" (v.37).

C. His alliance with Joram

Jehoshaphat was invited by Joram, a second son of Ahab, to fight together against Moab (2 Kings 3:7-19). They consulted the prophet Elisha about the battle and they won. A popular saying goes that man is the only animal capable of tripping up twice (and even more times) on the same stone. It seems that Jehoshaphat was unable to recognize his own mistakes. Could it be that Ahab's family had him trapped?

Ask: What are some of the mistakes that we as human beings repeat? Why do we do it? What would be the strategy to break that circle?

Optional Questions:

I. King Jehoshaphat's successes

- How would you describe the reign of Jehoshaphat, according to 2 Chronicles 17:1-6?

- What system did Jehoshaphat introduce to teach the law of God and to do justice in Judah, according to 2 Chronicles 17:7-9?

- Is there anything your church can do in your neighborhood or city so there is less injustice? What should be the prophetic role of the church?

- What was the action of Jehoshaphat against Moab and Ammon; And what was the result?

- What is the role of true worship of God in the life of the believer and the church?

II. King Jehoshaphat's misdeeds

- What alliances did Jehoshaphat make? What were the consequences of these acts of the king, according to 2 Chronicles 18:1-34?

- What are the wrong alliances we can make? What could be the consequences of these decisions?

Conclusion

Jehoshaphat was a pious king of Judah. He was distinguished by his zeal for true religion, and his firm trust in God. He tried to rid the land of idolatry, restored the divine ordinances, and provided religious instruction to the people. But the great mistake of his life was to make alliances with the wicked Ahab and his two sons, Ahaziah and Joram.

Listening to good advice

Samuel Pérez (Puerto Rico)

Memory verse: "Trust in the Lord with all your heart and lean not on your own understanding; in all your ways submit to him, and he will make your paths straight" (Proverbs 3:5-6).

Lesson Aim: To learn the importance of listening to and taking good advice.

Introduction

1. Get a pair of shoes from that do not fit you well, and take them to the class to do a demonstration. When everyone is seated and ready to start, tell them, "I have a pair of shoes here. They look great, don't they? Well, the truth is that I regret buying them because they don't fit very well" (Try to put them on).

2. After a few seconds, tell your class: "When I entered the store, in reality, I wanted to buy another type of shoes; but the salesman who attended me told me that these were very comfortable, and convinced me that with use, they would become the most comfortable shoes I have ever worn."

3. Ask your students if someone has ever suggested to them or given them advice that later on cost them dearly.

4. To finish this introduction, mention the following: "I do not know why I listened to the vendor's advice, because now I suffer a lot with these shoes. I think he was more interested in selling me the shoes whether they fit me or not."

We begin this lesson by asking a question: When we are alone with God and do not have a spiritual counselor, can we remain faithful to God? We live in a time where mentors are fashionable. The relationship between the mentor and the apprentice or disciple is known as "mentoring" or "coaching." Through this link, the mentor shares his experience and knowledge with the other person so that they can be successful in their profession, as well as personally. Also, the term coaching is used to refer to an interactive process through which the coach helps the apprentice reach certain goals by using of their own abilities and resources in the most effective way.

In this lesson, we can analyze the dynamic of spiritual mentoring that the child king Joash received, recorded in 2 Kings 12:1-21. We will be able to see what effect it had on the King's life and performance over the years.

I. Listening to good counsel leads us to do God's work (2 Kings 12:1-3)

2 Kings 12:1 states the following: "In the seventh year of Jehu, Joash became king, and he reigned in Jerusalem forty years. His mother's name was Zibiah; she was from Beersheba."

Joash was a special king, rescued from a massacre initiated by his own grandmother. Some uncles protected and cared for him in such a way that when he assumed the role of king over the nation (2 Kings 12:1-6), he knew how to guide his people well. He received the instruction that prepared him properly for his life as king. There is a similarity between Joash's experience as narrated in 2 Kings 11, with the circumstances of Moses, besides the detail that both led the nation for 40 years.

The Bible does not necessarily explain what each number symbolizes, but scholars have come to point out some of their symbolisms and have tried to bring a new possibility to biblical episodes. The number 40 also has symbolic value. It represents the 'change' from one period to another, the years of a generation. Therefore, the flood lasted 40 days and 40 nights (since it was the change towards a new humanity). The Israelites spent 40 years in the desert (until the unfaithful generation changed to a new one). Moses stayed for 40 days on Mount Sinai, and Elijah pilgrimage was 40 days (from which time their lives would change). Jesus fasted 40 days (because it was the change from his private life to his public life). The reference to the 40 years is significant since it represents a lesson and teaching for the nation. The mission of both men did not necessarily conclude successfully. These two men, Joash and Moses, somehow rebelled and gave in; however, they were instruments in the work of God.

2 Kings 12:1 suggests the care that Joash's mother Zibiah, a Jewish princess, gave him. All we know about her is her name; however we can infer that she was a positive influence, encouraging him to please the Lord. The fact that her noble son was someone who did what pleased the Lord shows the importance of receiving the counsel of God from childhood. This king grew up in the temple under the care and spiritual instruction of the priest, Jehoiada, who was his mentor.

II. Following the Lord's counsel allows us to put God first (2 Kings 12:4-14)

2 Kings 12:4-14 contains the testimony of the narrator of the story regarding the work of Joash on behalf of the Lord. However, we should note that even though Joash was committed to the work of God, the high places were not eliminated and the people still sacrificed and burned incense to idols.

According to the narrative of the books of 1 and 2 Kings, on different occasions the phrase is repeated: "the high places were not taken away "(1 Kings 15:14;22:43; 2 Kings 14:4; 15:35). The Israelites had fallen into bad syncretistic practices, allowing themselves to be influenced by the pagan religions around them, including idolatry. Joash received good counsel from Jehoiada. Would he listen to his mentor? It is one thing to receive good advice, and quite another to collaborate in God's Work.

Joash's reign received praise from historians: "Joash did what was right in the eyes of the Lord" (2 Kings 12:2). What did he do to deserve this qualification? When we look more closely and exhaustively at the word 'right,' we understand that it comes from the Hebrew term "yashar." In the broadest sense of the word, this refers to the abilities of Joash to govern. This adjective can be translated as 'good' or 'apt', referring to Joash's qualities to carry out his reign, and in this way, become an instrument of God for the benefit of the people.

During Joash's long reign, the narrator points out his interest in the remodeling of the temple. It is very important to highlight the social, political, economic and religious significance of the temple.

a. It was considered the seat of the divine presence. The temple was the 'house' of God. In the dedication of the temple, Solomon said in a short poem that he had built a dwelling where the Lord would dwell forever (1 Kings 8:13).

b. God chose to live in the city and the temple. The temple was a visible sign of the divine election.

c. It was the place where God chose to forgive. It was central to the law. It was where God's glory could be found. God himself lived there. The fact that the temple existed was proof that God, a living God, dwelt among them in Israel.

We should not be surprised by Joash's concern and interest in the restoration and renovation of the temple. Evidently, Joash had to face a prominent group of religious leaders who were corrupt and did not comply with Joash's guidelines. Joash was eager to repair the temple of God, so he asked the priests to collect money and offerings for that purpose. The years passed, but the repair work was not done. So Joash ordered the priests to begin work immediately.

It is interesting to see how the money was handled during the time of the kings. Poorly managed money can cause pain and suffering for many (1 Timothy 6:10). The Scriptures identify and recommend various ideas to help us manage God's resources that He has entrusted to us more efficiently.

In 2 Kings 12:1-21 there are a series of recommendations:

a. A type of special ark was established for the collection of the offerings.

b. The priests guarded the entrance.

c. The money was accounted for, taken to the temple and put into bags.

d. A specific amount was determined for the salary of the human resources employed.

e. The money received was given to the supervisors to pay salaries and everything else related to the repair of the temple.

f. The use of the money was determined, and that could not be changed.

All these measures had to be strictly followed to ensure that financial resources were properly managed. 2 Kings 12:15 tells us, "They did not require an accounting from those to whom they gave the money to pay the workers because they acted with complete honesty."

These measures of sound administration were vital so that the temple could be repaired and restored. This experience in the reign of Joash provides an excellent example of good management of God's work even for us today as we administer the offerings of God's people in our churches, districts and at the global level.

III. Abandoning the counsel of the Lord leads us to apostasy (2 Chronicles 24:17-27)

After the death of his mentor Jehoiada, Joash's life took a vertiginous turn downwards. According to the editor, bad company influenced him to go astray. 2 Chronicles 24:17-18 tells us, "After the death of Jehoiada, the officials of Judah came and paid homage to the king, and he listened to them. They abandoned the temple of the Lord, the God of their ancestors, and worshiped Asherah poles and idols. Because of their guilt, God's anger came on Judah and Jerusalem."

The king who previously humbled himself before God was now flattered by the evil men who paid him reverence. He listened to the wrong people (Psalm 1:1). By following their counsel, Joash turned away from God, forgetting the law that he had been taught in his youth. He began to practice evil until he influenced all of Judah to follow his evil ways. The good king who had sought to repair the temple, and thus encourage the worship of God by the people, became a careless king who led his subjects to idolatry (2 Kings 12:18).

Joash's life is an example of apostasy. Those who leave the Lord and cause others to deviate often are people who were once faithful to the Lord in their youth. Most of these leaders were raised by Christian parents or benefited from the influence of faithful lay leaders, pastors and preachers. The influence generated by these leaders manifests itself for a time and is capable of generating enthusiasm, passion and commitment in favor of the work of God. However, when the moments of adversity and crisis arrive, they leave the path of truth for the paths of error and falsehood. The fall of these leaders often occurs before the entrance of pride into their lives (Proverb 16:18, 29:23).

When a person listens to adulation of those individuals who seek to use their influence, the result is likely to be devastating. A brief look at history in more recent times and contexts shows similar attitudes and consequences. How many times have the most renowned and famous preachers and leaders strayed and distanced themselves from the path of ethical truth and justice as they listened to the adulation of those who seemed to be their worshipers? How many times did those who had a humble beginning begin to compromise the truth by listening to counsel against the Word of God?

When as Christian leaders we receive advice, we must be careful to discern good counsel from advice contrary to the values of the Kingdom. Bad advice often causes unimaginable damage. Good counsel is like a solid rock that edifies, while bad advice is like dynamite that destroys. To understand whether council is good or harmful, we need to consider its source and the integrity of the individual. As a young man, King Joash trusted the priest Jehoiada who advised him in God's ways, and he managed to restore the temple despite the conduct of the corrupt leaders, but when Jehoiada was not there, everything fell to pieces.

Optional Questions:

I. Listening to good counsel leads us to do God's work (2 Kings 12:1-3)

- According to 2 Kings 12:1-2, how was Joash brought up? Who influenced his life?

- What results did the mentoring of these people have in his life and reign (2 Kings 12:2-6)?

II. Following the Lord's counsel allows us to put God first (2 Kings 12:4-14)

- Why did he accept good counsel and mentoring (2 Kings 12:4-14)?

- What was he able to achieve?

III. Abandoning the counsel of the Lord leads us to apostasy (2 Chronicles 24:17-27)

- Who turned Joash off God's pathway?

- What might be the consequences of paying attention to advice from people who are not motivated by the values of the Kingdom and by the Word?

- Do you remember times when people, because they did not receive good advice, made the wrong decisions? Share.

Conclusion

Joash should have sought God's plan rather than that of bad counselors! God will always listen to us and answer us when we seek wisdom when we don't know what to do. How important it is to trust and listen to God's counsel! We can always count on Him! Listening to and following God's counsel blesses us and allows us to fulfill the mission that He has conferred upon us.

Three believers

Rita Barco (Peru)

Memory verse: "Dear friend, I pray that you may enjoy good health and that all may go well with you, even as your soul is getting along well" (3 John 2).

Lesson Aim: To learn to differentiate and evaluate between three types of believers.

Introduction

The third epistle of John offers us a bird's eye view of life in the early church. This epistle follows the second letter which was addressed to a Christian woman, so that they would know how to deal with the false teachers who existed in those days.

The third epistle of John was written to a Christian man about how he should support true teachers who traveled from one place to another, proclaiming the Word of God. Therefore, we find both a contrast and a certain similarity between these two epistles written by John, the apostle.

Also, this third epistle shows us something about the problem caused by the various personalities within the church. Three people are mentioned: A man named Gaius, to whom this epistle is addressed; a second man named Diotrephes; and a third named Demetrius. These three men represent three different kinds of Christians who are in the church at any time. As with all the epistles of the New Testament, 3 John is a very up-to-date and extremely important epistle.

I. Gaius, the kind Christian

To begin with, we have a man named Gaius. He may be one of the three Gaius's who are mentioned in other parts of the New Testament (although Gaius was a very common name in New Testament times, as was the name John). Be that as it may, it is evident that John knew him and addressed this letter in a warm and friendly tone. Judging by what we read, he knew that Gaius was an affable, cordial and generous man. It is important to look at three issues that John writes about him.

A. Stable both spiritually and physically

In the first place, Gaius was a man who had a strong foundation, and that is what made John feel a deep appreciation for him. Hence what we read at the beginning of this letter, "How truly I love you! We're the best of friends, and I pray for good fortune in everything you do, and for your good health—that your everyday affairs prosper, as well as your soul!" (3 John 2, The Message). I think those are wonderful words to say to a person. It seems that John is saying. "May you be equally strong in body as you are in spirit." It would be interesting to do a test to see how people react today if we use this expression.

Ask: If your physical appearance reflected your spiritual state, what would you look like? Would you be a strong person, strong and virile/feminine? Or would you be weak and decrepit, one who can barely move? Gaius was the kind of person the apostle John could say, "I wish your physical life was as strong as your spiritual life."

B. He was consistent in his actions

3 John 3 says, "It gave me great joy when some believers came and testified about your faithfulness to the truth, telling how you continue to walk in it." Gaius's life was a testimony of the truth. But what impressed John was not the fact that Gaius knew the truth, but that he followed it and lived it out. That is to say that this man had a consistent life, because he did not preach one thing, and then do something else. He walked in the truth and was generous in his way of life.

We can see his faithfulness in verses 5-6: "Dear friend, you are faithful in what you are doing for the brothers and sisters, even though they are strangers to you. They have told the church about your love. Please send them on their way in a manner that honors God."

One of the signs that shows that a person has been really touched by God is the fact that they are generous with their money. He was giving generously, with a good attitude, and with joy, as God likes. And this man, Gaius, was faithful (loyal) at the time of giving, which means that he gave in a continuous and systematic way. He did not give only when he let himself be carried away by his emotions, but he gave faithfully, continuing faithfully with the work.

Also, it is clear that this servant of God gave with joy, because John said he did it in a "manner that honors God" (v.6), or as a benefit to the work. From here we understand that God does not want us to give because we feel obligated, or because someone is collecting a special offering. We should not give because we feel that if we do not, other Christians will look at us with contempt. But it is God's will that we should give our offerings with an attitude like that of Gaius, who gave and was delighted in doing so.

II. Diotrephes a bad example

Verse 3 of John 11 says, "Dear friend, do not imitate what is evil but what is good. Anyone who does what is good is from God. Anyone who does what is evil has not seen God." In other words, John instructed Gaius not to follow those men who wanted preeminence. This warning is good for us too. If we meet someone who is always seeking power, wanting to occupy a position in Christian relationships, wishing to always be seen by others, we should not follow them, because they are following their own path and not God's.

A.   Who was Diotrephes?

In 3 John 9-11, we read, 'I wrote to the church, but Diotrephes, who loves to be first, will not welcome us. So when I come, I will call attention to what he is doing, spreading malicious nonsense about us. Not satisfied with that, he even refuses to welcome other believers. He also stops those who want to do so and puts them out of the church. Dear friend, do not imitate what is evil but what is good. Anyone who does what is good is from God. Anyone who does what is evil has not seen God.''

This is the first example in the early church of someone trying to run the church. He may have been a church board member, or perhaps a pastor. It is difficult to know, but the truth is that it was undoubtedly someone who considered his job to be telling everyone in the church what was to be done.

It seems that in the early church they had some kind of list of the members, and if there was a person who did not like Diotrephes, Diotrep heswould delete their name from the list and throw them out of the church. John was totally against that, clearly understanding that Diotrephes was guilty of four particularly wrong attitudes and actions that we will deal with next.

1. Diotrephes owed his faith to John

To begin with, John says that Diotrephes was guilty of denigrating him, because this man spoke malicious words against him, and denied the authority he had as an apostle. We know, based on what other epistles say, that the apostles played a unique role in the history of the church. They had to build the foundations of the church, and they had also been granted the necessary authority to resolve the issues concerning it. It is precisely this apostolic word that is passed on to us in the New Testament, and that is why it has such authority for Christians. So, in Diotrephes we have the case of a man who not only ignored the authority of the apostle John, but he also spoke against him, saying slanderous and malicious things against this servant of God.

2. He was not compassionate

Moreover in this epistle, it is said that Diotrephes refused to receive the ministerial brothers who arrived at the church. They were traveling from one place to another, speaking the truth of God. So, they came to the congregation, but Diotrephes wanted nothing to do with them, and then he threw them out of the church and refused to let them speak in the church.

3. He caused divisions

A third issue is that Diotrephes was expelling from the church those brothers who received the visiting ministers in their homes. Undoubtedly, this man took pleasure in what we might currently call 'secondary separation.' Not only was he against the men who came, but against those who were willing to receive them. Because of this tendency to deny Christian friendship to someone who does not like you, there was widespread dissensions in the church, doing irreparable harm. But of those three offenses, none of them was as serious as the one which John puts first. The most serious problem was that Diotrephes thought that he was the ultimate authority.

4. He kept hold of the power in the church

Diotrephes loved being the first. This clearly shows that he was acting according to the flesh. By acting in this way, he was depriving the Lord of His right to occupy the first place, for only He is the one who has the right to pre-eminence. He must occupy the first place; however in this case, this man placed himself at the top, and that is something really very serious.

Currently, unfortunately there are many people like Diotrephes in the churches who are always characterized by this attitude. That is, they want to always be first, and want part of the glory for themselves. Such people want to deprive God of his inheritance, stealing what belongs only to the Almighty.

III. Demetrius, another good example

Finally, a third man is mentioned here: Demetrius. All we know about him is what John tells us: "Demetrius is well spoken of by everyone—and even by the truth itself. We also speak well of him, and you know that our testimony is true" (v.12).

In this case, John speaks like an apostle who possesses the gift of discernment. In his words, he wanted to emphasize what everyone thought about Demetrio. This was a man who could be trusted, a man who was truthful and who had given good testimony in everything, making it very clear that he could be trusted. It is evident that Demetrius was the one who brought this epistle to Gaius, and probably was one of those missionaries who traveled from one place to another. John says of these itinerant ministers, "It was for the sake of the Name that they went out, receiving no help from the pagans. We ought therefore to show hospitality to such people so that we may work together for the truth" (vv.7-8).

At this point, John finishes this third epistle with

some personal words: "I have much to write you, but I do not want to do so with pen and ink. I hope to see you soon, and we will talk face to face. Peace to you. The friends here send their greetings. Greet the friends there by name" (vv.13-15).

What an intimate epistle! It seems to come from not only John, but from the Lord himself. I like to read this epistle as if it reflected what the Lord Jesus is saying to His own church. That is, something like this: "There is a lot I want to write to you about. Here I have written a whole book, but I have much more to tell you, but I do not want to do it by means of ink and pen. Rather I hope to see you soon and we will talk face to face."

Optional Questions:

I. Gaius, the kind Christian

- After reading 3 John 1-8, what characteristics can we infer about Gaius?

- How do you interpret this expression: "I pray that you may enjoy good health and that all may go well with you, even as your soul is getting along well" (3 John 2)?

- Do you think that Gaius' characteristics apply to your life? If you do not have them, what should you do to have them?

II. Diotrephes, a bad example

- What does 3 John 9-10 say about Diotrephes?

III. Demetrius, another good example

- What does 3 John 11-12 allow us to observe about Demetrius?

Conclusion

If the letter were to your church, which of these characters would you be? Let us invest in our spiritual lives and grow and mature so that our testimony shines before a world that is submerged in darkness.

Notes :

Lesson 45 — Caleb's positive attitude

Litzy Vidaurre (Spain)

Memory verse: "But because my servant Caleb has a different spirit and follows me wholeheartedly, I will bring him into the land he went to, and his descendants will inherit it" (Numbers 14:24).

Lesson Aim: To learn about faithfulness and commitment to the Lord from Caleb's example.

Introduction

At times, God reveals to us His plans and purposes for our lives, and all we have to do is believe and then act. This attitude may put us among the minority, and even bring us problems with others. However, trusting in the Word of God and believing in its promises will keep us faithful. Caleb had a different attitude than the others, and this helped him enter the promised land.

I. The sending of the spies

If we read Deuteronomy 1:19-46, we will notice a very interesting fact: The sending of spies to explore the promised land was not God's desire or plan, but rather was what the people wanted to do.

Moses clarifies this in Deuteronomy 1:22 where he mentions: "Then all of you came to me and said, 'Let us send men ahead to spy out the land for us and bring back a report about the route we are to take and the towns we will come to.'" At first glance, this does not seem like a bad plan. It even sounds like an innocent and strategic idea, but this idea reveals to us the true place that God occupied in the Israelites' lives. It was the people themselves who proposed the need to see before believing. What real need was there to go explore the promised land? Had God not already told them what it would be like? Why did God allow them to doubt His Word? God allowed this plan to be carried out to reveal to the people how their hearts really were.

Of course, there was no need to go exploring the land, for God had told them many times what Canaan was like and also what the inhabitants who dwelt there were like. Also, He had told them how the Canaanites would be defeated, and

most importantly, He had promised that land as an inheritance for them and their descendants. The word of God should have been enough for them, but it wasn't.

II. The spirit of the ten spies

After 40 days of spying in Canaan, the Israelite spies brought back their report and samples of the land (Numbers 13:23-33, 14:21-23). They brought a bunch of grapes so big that they had to carry it between two men. They also brought pomegranates and figs. It was evident that the land they had explored was just as God had told them. Next, we will see what this report reveals about them.

A. A negative spirit

Numbers 13:27-28 tells us the following: "They gave Moses this account: 'We went into the land to which you sent us, and it does flow with milk and honey! Here is its fruit. But the people who live there are powerful, and the cities are fortified and very large.'"

Up to this point, the report was relatively positive. The land was certainly how God had told them, and the description of the cities and their inhabitants also fit with what God had said. The report was revealing and confirming that God had given them this land.

Unfortunately, the ten spies were not satisfied with giving the report of everything they had seen; but they gave their own opinion, revealing what was in their hearts and the kind of spirit that lived in them. In Numbers 13:31, we see the conclusion reached by these men: "But the men who had gone up with him (Caleb) said, 'We can't attack those people; they are stronger than we are.'"

On the one hand, ten spies confirmed the truthfulness of the word of the Lord; but on the other hand, they completely nullified the promise of possession of the promised land. After seeing the fortified cities and the strength of their inhabitants, they doubted the supernatural power of God to fulfill His promise, and preferred to rely on their own strength.

B. They made the spirit of the people weaken

What these men expressed not only reveals a negative spirit that doubted the power of God, but it also revealed the report of exaggeration, falsehood and fear, since they spoke badly of the land they had visited saying: "And they spread among the Israelites a bad report about the land they had explored. They said, 'The land we explored devours those living in it. All the people we saw there are of great size. We saw the Nephilim there (the descendants of Anak from the Nephilim). We seemed like grasshoppers in our own eyes, and we looked the same to them'" (Numbers 13:32-33).

They terrorized the people with their statements, making them doubt the blessings of God's promises. Unbelief always makes us doubt the Word of God and makes us highlight difficulties and obstacles, while faith helps us see those difficulties as opportunities.

C. This spirit displeases God

The people doubted the fulfillment of God's promise. This made them surrender to the difficulties. They cried and complained against Moses and Aaron, even saying they would rather die in the desert or go back to Egypt. Clearly, we observe that the Israelites doubted God's power, and even accused God of having brought them to that place to die by the sword (Numbers 14:1-3). As a result, they missed the opportunity to enjoy the blessings that God had prepared for them in the promised land. In Numbers 14:21-23, we see God's response to the people's unbelief. It is evident that God deeply disliked the lack of faith and disbelief of His people. The incredulity of the people was truly irritating and displeasing to God. For that reason, He punished them severely without exception.

III. Caleb had another spirit

All those who had a negative attitudes of defeat and doubt, giving up before the battle had even began, and those who complained, did not go into the promised land.

Instead, let's look at what God said about Caleb in Numbers 14:24 where we read: "But because my servant Caleb has a different spirit and follows me wholeheartedly, I will bring him into the land he went to, and his descendants will inherit it."

Caleb had a totally different attitude. Ask: What spirit or attitude did Caleb show that pleased God so much?

A. Caleb had a spirit of courage

Numbers 13:30 states, "Then Caleb silenced the people before Moses and said, 'We should go up and take possession of the land, for we can certainly do it.' The ten spies and all the people were defeated before the battle began. In fact, they already gave it up for lost. They were lamenting and complaining that God had brought them to that place to die. They even preferred to die in the desert or in Egypt before going to possess the land that God had already promised them. However, Caleb did not remain silent in a corner, but rose up in front of the people. He was tired of hearing the complaints and reproaches of his countrymen. Therefore, he resolutely told them that they should go in and take possession of the land.

Why was Caleb so sure and braver? Caleb was not only a man of great courage, but also a man of faith in a great God. His courage rested in his knowledge of God, not in Israel's confidence to conquer the land. Surely, Caleb had witnessed all the wonders and miracles that God had done since they had left Egypt. This knowledge of God and His power gave Caleb the courage to face any circumstance.

When we are aware of what God can do in our lives and in all the situations we face, we can be like Caleb and face multitudes and act with the certainty that we can overcome, because God is with us.

B. Caleb had a spirit of faithfulness

Caleb decided to follow God; he preferred to trust in God rather than in the opinion of the majority. The easiest thing would have been to give in to the pressure and get carried away by what others said, but Caleb could not do that because it went against his principles. He preferred to trust in God.

How many of us prefer to remain faithful to God in the midst of adversity? Against all prognosis? Against all the other voices that tell us we are taking the wrong pathway? How many of us truly trust in

God, even when everything seems to be going badly wrong?

Faithfulness is standing firm even in the midst of problems and adversities. The best example that comes to mind is a tree well planted and grounded in good soil. Although winds and storms come, that tree does not move. To be faithful implies being firm even in the midst of great storms and opposition, like strong trees, well planted in the promises of God.

C. Caleb had a spirit of perseverance

Caleb had a different attitude because he had been a faithful servant all his life. The years passed, and they were already in the promised land. The Bible tells us that only Joshua and Caleb entered the Promised Land. Some 45 years later, the 85-year-old Caleb came to Joshua with a very special request. Let's look at this carefully in the passage from Joshua 14:6-12 where we read the following: "Now the people of Judah approached Joshua at Gilgal, and Caleb son of Jephunneh the Kenizzite said to him, 'You know what the Lord said to Moses the man of God at Kadesh Barnea about you and me. I was forty years old when Moses the servant of the Lord sent me from Kadesh Barnea to explore the land. And I brought him back a report according to my convictions, but my fellow Israelites who went up with me made the hearts of the people melt in fear. I, however, followed the Lord my God wholeheartedly. So, on that day Moses swore to me, 'The land on which your feet have walked will be your inheritance and that of your children forever, because you have followed the Lord my God wholeheartedly. Now then, just as the Lord promised, he has kept me alive for forty-five years since the time he said this to Moses, while Israel moved about in the wilderness. So here I am today, eighty-five years old! I am still as strong today as the day Moses sent me out; I'm just as vigorous to go out to battle now as I was then. Now give me this hill country that the Lord promised me that day. You yourself heard then that the Anakites were there and their cities were large and fortified, but, the Lord helping me, I will drive them out just as he said.'"

Caleb had not forgotten the promise God had given him 45 years ago; he remained faithful and persevering until he saw it fulfilled in his life. He had waited for this moment. Not only did he not forget the promise of God, but he was just as willing to go to conquer what God had promised him. At 85, he had the same strength as at the beginning. He was already old, but he did not let time or age prevent him from seeing God's promise fulfilled in his life.

Ask: Have you forgotten about the promise God has given you? Or are you still struggling and willing to go for what God has prepared for you?

Optional Questions:

I. The sending of the spies

- Whose idea was it to explore the land before them, according to Deuteronomy 1:22?

- What need was there to go explore the land if God had already told them what it would be like?

- What was God's purpose in allowing them to send spies to spy out the promised land?

II. The spirit of the ten spies

- What spirit revealed the report of the ten spies? (Numbers 13:23-33, 14:21-23)

- What produced this among the people? (Numbers 14:1-3)

- What was God's response to the spirit of the people? (Numbers 14:21-23)

III. Caleb had another spirit

- What was the courage of Caleb? (Numbers 13:30, 14:24)

- Caleb waited 45 years to see the fulfillment of God's promise to him. What does this reveal about him? (Joshua 14:6-12)

Conclusion

God has great promises prepared for us, but the spirit that we show will determine if we will see them fulfilled in our lives or not. The ten spies and the people missed the opportunity to enter the promised land because of their negative spirit and doubting. However, Caleb, who had a positive attitude, enjoyed all the blessings that God had promised him. What attitudes do we have?

The return of the slave Onesimus

Flavio Martínez (Mexico)

Memory verse: "There is neither Jew nor Gentile, neither slave nor free, nor is there male and female, for you are all one in Christ Jesus" (Galatians 3:28).

Lesson Aim: To discover the experience of the transformation and freedom that comes to us when Jesus forgives our sins.

Introduction

The key to this letter to Philemon is found in verse 16. Paul told Philemon that he is sending Onesimus back to him "no longer as a slave, but better than a slave, as a dear brother. He is very dear to me but even dearer to you, both as a fellow man and as a brother in the Lord."

When looking for a job, everyone should bring with them a letter of recommendation which will introduce them to their new possible boss. Many companies that recruit employees request one or more recommendation letters as requirements to fill a vacancy.

The background to this story is very interesting. This epistle was written when the apostle Paul was already old and imprisoned for the first time in the city of Rome. This letter needs to be considered alongside the Epistle to the Colossians (Colossians 4:8-9). Probably, Paul's letter to Philemon was written at the same time as the Epistle to the Colossians, approximately in the year 62 A.D. This letter was sent to Philemon, one of Paul's Christian friends, living in Colossae.

I. Onesimus did wrong to Philemon

We are not sure what Onesimus did to Philemon (v. 18). It is possible that Onesimus became a fugitive after stealing from Philemon to pay for his escape to Rome, where he planned to go unnoticed among the masses. In the Greco-Roman world, fugitives were a problem of great proportions. Not only for their owners, but also for the Roman public administration. Rome was reputed to be a regular place of refuge for runaway slaves.

It is possible that Onesimus was working for Philemon in order to pay off a debt he had. Back then, if someone had unpaid debts, he could be imprisoned. To avoid this, sometimes they made an agreement with some rich man to work for free for a period of time in exchange for paying off their debt. Or perhaps, Philemon had entrusted Onesimus with his possessions, and he could not resist the temptation to steal something and escape.

II. Onesimus arrived in Rome

At that time, Rome was very far from Colossae. Onesimus was more than 1,400 kilometers from his house. He knew that he had done wrong and tried to escape the consequences of his crime (vv. 10-12). Maybe he used the money he stole from Philemon to travel, and then, he did not have any money left. The intentions and desires of men come to naught when there is no money.

Probably, Onesimus thought about starting a new life there through the opportunity that a large city offered, especially in education and culture. Or maybe he thought, "I'm going to learn a trade; I'm going to be someone in life." Many people had begun to emigrate to the big cities for that purpose. However, life in Rome was worse than in Colossae.

Life is very lonely for a foreigner in a big city, and it was no exception for Onesimus. He had abandoned his relatives and friends from Colossae, and every contact he had with people was impersonal.

III. The conversion of Onesimus

Onesimus found a new life in Rome (vv. 10-14).

A. He came to Paul's door

It is very possible that Onesimus had met Paul, or at least he would have heard of him through Philemon. Although it is not specifically mentioned that Paul visited Colossae on his missionary tours, he traveled through that area and knew Philemon.

How did Paul and Onesimus find each other? The Bible does not give us that information. However, when freedom ceased to be a novelty for Onesimus, it is likely that he realized that he had entered into a very compromising situation.

In the city of Rome, there was a special police corps chasing runaway slaves whose offense was one of the most serious in the laws of antiquity. The fugitive slaves who were caught were marked on their foreheads with red-hot iron. They were often tortured, thrown to the beasts in the circus, or crucified to discourage other slaves from following their example. Most likely, when he ran out of money and could find no hiding place or get a job, Onesimus sought the protection and intercession of Paul, whom he had heard of in the house of Philemon.

B. He asked for Paul's help

Paul knew that the best help he could give Onesimus would be to put him on the path of Christ. Onesimus, who had previously been a slave, realized that there was a bondage in freedom, and that there was a freedom in slavery. When he was a slave, he did not care about where he was going to sleep, or about what he was going to eat, because his master owned him. But once free and in Rome, he had a real problem. We can imagine Onesimus walking along a Roman street one day, and seeing a group of people gathered listening to a man. It may be that Onesimus infiltrated the group, made his way to the front, and there he saw that the man (Paul) was in chains. Onesimus had fled the chains and thought he was free, but when he heard this man whose name was Paul, he surely thought: "This man is free and I am still a slave of hunger, poverty and anguish. I am still a slave, but that man, although he is chained, is free."

After the people left, Onesimus approached Paul. He wanted to know more about what he was preaching, and the apostle led him to Christ. He presented the gospel to him, told him how Jesus had died for him, how he had been buried, and then rose again on the third day. He asked Onesimus to place his trust in Christ, and he did so. From that moment, Onesimus became a new creature in Christ Jesus.

The best we can do for people is to help them know Christ. Social problems have their roots in spiritual problems. The human being always wants freedom, but at present, there are millions of people who are slaves of alcohol or drugs. Others are slaves of money. They are not free, although they may seem so. In our time, people take pride in being free. They think they are free. Christ offers a freedom that is above all the slaves of the world. It is the freedom that each person should enjoy.

IV. Onesimus goes back

A. He returned because he wanted to

We have something really extraordinary here, a slave, a thief who returns of his own volition to his employer from whom he fled, without knowing the kind of reception he would receive (vv. 15-17). Recall that according to the laws of the time, Onesimus was obliged to return to his master and that his master could do what he pleased with his slave, subjecting him to severe punishments, even taking his life. It was hard on Paul to part with Onesimus (v.13); he was asking Onesimus to take a great risk. However, his new concept of life and interpersonal relationships urged him to return to the house of Philemon.

Imagine the scene at Philemon's home when this letter arrived. We can imagine Philemon standing in his garden, looking towards the road, when he sees someone approaching. He tells his wife: "Dear, someone is coming to see us." While he watches the person approaching, he thinks he knows who he is and says, "Do you know something, dear? I hope I'm wrong, but I get the impression that the one who approaches on the road is that thief Onesimus coming back again." As he gets closer and closer, Philemon sees that it is Onesimus. He is that runaway slave who fled and dishonored the family, a fugitive from justice. Philemon raises his arms in the air and says, "Oh, so you have come home at last! What brings you here this time?" We can imagine then that Onesimus says absolutely nothing, knowing that it is useless to try to defend himself, but only to deliver Paul's recommendation. Philemon opens the letter that was written in the form of a scroll and begins to read.

B. He is recommended as someone different

Paul tries to create in the mind of Philemon a favorable impression about this person, and also a sympathy for the one of whom he writes. The description is very tender: "yet I prefer to appeal to you on the basis of love. It is as none other than Paul—an old man and now also a prisoner of Christ Jesus— that I appeal to you for my son Onesimus, who became my son while I was in chains" (vv. 9-10). Paul was Onesimus's spiritual father.

With such a recommendation, it is not difficult to imagine that Onesimus had changed. Undoubtedly, he was willing to give Philemon the same care and attention in services that he had voluntarily rendered to Paul. The name Onesimus means profitable or useful. He would no longer be a useless slave but would do honor to his name. His uselessness disappeared because he had been transformed by the grace of God. Dishonesty, selfishness, falsehood were taken away by the power of true freedom. Now as a Christian, he would work with a new attitude, trying to please for Christ's sake.

Onesimus became a reliable person. Before, he was useless, careless in his duties, a scoundrel and a fugitive, and therefore totally unfaithful. But now, Paul said that he was useful both for Paul and Philemon (v.11). It is probable that when Philemon remembered the name of Onesimus, his mind made him think of him as an unworthy demon. Paul, in a funny and skillful word game, says that Onesimus is useful to Philemon and him: "Formerly he was useless to you, but now he has become useful both to you and to me. I am sending him—who is my very heart—back to you (vv.11-12).

Onesimus had become useful to the apostle during his imprisonment. In fact, had it not been a violation of the law and an abuse of Philemon's rights, Paul would have allowed him to stay with him (vv.13-14). In another letter, written more or less at the same time and addressed to the congregation that met at the house of Philemon, Paul said that Onesimus was "a faithful and beloved brother, who is one of you" (Colossians 4:9a). These words imply that Onesimus had already proved his reliability.

However, it is necessary to understand that Paul did not free Onesimus from his guilt (vv. 15-16); but he wants Philemon to see and consider the glorious and sovereign providence of God. It seems as though he is saying that God was working in all of this because He used Onesimus' evil action to do something good. This was true both for the fugitive himself and for Philemon. The latter had been removed from being a slave for a short time. Now they would be united again. The bond that existed between master and slave had been broken during that brief time that elapsed between the flight and the return. The union now between these two men would be like brothers in Christ, an unbreakable relationship, now and forever. That was God's purpose, His wonderful plan.

In any case, Onesimus returned to Colossae with a new personality, transformed in his way of thinking, thanks to the power of the gospel. Undoubtedly, this man became a faithful Christian of the congregation of that city. The Scriptures do not reveal to us whether Philemon, in time, freed Onesimus from servitude. However, seen from a spiritual perspective, the previous fugitive had become a free man (1 Corinthians 7:22). Nowadays, similar transformations take place. When we put into practice the biblical principles of the gospel, our situation changes.

According to St. Jerome, Onesimus became a preacher of the gospel, Bishop of Ephesus by order of the Apostle Paul. Subsequently, Onesimus was taken prisoner and taken to Rome, where he was stoned to death and beheaded.

Optional Questions:

I. Onesimus did wrong to Philemon

- Describe what you think was the wrong that Onesimus did to Philemon? (v. 18)
- These days, what kind of wrongs can we cause our bosses?

II. Onesimus arrived in Rome

- What do you consider to be the reasons that caused Onesimus to flee to Rome? (Philemon 10-12)

III. The conversion of Onesimus

- How did Onesimus change after his conversion? (vv. 10-14)
- How did you change after you accepted the Lord?

IV. Onesimus goes back

- How do you think Onesimus felt as he travelled back to Colossae?
- How important to him was Paul's recommendation? (vv. 17-17).
- To what extent do you seek to make up for the mistakes you made before becoming a Christian?

Conclusion

When a sinner repents, his life is transformed by the power of God. After being a useless person for himself and for others, he becomes a blessing to others. This story is a beautiful picture of Calvary. Christ found us as runaway slaves who had broken the law, rebelling against Him. But he forgave us and made us part of His household. He went to the cross and paid our debt. And today, He calls us to be useful in fulfilling His mission.

Steps in the training of John Mark

Marcos Cisneros (U.S.A.)

> **Memory verse:** "Only Luke is with me. Get Mark and bring him with you, because he is helpful to me in my ministry" (2 Timothy 4:11).
>
> **Lesson Aim:** To learn that although sometimes we do not see all the desired results, we should not get discouraged, but keep moving forward until God's plans for our lives are fully realized.

Introduction

The opposite of helpful is useless, a word that makes us uncomfortable since nobody wants to be useless. However, sometimes we have to face our own incompetence in fulfilling our responsibilities or tasks that others expect us to perform.

In today's lesson, we will learn and be challenged to keep going forward and not give up. We should never let the circumstances, or the opinion of other people, define what we truly are, or what God has carefully planned that we should become. Our purpose in life is clear: to become all that God expects us to be, and to become all that God has planned for us to be, and not settle for anything less.

I. Meet John Mark

Does it make any difference to call a person by a nickname rather than his given name? Do you have or did you have a nickname? John's nickname was Mark. In the Bible he is usually referred to as Mark. He was a young man from a family who belonged to the wider group of Jesus' disciples. Like most young people, he was still a bit immature. He was very interested in discovering the world.

According to Acts 12:12, John Mark was the son of Mary. And according to Colossians 4:10, John Mark was also Barnabas's relation. Later in this lesson, we will look at these two verses more closely.

II. John Mark and Mary

Acts 12:12 says, "When this had dawned on him, he went to the house of Mary the mother of John, also called Mark, where many people had gathered and were praying." Until that moment, it had not been easy for Barnabas and Paul as they had faced tribulations and sufferings during their first missionary journey. The young John Mark accompanied them, but after seeing all the situations they were facing during their missionary journey, decided to return to the home of his mother, Mary.

We see this evident in the following verse: "From Paphos, Paul and his companions sailed to Perga in Pamphylia, where John left them to return to Jerusalem" (Acts 13:13). Who was Mary, John's mother? When the church was started in Jerusalem, the disciples took meeting together very seriously, regardless of number, adversity, or even persecution. The new Christians, sanctified by the presence and power of the Holy Spirit, always found opportunities to be together: "Every day they continued to meet together in the temple courts. They broke bread in their homes and ate together with glad and sincere hearts" (Acts 2:46). They met together in the temple and in houses.

One of those houses was the home of Mary, John's mother. She had opened her house for the brothers and sisters to meet together to pray, celebrate the Lord's Supper, study the doctrine of the apostles, worship the Lord, to have fellowship, among other things (Acts 2:41-47).

During the persecution of the church, Peter was put in jail. Many were afraid, and several houses were closed. However, the disciples met secretly in Mary's house to pray together (Acts 12:12). Even during the persecution, Mary's house remained open for these prayer meetings. This shows that she was a wise sister who loved the Lord very much. Her house was a meeting point for the apostles as we can see when Peter was released from prison, he went straight to Mary's house (Acts 12:12-16).

Coming back to the incident in the first missionary journey, the fact that John Mark returned home because he found that it was too hard for him is understandable; he was a young man. His mother probably had to comfort him and encourage him to continue serving the Lord.

If you had been John's mother, what would you have done in this situation? She would have told her son not to give up in the face of hardship. She probably motivated him to go on another mission trip with the apostles, and helped him set out again with his uncle Barnabas. Mark listened to his mother's words, obeyed and returned to Antioch. Although rejected by Paul, he worked alongside Barnabas in Cyprus (Acts 15:37-40).

III. John Mark and Barnabas

In Colossians 4:10, Paul wrote, "My fellow prisoner Aristarchus sends you his greetings, as does Mark, the cousin of Barnabas. (You have received instructions about him; if he comes to you, welcome him)."

John Mark was related to Barnabas but he was also his spiritual son, which is why Barnabas had a particular desire for this young man to be part of the missionary work in those days, although this later caused a little conflict within the missionary team led by Paul. Through the story, we see that Barnabas brought John Mark even without Paul's consent. On one occasion later, Barnabas wanted to take John Mark back on the team, however Paul was strongly opposed. So in then end, there was a disagreement between Barnabas and Paul, and they went in different directions. Barnabas and Mark went to Cyprus, and Paul and Silas went to Syria and Cilicia.

It is worth mentioning that after this incident, Barnabas is not mentioned any more in Acts, and is mentioned only twice in Paul's letters (Gal. 2:11-13, 1 Corinthians 9:6). What do you think happened? Was this the price that Barnabas had to pay to let Mark continue in the ministry? Of course, these are only ideas, we do not know the real situation. However, what we do know with regard to Barnabas is that he fulfilled his purpose and his ministry.

IV. Mark and Paul

Perhaps the master-disciple relationship between Paul and John Mark was not exactly the same as that of Paul and Timothy, or even Titus. The latter were two young companions and assistants of the Apostle Paul. However, through different stages and different avenues, these three young people -Timothy, Titus and John Mark - became helpful servants and collaborators with Paul in the ministry.

Let's see the salient aspects in the life of Mark and his relationship with the apostle Paul. These aspects will help us see the process and progress in his life. We can note an increase of confidence, commitment and devotion. In our difficult moments, we must always remember that God has not finished His work in us yet. A failure does not determine the rest of our lives. Every crisis presents a new opportunity.

A. Paul asks that John Mark not go with them, because he left them in Pamphylia

Acts 15:38 says, "but Paul did not think it wise to take him, because he had deserted them in Pamphylia and had not continued with them in the work." In spite of Barnabas' insistence, Paul did not want to take John Mark with them. Although both took different itineraries, the reality is that Mark was the reason for the disagreement. Paul saw the risk, Barnabas saw the possibility. Life is a constant risk. So, we must always ask God to give us His direction and help us take the "most viable risk."

B. Paul asks that they receive Mark

Several years later, Paul wrote in a letter: "My fellow prisoner Aristarchus sends you his greetings, as does Mark, the cousin of Barnabas. (You have received instructions about him; if he comes to you, welcome him)" (Colossians 4:10). Can you see the change in the relationship between Paul and Mark? By then, he was no longer the young man that Paul refused to take with him on the trip. He was a well-known leader and someone who carried messages. Paul tells the Colossians to receive him. Undoubtedly, he had gained the confidence of the great apostle. Paul, in his wisdom, had a humble spirit to accept and recognize what God had done in the life of John Mark. Perhaps it was the pressure of the moment and the urgency of the need that did not allow the great apostle to see all the potential in the young disciple, especially what God wanted to do in both of them.

C. Mark - Paul's helper in ministry

2 Timothy 4:11 says, "Only Luke is with me. Get

Mark and bring him with you, because he is helpful to me in my ministry." At that moment, Paul himself asked that they bring Mark. What a big difference! He had previously asked this young man to leave. Now he was calling for him. It is really special to think that Paul could see that Mark was necessary for him to complete his ministry. Someone who failed one moment but now was indispensable. God had worked in John Mark's life, maturing him and developing his gifts.

On one occasion, one of my professors said, "We are all important; nobody is dispensable." John Mark was never dispensable for the work of the ministry; he was a very important leader in the early church.

D. Mark remains as one of Paul's collaborators

Paul wrote to Philemon: "Mark, Aristarchus, Demas and Luke, my fellow workers"(Philemon 24). That young man who fled, leaving the missionary trip half-way through, was now one of Paul's fellow workers. What a difference the years of experience make! What a difference it makes to remain firm and faithful, seeing what God can do in a person's life! Think for a moment about this:

If Mary had given up on her son, if Barnabas had given up on him and had not invited him to Cyprus, if Paul had never invited John Mark again, and if John Mark himself had thrown in the towel and never again tried again, Mark would not have been able to become what he did. Have we given up on someone, or are we about to give up on ourselves? Mark's life teaches us to persevere. But there is still more ...

V. John Mark and Peter

1 Peter 5:13 says the following: "She who is in Babylon, chosen together with you, sends you her greetings, and so does my son Mark." Peter calls Mark his son, and he is with Peter, probably in Rome. Most scholars say that there is real evidence that Mark wrote his gospel using Peter as his source. Mark, who was formerly known as John, son of Mary, cousin/nephew of Barnabas, disciple of Paul and spiritual son of Peter, became the writer of the holy gospel according to St. Mark. The one who at first was not useful, later was used by God to write such a beautiful and important book in the Bible, the first Gospel. Yes, God took him through different chapters in his life, but always with a clear purpose! This should fill our hearts with hope, encouragement and inspiration.

Optional Questions:

I. Meet John Mark

- According to Acts 12:12, 13:13 and Colossians 4:10, who was John Mark?

II. John Mark and Mary

- Mary was a faithful person (Acts 12:12-16). What role did she play when a dejected Mark returned home?

III. John Mark and Barnabas

- According to Colossians 4:10, what relationship was there between Barnabas and Mark?

- What happened in Acts 15:37-40?

- Think and write three names of people who have contributed to your spiritual growth.

- What are the three biggest challenges we face in trying to be someone's mentor?

IV. Mark and Paul

- According to Colossians 4:10, 2 Timothy 4:11, and Philemon 24, what was Paul's attitude?

V. John Mark and Peter

- What does Peter say in 1 Peter 5:13 to John Mark? What does that say?

- Who is discipling you? And who are you discipling? Share.

- Based on the lesson we studied today about Mark, Paul and Barnabas, what are the benefits of investing time, confidence, effort and dedication in the life of another person?

Conclusion

Do we believe that God can do great things in our lives? We must remain faithful, strive, and learn from the leaders and mentors that God has placed around us. There will always be a 'Mary', a 'Barnabas', a 'Paul', and a 'Peter.' God will provide someone to help us on His way, so that we too can become useful for the ministry. God will take us to higher levels, or help us to move one step further in our life. Perhaps God has prepared for you a 'John Mark'. Don't give up! Don't settle for less!

A Miracle with purpose

José Barrientos (Guatemala)

> **Memory verse:** "Go, he told him, wash in the Pool of Siloam (this word means "Sent"). So, the man went and washed, and came home seeing" (John 9:7).
>
> **Lesson Aim:** To understand that God's miracles are part of his redemptive plan and go beyond just mitigating a physical need, but also affecting spiritually not only those who receive them, but also those who observe them.

Introduction

One of the hymns that has blessed the church throughout history is entitled 'Amazing Grace'. Its author, John Newton, was captain of slave ship. After accepting Jesus, he abandoned his profession and devoted his life to work in the church. Although he ended up blind, in the lyrics of the hymn, he wrote a revealing phrase: 'I was blind but now I see.' John 9 tells about a blind man who, by diligently obeying what Jesus told him, received his sight. After receiving this miracle, he was expelled from the synagogue; but Jesus showed him about those who, being able to see, are blind. We will see various lessons that emerge from this miracle of Jesus which will help us affirm our faith and long for the touch of Jesus in our lives.

I. Jesus heals blind man

After being tempted in the desert, the Lord began his ministry by quoting the passage he read in the synagogue, which describes his mission (Luke 4:18). From the beginning of his ministry, Jesus performed many miracles of healing. In this passage we are dealing with one of them, which is told with many details. It is the case of a blind man, who was on the road where the Master was walking, who received different comments from the passers-by (John 9:1-6, 12).

A. The blind man and the disciples (vv.1-5)

Jesus was focused on fulfilling his mission. For this reason, he identified what in his environment allowed him to execute his redemptive plan. For Jesus, that blind man was a person who had a need, and for that reason, Jesus looked at him with compassion. Jesus was concentrated on his mission as we see clearly in what he said to his disciples: "As long as it is day, we must do the works of him who sent me" (John 9:4a). The Lord met the need of the blind man as well as using the incident as an opportunity to teach some truths regarding wrong Jewish teaching of those times. Jesus also communicates a cause in this man's blindness which challenges our understanding of what happens on earth.

The question was: why was this man blind from birth? Using the Jewish belief of those times, the disciples asked him, "Rabbi, who sinned, this man or his parents, that he was born blind?" (v. 2). They had been taught that blindness and other such illnesses were the result of sin.

Perhaps this teaching was based on texts from the Pentateuch (Exodus 20:5; Deuteronomy 5:9), where God told the people that wickedness will affect several generations. However, Ezekiel made it clear that each one is responsible for his own sins: "The one who sins is the one who will die" (Ezekiel 18:4).

It seems that rather than have compassion on this blind man, they saw the opportunity to satisfy their theological curiosity. Jesus answers this in a simple yet very profound way: "Neither this man nor his parents sinned…but this happened so that the works of God might be displayed in him" (John 9:3). With this said, he acted on the life of the blind man.

B. The blind man and Jesus (vv. 6-7)

The blind man was listening to the conversation. However, the conversation suddenly became hopeful. A voice said something unexpected about the question of who had sinned. It was the Master's voice that said, "Neither this man nor his parents sinned" (John 9:3). How would those words have sounded in that man's ears? Maybe they freed him from the guilt that had been attributed to him or his parents all that time.

Jesus saw his deep need and healed him: "After saying this, he spat on the ground, made some mud with the saliva, and put it on the man's eyes. "Go," he told him, "wash in the Pool of Siloam" (this word means "Sent"). So, the man went and washed, and came home seeing" (vv.6-7). Then the blind man was attentive, and when Jesus put the mud in his eyes and sent him to the pool of Siloam, he had already believed. He did not doubt. He obeyed diligently, and at the end he came back seeing.

C. The 'blind man' and his neighbors (vv. 8-12)

In the face of what happened, the observers were challenged. Those who saw him blind before now saw him with sight. When the neighbors saw him, they began to ask questions: "His neighbors and those who had formerly seen him begging asked, 'Isn't this the same man who used to sit and beg?' Some claimed that he was. Others said, 'No, he only looks like him'" (vv. 8-9). They overwhelmed him with questions. Then, in response to the demand of the crowd, he replied, "The man they call Jesus made some mud and put it on my eyes. He told me to go to Siloam and wash. So, I went and washed, and then I could see" (v.11).

D. The 'blind man' and the Pharisees.

The neighbors took the young man to the Pharisees (v. 13). If the disciples looked at the blind man as a way to answer their theological doubts, and the neighbors were filled with curiosity, the Pharisees were filled with indignation. Jesus had healed the man on the Sabbath (v. 14). "Some of the Pharisees said, 'This man is not from God, for he does not keep the Sabbath'" (v. 16a). Some of the other Pharisees asked, "How can a sinner perform such signs?" (v. 16b).

They called the young man who testified to the way that Jesus had healed him, and because they still did not believe what had happened, they called his parents who said, "We know he is our son…and we know he was born blind. But how he can see now, or who opened his eyes, we don't know. Ask him. He is of age; he will speak for himself" (vv. 20-21).

The leaders called the man again to tell his story. They insulted him (v. 28) and he gave an incredible answer: "Now that is remarkable! You don't know where he comes from, yet he opened my eyes. We know that God does not listen to sinners. He listens to the godly person who does his will. Nobody has

ever heard of opening the eyes of a man born blind. If this man were not from God, he could do nothing" (vv.30-33). The result was that they expelled him from the Synagogue which was a serious thing. This was not easy to face as it meant humiliation and isolation.

II. Spiritual blindness (John 9:35-41)

From the beginning of the event, Jesus had expressed that the blindness of this man was so that the grace of God would be manifested. So, nothing was ever out of God's control, but in the face of the expulsion, it was possible to give new lessons.

A. The healed man received spiritual sight

Jesus knew that he had been expelled from the Synagogue. So he found him and questioned him about his faith by saying, "Do you believe in the Son of Man?" (v. 35b). The healed man answered him with a question: "Who is he, sir? Tell me so that I may believe in him" (v. 36). Jesus told him the person who had healed him was the Son of God. In this way, he opened his spiritual eyes, and the man who had been blind now understood or saw this great truth. He did not need another test, for he knew that Jesus had healed him and that undoubtedly, He was and is the Son of God. He said, "Lord, I believe, and he worshiped him" (v. 38). The grace of God had manifested itself in him.

B. The Pharisees are condemned for their deliberate blindness

The dialogue narrated above was between Jesus and the healed man, but the Pharisees who listened felt accused. Jesus told the blind man, "For judgment I have come into this world, so that the blind will see and those who see will become blind" (v. 39). The Pharisees listening asked, "What? Are we blind too?" (v.40). Jesus answered them directly: "If you were blind, you would not be guilty of sin; but now that you claim you can see, your guilt remains" (v.41).

C. Definition of spiritual blindness

In this way, our Lord Jesus defines what spiritual blindness is, and which is reiterated in Revelation 3:17-18. From the healing of the blind man, we can learn the following:

1. The circumstance of life that we experience, whether desirable for us or undesirable, do not escape God's sight. Jesus saw the blind

man and did not ignore his circumstances. He also knew the effects that his healing would produce. These were positive for the blind man, but negative for the Pharisees, showing up their improper conduct.

2. The purpose of the miracles God performs is to bless the lives of people by meeting a need, and at the same time, this is a testimony to those who observe, which strengthens the convictions of those who believe. The blind man was expelled from the synagogue but he joined the family of God.

3. The blind man humbly obeyed Jesus in every detail and was healed and received salvation, while the Pharisees were arrogant, spiritually blind and in danger of condemnation.

Optional Questions:

I. Jesus heals the blind man

- Are we sick as a result of our sins or as a result of the sins of our fathers?

- How did the blind man react to Jesus' instructions? What does this say about him.
- How did the man testify to the neighbors?
- What was the reaction of the Pharisees? Why did they react like that?
- Are there "Pharisees" in our churches today?

II. Spiritual blindness

- In this narrative, who are the really blind people? Why?
- How did his healing affect the young man?
- Who are the spiritually blind groups today?

Conclusion:

God's miracles are within his redemptive plan, but we must remember that these go beyond just meeting a physical need. These happen so that those who have received the miracle, and those around them, understand and recognize that God is the only true God, and there is no other besides Him.

Notes :

A disciple like Christ

Eudo Prado (Venezuela)

Memory verse: "But they could not stand up against the wisdom the Spirit gave him as he spoke" (Acts 6:10).

Lesson Aim: To identify the main elements of Christian discipleship, examining the life of Stephen.

Introduction

If we had to describe exactly the characteristics of a disciple of Jesus, what aspects would we include? Do we fill the biblical requirements of the disciple? Stephen was an extraordinary disciple among the crowd of believers. The characteristics that distinguished him mainly were his holy character and his willingness to serve. Looking at the life of this servant of God from different angles, we can identify three main characteristics of a disciple who follows Jesus: Service, witness and sacrifice.

I. A disciple serving with love

Discipleship makes us protagonists in a marvelous story. It is not a fictional story, but a very real one of passion and total surrender to the One who gave his life for us: Jesus Christ.

The heart of a disciple is one that overflows with the love of Christ and it is, therefore, a heart willing to serve. Without service there is no discipleship. This is the first element of discipleship that we can identify in Stephen's amazing life.

A. Imitating Jesus in service

When the conflict recorded in Acts 6 was presented, the church chose as deacons seven men who radiated the character of Christ. That is to say, they were disciples similar to Him.

This first part of the lesson is recounted in Acts 6:5: "This proposal pleased the whole group. They chose Stephen, a man full of faith and of the Holy Spirit; also, Philip, Procorus, Nicanor, Timon, Parmenas, and Nicolas from Antioch, a convert to Judaism."

We know very little about Stephen. In Greek, his name "Stephanos" meant "crown", and was very common in the Hellenic world. Tradition affirms that Stephen and Philip were among the 70 sent by Jesus.

If so, undoubtedly that experience had marked their lives. The other six chosen also had Greek names, which seems to indicate that they were Jews of the Diaspora. This group is known as the first seven deacons, since they were dedicated to the office of diaconia (service to the needy recorded in Acts 6:1-2).

According to most commentators, the function of 'serving the tables' (v. 2) should not be taken literally. Rather, it was a task that consisted of distributing resources with prudence and justice to the needy. These seven men were a kind of stewards who wisely administered the Lord's goods.

Before Stephen was chosen for this function, he had undoubtedly shown his capacity. So, his appointment was a confirmation of his calling by the whole crowd of believers.

Service to others is an expression of Christ's love in us (Galatians 5:13), and therefore it is an indispensable mark of discipleship. Any service that we perform, whether in the context of society or within the church, has a fundamental parameter: "Serve wholeheartedly, as if you were serving the Lord, not people" (Ephesians 6:7).

B. The character of a server is everything

Some requirements were clearly enumerated by the apostles to choose those whom the church would dedicate to the important task of serving the needy. They needed to define well the capacities that are required for any function in the work of God, but service demands a fullness of love.

Although all the chosen group complied with the indicated requirements, it seems that Stephen was emphasized for his holy character and extraordinary trust in the Lord. Looking closely at the daily life of

Stephen, we can find the reason for his effectiveness. Luke highlights that he was "a man full of faith and of the Holy Spirit" (Acts 6:5).

Are we people who are full of the Holy Spirit? Everyone could clearly recognize Stephen's holiness! Sometimes we lower the standards too much and are very superficial when choosing candidates for ministry jobs. The case of Stephen and his companions' selection teaches us a different standard: No task in the church is so unimportant that it does not require consecration to perform it. Precisely because we serve the Most High God, three times Holy; everyone who approaches His altar must do so in a condition of complete moral purity (Psalm 15).

II. A disciple testifying with power

Shortly after being assigned by the church to distribute resources among the poor, Stephen transcended that original responsibility. He went on to play a more prominent role, one full of a lot of risks, i.e., giving public testimony of the faith.

In Acts 6:8-15, we observe his public testimony, his dispute with the Jewish teachers, his arrest, and finally, his judgment. Chapter 7 shows us his defense to the Council and his martyrdom.

Stephen was a disciple who testified with courage and power. Although his testimony meant death, he remained faithful to his beloved Lord and Master to the end, reflecting Christian love in all aspects of his life. Testimony is the second element of discipleship that we are going to identify in the life of Stephen.

A. Witnessing with signs and wonders

Stephen was a deacon, and not one of the twelve apostles. However, God used him in a powerful way. This means that the manifestation of God is not restricted to a select group of leaders, but to all those believers with a holy character who are willing to be used by God as He wills.

Acts 6:8 declares, "Now Stephen, a man full of God's grace and power, performed great wonders and signs among the people." The images we see in this passage are very beautiful, but at the same time, very challenging. First, Stephen appears surrounded by the people, ministering to many sick and demonized people who were freed by the Lord. It is clear that Stephen gave priority to the preaching of the gospel, and miracles happened as a kind of manifestation of God over those afflicted beings.

Miracles do not have to be constant today in every evangelizing work. However, God continues to respond to the prayer of faith of his people. As in the life of Stephen, the Holy Spirit supernaturally manifests himself in disciples obedient to the command to "Go ... and preach the gospel" (Mark 16:15).

B. Presenting a wise defense of faith

Subsequently, another impacting image is presented to us. Stephen victoriously resists the immense pressure of a horde of Jewish people attacking him (Acts 6:9-15). Christian witness is not always accepted with approval, but sometimes it receives fierce opposition. In such circumstances, we have the promise of divine help (Mark 13:11). However, sometimes God's help does not imply liberation from the suffering that faithful witnessing can bring. God allows in some cases that his enemies apparently triumph, eventually bringing greater glory to his holy name.

Probably, Saul was among those who attacked Stephen. Saul's native city (Tarsus) belonged to the Roman province of Cilicia mentioned in Acts 6:9. In any case, neither Saul, the outstanding disciple of the great Rabbi Gamaliel, nor any of his companions, could resist the wisdom with which Stephen spoke.

Stephen's defense was a historical summary of God's covenant with Israel, His people. It was a quick summary of the experiences of God with the people of Israel and with the Gentiles throughout history up to that time. All of Stephen's exposition was from the Scriptures, but with a clearly Christological emphasis. This man demonstrated that the cross of Christ is the center of the history of salvation narrated in the Old Testament. We too need to point out the importance of grounding our message about Christ in a full understanding of his person through the thread of the progressive revelation of the Bible.

Finally, after making a series of false accusations against Stephen, and obstinately rejecting his testimony, those who judged him saw something very shocking: Stephen's face shone "like the face of an angel" (Acts 6:15). And yet, in spite of this supernatural manifestation, the attackers continued to judge him, behaving like true wild beasts, dominated by the hardness of their hearts (Acts 7:54).

III. A disciple willing to sacrifice

Tertullian compared the blood of the martyrs to an effective seed for the multiplication of new Christians. Wherever the church has been persecuted, it has resulted in revival and extension of the Kingdom of God.

The last scene of chapter 7 (vv. 55-60) is the basis for the study of this part of the lesson. Stephen's martyrdom is probably one of the most dramatic stories in the New Testament. Although the possibility of martyrdom is not usually a reality in our cases, as disciples of Jesus, we must be willing to bear the cost of sacrifice. It is not only about being prepared for the loss of life as such, but also of the daily sacrifice for the cause of Christ. Remember what our Lord told us: "Whoever wants to be my disciple must deny themselves and take up their cross daily and follow me" (Luke 9:23). Sacrifice is the third element of Christian discipleship that we can clearly observe in Stephen.

A. A vision of the glory of God

In the midst of his martyrdom, Stephen saw the glory of God, and Jesus sitting at his right hand. His confrontation with death was transformed into an overflow of divine presence and manifestation in his life. His mind and emotions were clothed with the vision of God's greatness.

In this way, God brought greater faith and strength to his servant in such a bitter moment.

Here we see how a full understanding of the sanctity and sovereignty of God becomes the key element that gives us security before the tribulations of life. Disciples are willing to give their life for their Master because they have experienced the filling of the Holy Spirit.

In other words, the small devotion we observe today to the cause of Christian witness is, to a large extent, a reflection of the spiritual inconsistency and the lack of intimate communion with God.

B. A prayer of forgiveness for enemies

The martyrdom of Stephen was similar to the death of our Lord Jesus himself; for he delivered to the Lord his spirit, and he prayed for the forgiveness of his murderers (Acts 7:59, 60; Luke 23:34, 46).

Let's see what Acts 7:60 says: "Then he fell on his knees and cried out, 'Lord, do not hold this sin against them.' When he had said this, he fell asleep." Stephen literally gave his life as an act of worship to God. This also reminds us of Paul's disposition in prison. He considered his impending death a libation on the sacrifice of believers (Philippians 2:17).

On the other hand, the story of Stephen's death points out the biblical principle that we should not take revenge in our hands. We must leave it in the hands of our righteous God (Romans 12:19). The natural man's tendency is to respond to violence with violence; but this violates the law of Christian love. In the times of the primitive church, the persecuted believers rejected the temptation to take justice into their hands. Therefore, the apostles in their writings often warn the believers not to seek revenge. The admonition of Hebrews 10:26 about not sinning voluntarily after having received the knowledge of the truth is given to believers showing how they could be tempted to respond wrongly (Hebrews 10:26-39). A disciple of Jesus must always respond patiently and kindly to the offenses of lost sinners, understanding that our attitudes can be the key element for their acceptance or rejection of the gospel message (2 Timothy 2:24- 26).

It is appropriate to ask ourselves how we are responding to the pressures we receive from the world due to our Christian faith. Or also, how easily have we given in or fought back? Do we forgive offenses and pray for the salvation of opponents of the gospel?

Optional Questions:

I. A disciple serving with love

- What did the "serve tables" function imply? (Acts 6:1).
- What was the reason for Stephen's efficiency in service? (Acts 6:2-8).

II. A disciple testifying with power

- What happened to Stephen, according to Acts 6:8-15?
- Have you ever found yourself in a situation where you were attacked while defending the principles of God? How did you react?
- Does God always totally free us from suffering, according to Acts 7:51-60? Explain.

III. A disciple willing to sacrifice

- What enables a disciple to be willing to give his life for Christ?
- How should a disciple respond to the offenses of lost sinners? Why? Do you have an example? If so share it.

Conclusion

Living and being like Jesus as His disciples is not easy, but it is what God wants from us. Stephen's life has taught us that the filling of the Holy Spirit is indispensable in being a true disciple.

May God help each of us to be disciples like Christ, and shine with the light of the gospel and the presence of God in a world increasingly filled with darkness.

The correct request

Scarlet Jimenez (Ecuador)

Memory verse: "The fear of the Lord is the beginning of knowledge, but fools despise wisdom and instruction" (Proverbs 1:7).

Lesson Aim: To understand that the correct petition to God is the one which can lead us to greater blessing.

Introduction

Something we have to remember is that from his birth, Solomon pleased God. His other name, Jedidiah, means 'beloved of the Lord' (2 Samuel 12:25). In spite of this, the story of Solomon is full of ups and downs and somber matters. But in this lesson, we will focus on his best decision when he was still young.

His mother, Bathsheba, was the former wife of Uriah, whom David sent to his death in order to cover up his sin. Solomon was the son of David and Bathsheba, and his name means 'peaceful', because he was born in a moment of peace, and the name resembles the word Shalom. Other commentators also claim that the name Bathsheba gave her son is derived from the Hebrew root meaning 'to replace or restore,' because he came to replace her first son, who died after the visit of the prophet Nathan. We see this story of Solomon in 1 Kings 3:1-28 and 2 Chronicles 1:1-13).

I. Solomon asks for wisdom

At the beginning of His reign Solomon made an alliance with Pharaoh king of Egypt and married his daughter (1 Kings 3:1). In this way, he was trying to strengthen political and commercial treaties. He built a palace for her.

Solomon loved the Lord and fulfilled all His laws, following the example of his father David. The temple had not yet been built and the Ark of the covenant was in Gibeon. 2 Chronicles 1:2-3 tells us, "Then Solomon spoke to all Israel—to the commanders of thousands and commanders of hundreds, to the judges and to all the leaders in Israel, the heads of families— and Solomon and the whole assembly went to the high place at Gibeon, for God's tent of meeting was there, which Moses the Lord's servant had made in the wilderness." 1 Kings 3:4 tells us, "Solomon offered a thousand burnt offerings on that altar."

A. Solomon meets with God

It seems that after making these sacrifices, Solomon and the people stayed in Gibeon overnight. Solomon had a powerful dream that night. God said to him, "Ask for whatever you want me to give you" (2 Chronicles 1:7). Solomon could have asked for anything: wealth, victory over his enemies, expansion of his domain, peace and lots more. But Solomon shows that he has a correct evaluation of himself. He said, "But I am only a little child and do not know how to carry out my duties" (1 Kings 3:7-8). David had said before he died: "My son Solomon is young and inexperienced" (1 Chronicles 22:5a).

It is beautiful to be young, but at the same time, it can be extremely challenging. Adults do not always trust the generation of young people. We can imagine some of Solomon's anxieties: Would the elders trust him? He had brothers who were older than him who wanted to take away his throne. David had commissioned him to build a house for God - the temple, but under these conditions would he be able to do it? Different groups could scheme to murder him to achieve their purposes.

Solomon was humble and intelligent and he trusted God. But above all he recognized that he did not have the experience and enough knowledge to be a king. Have you ever had to take on a task for which you didn't feel capable? How did you react?

B. Solomon's desire

What Solomon needed was a sensitive heart, and the understanding to govern with justice. He wanted to have the wisdom to be able to distinguish between good and bad, fairness and injustice, right and wrong. Solomon wanted to govern his people in a correct and just way. Leading this people was a daunting task. He would have to lead the people into battle if necessary. He was the leader of a huge army: "In all Israel there were one million one hundred thousand men who could handle a sword, including four hundred and seventy thousand in Judah" (1 Chronicles 21:5-6).

Solomon did not ask God for a long life or freedom from his enemies. He did not ask for riches, which many of us might have done. His main concern was to be able to govern correctly. Solomon said to God, "Give me wisdom and knowledge, that I may lead this people, for who is able to govern this great people of yours?" (2 Chronicles 1:10). Wisdom isn't simply intelligence or knowledge or even understanding. It is the ability to use these to think and act in such a way that common sense prevails and choices are beneficial and productive. Wisdom is the ability given by God to deal intelligently with the varied experiences of life, which results in blessing for those involved. Job, a God-fearing person, said, "The fear of the Lord—that is wisdom, and to shun evil is understanding" (Job 28:28). Fearing God does not mean being afraid of Him, but implies an attitude of submission and obedience to Him.

God granted him his request; he was unequaled in wisdom (1 Kings 3:12, 4:29-31). It is interesting to note that this young man did not ask for riches or glory, but these came; it was a gift that God added (1 Kings 3:13). He also lived a long time. When he went back to Jerusalem, Solomon showed his gratitude by offering sacrifices to God (1 Kings 3:15).

II. Evidence of Solomon's wisdom

In 1 Kings 3:16-28, we read that two women came to Solomon. They went before the king so that he could give them justice. Although they were prostitutes, and this was a poorly viewed practice, they came before him. This was because at that time, the custom was that the king was accessible to his subjects, especially the poor.

In his role as judge, Solomon heard the plea. The first mother presented her case: "This woman and I live in the same house, and I had a baby while she was there with me. The third day after my child was born, this woman also had a baby. We were alone; there was no one in the house but the two of us. During the night this woman's son died because she lay on him. So, she got up in the middle of the night and took my son from my side while I your servant was asleep. She put him by her breast and put her dead son by my breast. The next morning, I got up to nurse my son—and he was dead! But when I looked at him closely in the morning light, I saw that it wasn't the son I had borne" (1 Kings 3:17-21).

The other lady said that the first woman was lying and that the baby was hers. Solomon had to work out which of them was telling the truth to be able to connect the baby to its rightful mother. It was a difficult case. After stating their cases, each woman affirmed that she was the mother of the living child. Solomon asked for a sword and commanded his servants to cut the baby in half. This was a very wise decision.

The ladies answered at once: "The woman whose son was alive was deeply moved out of love for her son and said to the king, 'Please, my lord, give her the living baby! Don't kill him!' But the other said, 'Neither I nor you shall have him. Cut him in two!'" (v. 26). It became clear who the real mother was. Solomon had made a good judgement and the real mother got to have her baby. "When all Israel heard the verdict the king had given, they held the king in awe, because they saw that he had wisdom from God to administer justice" (v. 28).

With this, his reign began to prosper. Wisdom was not only limited to his role as the people's judge, but also to the business that he carried out with other countries in order to obtain the materials for the construction of the temple of God and the palace. Finally, the nation enjoyed a time of peace and stability.

Solomon teaches us that fearing and putting God first helps us to be successful. The New Testament says that we must first seek the Kingdom of God (Matthew 6:33). The example we receive from our parents is important, because it marks our life, but the decision about how we want to live our lives depends on each one of us. These decisions mark the course of our lives. If we walk with God in every way, He will grant the requests of our heart. As human beings, we all have limits, but with God's important thing is that whenever we ask God for something, we do it with a simple and humble heart. Solomon recognized his limits, and asked for the help he needed, which could only come from God. God is the only one who has the power to take us beyond what we could even hope for. Solomon made the right request, and was blessed with much more.

If we are leaders, or feel that God is calling us to serve the church, first we must ask God to enable us, and we will see that with divine guidance and our obedience, we will be able to do it.

Solomon's request was to have wisdom. We should follow the example of this humble and fearful young man of God who was able to carry out God's purpose. How can we recognize God's wisdom? James 3:17 tells us: "But the wisdom that comes from heaven is first of all pure; then peace-loving, considerate, submissive, full of mercy and good fruit, impartial and sincere."

Optional Questions:

I. Solomon asks for wisdom

- What do we read about Solomon in 1 Kings 3:1-5?

- What other person was recognized for his wisdom according to Genesis 22:12?

- What was the difference between the wisdom of Solomon and of others, according to 1 Kings 3:12, 4:29-31?

- Have you made any request to God? What was your motivation? If you have not made any, what would you ask for today?

II. Evidence of Solomon's wisdom

- What teaching can you take from this story recorded in 1 Kings 3:16-28?

- What characteristics does the wisdom of God have in a person, according to James 3:17? Mention some examples.

Conclusion

God is willing to give us what we ask of him, but before asking, let's examine our motivation. Our request should not be capricious or self-centered, but with a desire to bless others and serve the Lord wholeheartedly.

Notes :

Nehemiah's huge request

Marco Rocha (Argentina)

Memory verse: "Lord, let your ear be attentive to the prayer of this your servant and to the prayer of your servants who delight in revering your name. Give your servant success today by granting him favor in the presence of this man" (Nehemiah 1:11).

Lesson Aim: To discover some of the distinctive features of the life of Nehemiah.

Introduction

One of the attitudes that reflects much of our personality is how we react in the face of problems and difficulties of life. Ask your students to collaborate in making a list of different ways in which people react to bad news or a problem. Then, conclude this introduction by explaining that although it is normal for us to react to the difficulties of life with pain and grief, the Bible teaches us through the life of Nehemiah that we can do more than just have those feelings, whatever the situation we are going through. This study covers the first two chapters of the book of Nehemiah.

I. Transforming sorrow into action

The name "Nehemiah" means 'comfort of the Lord.' This prophet lived during the years of Persian domination over the Jewish people. He was a member of a Jewish family brought to Babylon during the exile at the beginning of the sixth century. There he served as cupbearer to the king. Ask: What advantages and disadvantages could Nehemiah have as a cupbearer?

A. Receiving bad news

Bad news hits us hard, and so it was with Nehemiah. A group of Jerusalem pilgrims presented to Nehemiah the serious condition of the Jews in the city, especially the deplorable state of the wall, which had long served as protection for the people. However, now "the wall of Jerusalem was broken down, and its gates have been burned with fire" (Nehemiah 1:3).

Although Nehemiah was more than 1,200 kilometers away, this harsh description generated a deep sorrow that led him to mourn, fast and pray (v. 4). It is important to note that in Nehemiah, we find a person who does not deny nor represses their feelings before the evil that is approaching, but he directs them towards the search of God in worship. It is not the same to mourn and moan without faith or hope, as to bring our grief to God in fasting and prayer.

B. Nehemiah's prayer (Nehemiah 1)

Nehemiah teaches us that, faced with the difficulties of life, we do not have to deny how we feel. On the other hand, we must take our pain before God. And the way to do that is by praying. If we decide to start doing something to change the situation of grief in which we find ourselves, then we must begin with prayer.

Nehemiah's prayer begins with words of adoration: "Lord, the God of heaven, the great and awesome God, who keeps his covenant of love with those who love him and keep his commandments..." (v. 5) When we begin our prayer focusing on who God is, and not on our problem or difficulty, then we focus on who can really come to our help at such a time - God. Nehemiah knew that he would find no answer for his grief in any other than the true and original builder of the city and the wall that would protect the chosen people.

In verses 6-7, Nehemiah's prayer teaches us that sin brings desolation and destruction in its wake: "let your ear be attentive and your eyes open to hear the prayer your servant is praying before you day and night for your servants, the people of Israel. I confess the sins we Israelites, including myself and my father's family, have committed against you. We have acted very wickedly toward you. We have not obeyed the commands, decrees and laws you gave your servant Moses."

Nehemiah presents us with Israel's disobedience, when instead of complying with the commandments of God given through Moses, they had persisted in erring again and again, offending and betraying divine love and faithfulness. However, we need to emphasize that Nehemiah did not blame others in his prayer, nor did he point out the errors of past generations. But he identified with his people, being responsible for sins and confessing them before God. This attitude of Nehemiah teaches us that there is no principle of restoration without sincere repentance.

In verses 8 and 9, Nehemiah's prayer teaches us about the importance of divine promises. Let's read what the verses say: "Remember the instruction you gave your servant Moses, saying, 'If you are unfaithful, I will scatter you among the nations, but if you return to me and obey my commands, then even if your exiled people are at the farthest horizon, I will gather them from there and bring them to the place I have chosen as a dwelling for my Name.'"

Although the description of the situation of Jerusalem and its wall was regrettable, and the pain was great in Nehemiah's heart, he did not look at the problem with sorrow alone, but also with faith in the promises that God had given to his people. He was convinced God would fulfill them. Ask: Why do you think it is important to know the Scriptures, and especially the promises of God? Do you remember any promise that came to your memory at some difficult time in your life?

II. Nehemiah acts (Nehemiah 2)

A. Fulfilling a great mission

In the final part of Nehemiah's prayer, we read: "They are your servants and your people, whom you redeemed by your great strength and your mighty hand. Lord, let your ear be attentive to the prayer of this your servant and to the prayer of your servants who delight in revering your name. Give your servant success today by granting him favor in the presence of this man" (vv.10-11). As we can clearly see, we find a specific request. The bad news and grief in Nehemiah's heart had led him to commit himself to a goal, which the influence he had gained

as the king's cupbearer could help him to achieve. And that goal was the reconstruction of Jerusalem and its walls.

The first step that Nehemiah had to take was to speak with the king of Persia, and request his favor. But he knew that the will of the king would not depend on his mood on that day, but on God's sovereignty. It was God who could grant him good success, and it would only depend on God if he could find grace before the eyes of the king.

In our lives, we also go through situations in which our success seems to depend on the decision of certain people or situations, but Nehemiah teaches us to recognize in prayer that God is sovereign and that every situation is subject to the His will. Our future depends on Him, and even in pain and difficulty, we must rest in Him knowing that He takes care of us.

B. Nehemiah before the king

In Nehemiah 2:1-2, Nehemiah's presentation to the king is described in this way: "In the month of Nisan in the twentieth year of King Artaxerxes, when wine was brought for him, I took the wine and gave it to the king. I had not been sad in his presence before, so the king asked me, 'Why does your face look so sad when you are not ill? This can be nothing but sadness of heart.' I was very much afraid." It had been about four months since Nehemiah had received the bad news from Jerusalem, and the time had come to present his petition before King Artaxerxes. It is important to note that it was the duty of all servants to be cheerful in the presence of the king. Hence, the great fear expressed by Nehemiah when Artaxerxes noticed his sadness.

However, Nehemiah teaches us that it is possible to transform fear into an opportunity, taking advantage of this moment to present to the king his request, as described in Nehemiah 2:3-5 where we read: "but I said to the king, 'May the king live forever! Why should my face not look sad when the city where my ancestors are buried lies in ruins, and its gates have been destroyed by fire?' The king said to me, 'What is it you want?' Then I prayed to the God of heaven, and I answered the king, 'If it pleases the king and if your servant has found favor in his sight, let him send me to the city in Judah where my ancestors are buried so that I can rebuild it.'"

In this petition, we observe that Nehemiah did not hide his intentions from the king. He faithfully described the situation that his land was going through, although the consequences of his sincerity could cause problems which could not be measured at that moment. Nehemiah came out of his comfort zone, from his place of security that he had with the king, enjoying his favor. He did so to express what he had been carrying in his heart for months, that which he was convinced came from God. Nehemiah knew that this moment was not a fortuitous one, but a time prepared by God to make known his mission and for Him to show His glory by granting the favor that he had previously requested in prayer.

Ask: How many times does lack of faith make us lose opportunities to move forward in our spiritual growth?

Without faith it is not possible to please God. Therefore, we must be like Nehemiah and learn to depend on the Lord, recognizing that our times are in His hands and that He is the one who prepares the path through which we must travel. Like Nehemiah, let us seek Him in prayer and align our will with His to experience His glory in our lives. Only He can transform a moment of fear and uncertainty into one of victory and hope.

C. Nehemiah and the hand of God

In Nehemiah 2:6-8, the final scene of Nehemiah's encounter with the king is described: "Then the king, with the queen sitting beside him, asked me, 'How long will your journey take, and when will you get back?' It pleased the king to send me; so, I set a time. I also said to him, 'If it pleases the king, may I have letters to the governors of Trans-Euphrates, so that they will provide me safe-conduct until I arrive in Judah?'"

King Artaxerxes' answer proved to Nehemiah that this attitude could not come from his own will, it came from God himself. His request was fulfilled, including contributions that the governors had to make for the construction. In Nehemiah 5:14, we read that the king gave him army captains and horsemen, and the king also made him governor of the province of Judah. All this was possibly much more than Nehemiah expected from the king's hand, but it was a confirmation that God's hand was on him and his project.

Nehemiah teaches us that everything that had happened up to that point was a product of the favor of God, who even influenced the king to do what Nehemiah had asked of God in prayer. Today, we must also recognize, like Nehemiah, that when God works, He moves because in the end, His will will be done.

In these first passages of the book of Nehemiah, we find a man who teaches us the correct way to face the difficulties of life. From his prayer and his perception of what God was doing during his encounter with the king, we learn to turn to God in worship, to ask correctly, and to recognize with courage that His will and sovereignty prevail over any person or situation that we have to go through. In the midst of conflict and difficulty, are you ready to seek God in the style of Nehemiah?

Optional Questions:

I. Transforming sorrow into action

- What was the bad news that Nehemiah received (Nehemiah 1:3)?

- What was Nehemiah's reaction to this difficult situation (Nehemiah 1:4)?

- What is your reaction to bad news? Do you remember any difficult situation? What was your reaction? Share.

II. Nehemiah acts

- What was the goal that Nehemiah wanted to achieve (Nehemiah 1:10-11)?

- What lessons did you learn from Nehemiah's encounter with the king (Nehemiah 2:1-2)?

- In what practical ways are you applying, or will you apply, what you learned in these passages about the life of Nehemiah?

Conclusion

From Nehemiah we can see the importance of going to God in difficult situations and waiting for His direction and the opportune time for things to happen. We must never act according to our impulses, but wait for the guidance and direction of God.

The married couple that served God together

Ela González (Guatemala)

> **Memory verse:** "One night the Lord spoke to Paul in a vision: "Do not be afraid; keep on speaking, do not be silent. For I am with you, and no one is going to attack and harm you, because I have many people in this city" (Acts 18:9-10).
>
> **Lesson Aim:** To learn from the example of a married couple that served the Lord, leaving everything, even risking their lives.

Introduction

During the history of the church there have been many martyrs who have been bold, stood up for Christ, and as a result have been persecuted and often times killed for what they believe. Even today, many people are suffering for their faith. How many of us are ready be counted for Jesus, and even to lose our lives for the sake of the gospel? Priscilla and Aquila were willing to suffer for Christ, but they were also willing to suffer to help Paul. How many of us are ready and willing to suffer for Jesus, and would we suffer for someone else?

I. Biographical sketch of Priscilla and Aquila

Sacrificing our lives for someone else is not often part of our thinking or our culture. Romans 16:3-4 says, "Greet Priscilla and Aquila, my co-workers in Christ Jesus. They risked their lives for me. Not only I but all the churches of the Gentiles are grateful to them." We do not know what the couple did to save the Apostle, but this statement indicates that they somehow decisively intervened to spare Paul from harm.

The Lord Jesus told his disciples that only out of love can someone give his life for his friends. John 15:12-15 says, "My command is this: Love each other as I have loved you. Greater love has no one than this: to lay down one's life for one's friends. You are my friends if you do what I command. I no longer call you servants, because a servant does not know his master's business. Instead, I have called you friends, for everything that I learned from my Father

I have made known to you."

The apostle Paul, in his letter to the Romans, also refers to the fact of dying for another. Romans 5:7-8 says, "Very rarely will anyone die for a righteous person, though for a good person someone might possibly dare to die. But God demonstrates his own love for us in this: While we were still sinners, Christ died for us."

We do not know how this married couple came to be Christians. All that we know about them is that they were Jews, and they are always named together.

A. Priscilla

She was Aquila's wife. A very peculiar detail is that in most of the occasions where this couple is spoken about, Priscilla is mentioned first, which is very unusual in the culture of the time. Commonly they would put the man's name first. Possibly, the apostle Paul recognized that she was more influential than her husband in ministry and commitment to the church. In all the passages, she is always mentioned with her husband Aquila. They obviously served the Lord together. She was an admirable, enterprising woman who worked alongside Paul in his ministry. He calls them "co-workers" (Romans 16:3). We do not know if they had children or not.

B. Aquila

In Acts 18:2, we read: "he met a Jew named Aquila, a native of Pontus, who had recently come from Italy with his wife Priscilla because Claudius had ordered all Jews to leave Rome. Paul went to see them." Aquila worked in the same trade as Paul. He was a tentmaker. Initially, this couple worked and lived in Rome, but as the result of the edict of the Emperor Claudius in 50 A.D., accusing the Jews of provoking religious riots, they were forced to flee from Italy. This situation caused them to migrate to Corinth, where they met with the Apostle Paul.

II. A couple well-grounded in the faith

A. Paul disciples his companions and fellow servants

Acts 18:11 tells us: "So Paul stayed in Corinth for a year and a half, teaching them the Word of God." No doubt that during that time Priscilla and Aquila learned a great deal from Paul as they worked alongside him in the ministry in Corinth.

B. Reproducing the teaching

Later, Priscilla and Aquila traveled with Paul to Asia Minor, and arrived in Ephesus, where they settled. While they were in this city, Apollos arrived, a Jew from Alexandria. He was very eloquent, knowledgeable and a teacher of the Scriptures. He had become a Christian, was very enthusiastic, but he had only grasped half of the truth about Jesus from some of the disciples of John the Baptist, who emphasized John's teaching about baptism. He began to preach in the synagogue, but when Priscilla and Aquila listened to him, they noticed that his teaching was not complete. So they took him aside to complete his knowledge about the gospel (Acts 18:24-26). The way they handled Apollos is noteworthy; they took him aside and filled him in with the facts. They did not argue with him publicly. They had learned from Paul, and taught Apollos what they had learned. Apollos, with his great gift of oratory, was able to teach more effectively the whole message about Jesus as the Christ, arguing from the Old Testament Scriptures.

C. Missionary work

The apostle Paul was a great missionary who made many trips outside of Palestine to make known the gospel of Jesus Christ. After he had been in Corinth for a year and a half, preaching and teaching, supporting himself with tentmaking alongside Priscilla and Aquila, he decided to move his team to Asia Minor.

Acts 18:18-19 says, "Paul stayed on in Corinth for some time. Then he left the brothers and sisters and sailed for Syria, accompanied by Priscilla and Aquila…They arrived at Ephesus, here Paul left Priscilla and Aquila." Paul's visit on this occasion was brief. After preaching in the Synagogue, he continued his journey to Antioch, leaving Priscilla and Aquila in charge of the church in Ephesus.

III. A couple who opened their home to God

Priscilla and Aquila had a fervent love for the Work of God. They were co-workers of the Apostle Paul, both in the daily work for sustenance as well as in the ministry. Although they moved from one place to another, they always opened their doors to welcome the church into their home.

A. In Corinth
During the long period in Corinth, although the Bible doesn't specifically mention it, it is possible that they opened their home as a meeting place for the church.

B. In Ephesus

When the apostle Paul writes the first letter to the Corinthians from Ephesus, he sends greetings to the brothers of Corinth. He mentions specifically the church group meeting in Priscilla and Aquila's home. 1 Corinthians 16:19 says, "The churches in the province of Asia send you greetings. Aquila and Priscilla greet you warmly in the Lord, and so does the church that meets at their house."

C. In Rome

Apparently, Priscilla and Aquila returned to Rome, because when the apostle Paul writes his letter to the Romans, he says, "Greet Priscilla and Aquila, my co-workers in Christ Jesus. They risked their lives for me. Not only I but all the churches of the Gentiles are grateful to them" (Romans 16:3). Since there had been a change of government, they could go back to their business in Rome.

D. Again in Ephesus

The apostle Paul, almost reaching the end of his journey, writes his second letter to Timothy. Once again, he mentions Priscilla and Aquila: "Greet Priscilla and Aquila and the household of Onesiphorus" (2 Timothy 4:19). This letter was written probably when Nero was emperor, after the fire of Rome. It is his last letter before he was martyred.

The Apostle Paul describes Aquila and Priscilla as fellow workers in Christ Jesus. This couple was very missionary minded. They opened their home so that the believers could gather to remember the Lord, pray, and have fellowship as they were instructed in the Word of God. They also were engaged in secular employment so that they were not a financial burden on the churches.

They represent an example of how a married couple can minister together. Priscilla and Aquila are always mentioned together. They knew how to disciple together, teach together, host together, share their house with the church fellowship and encourage together. They served Jesus and helped Paul ... together.

Many, like Paul, lose their lives for sharing the Word of God. We who live in places where there is freedom of worship, with free access to the Bible and possibility to preach the gospel, must make a commitment to expand the Word. We need to follow the example of Priscilla and Aquila, who were always willing to open their homes to the church, teach sound doctrine, and even expose their lives for the sake of the gospel.

Optional Questions:

I. Biographical sketch of Priscilla and Aquila

- What was their nationality?
- How did they earn their living?
- What can we learn about them from Romans 16:3-4?

II. A couple well-grounded in the faith

- How did this couple correct Apollos? (Acts 18:24-26)
- How do you react when you hear someone say something that is not right?

III. A couple who opened their home to God

- What do 1 Corinthians 16:19 and 2 Timothy 4:19 tell us about them?
- What is involved in opening a home for God's work?
- How can you use your home for God's work?

Conclusion

We must learn from the example of a married couple who served the Lord wholeheartedly and without counting the cost, even risking their own lives. They served God in some of the major city centers of the Roman Empire. Together, Aquila and Priscilla made their home a place where Christ was honored and served.

Notes :

www.ingramcontent.com/pod-product-compliance
Lightning Source LLC
Chambersburg PA
CBHW081512040426
42447CB00013B/3195